UTOPIA

THOMAS MORE
UTOPIA

With Erasmus's
The Sileni of Alcibiades

Edited and Translated,
with an Introduction, by
David Wootton

Hackett Publishing Company
Indianapolis/Cambridge

Copyright © 1999 by Hackett Publishing Company, Inc.

05 04 03 02 01 00 99   1 2 3 4 5 6 7 8 9

For further information, please address
Hackett Publishing Company, Inc.
P.O. Box 44937
Indianapolis, IN 46244-0937

Cover design by Brian Rak and John Pershing
Interior design by Meera Dash

Library of Congress Cataloging-in-Publication Data

More, Thomas, Sir, Saint, 1478–1535.
    [Utopia. English]
    Utopia / Thomas More: translated, with introduction
and notes, by David Wootton.
        p.   cm.
    Includes bibliographical references (p.   ).
    ISBN 0-87220-377-8.—ISBN 0-87220-376-X (pbk.)
    1. Utopias. I. Wootton, David, 1952– . II. Title.
HX810.5E54   1999
335′.02—dc21   98-47076
                                                        CIP

CONTENTS

Utopia: AN INTRODUCTION

UTOPIA

Thomas More's *Utopia* was published in Latin, in Louvain (now in Belgium) in December 1516.[1] It was clearly intended for an educated, European readership and dealt with themes—the nature of a good society, the evils of warfare—that were not uncommon in the literature of the day.[2] At first *Utopia* appears to be a description of a real country, and More obviously drew his inspiration from contemporary travel literature describing the discovery of new worlds; at the same time *Utopia* claims to be a description of the best possible society, and in Greek the invented name "Utopia" would mean "Nowhere." By producing a realistic, fictional account of an ideal, More invented a new literary genre, the Utopia.[3] But More could scarcely have known that there would be numerous later Utopias modeled on his own, and there is no general agreement as to how we should read *Utopia*. Is it, as it appears to be, a portrait of the ideal political community? The majority of contemporary scholars argue that *Utopia* is, paradoxically, not a Utopia at all, but a demonstration of the inadequacy of Utopian thinking; that More intends to criticize, not endorse, Utopianism; that he invents Utopianism but at the same time ironically distances himself from it.[4]

---

1. Thomas More, *Utopia: Latin Text and English Translation*, George M. Logan, Robert M. Adams, Clarence H. Miller, eds. (Cambridge: Cambridge University Press, 1995), pp. 270–271 [hereafter cited as C]. I am grateful to Quentin Skinner and J.C. Davis for commenting on an earlier version of this Introduction. The faults are mine; the care and consideration theirs.

2. On the nature of the good society, Quentin Skinner, "Sir Thomas More's *Utopia* and the Language of Renaissance Humanism," in *The Languages of Political Theory in Early-Modern Europe*, Anthony Pagden, ed. (Cambridge: Cambridge University Press, 1987), pp. 123–57; on warfare, Robert P. Adams, *The Better Part of Valor: More, Erasmus, Colet, and Vives on Humanism, War, and Peace* (Seattle: University of Washington Press, 1962).

3. On Utopianism see Frank E. and Fritzie P. Manuel, *Utopian Thought in the Western World* (Oxford: Basil Blackwell, 1979); and J.C. Davis, *Utopia and the Ideal Society* (Cambridge: Cambridge University Press, 1981).

4. For example, R.S. Sylvester, "*Si Hythlodaeo credimus:* Vision and Revision

Utopia is a complex and subtle construction, deliberately intended to be open to numerous interpretations. In this Introduction I present a new account of how the book was written and what it was originally intended to mean. I seek to explain why More wrote a defense of communism, and why his ideal society seems full of what More himself called "near-absurdities" (*subabsurda;* below, p. 167). Explaining why *Utopia* is the sort of text it is, however, is not the same as fixing its meaning, for the whole point of *Utopia* is that whenever we feel we have a good grip on it, it slips from our grasp.

A MAN FOR ALL SEASONS

In 1511 Desiderius Erasmus of Rotterdam (c. 1469–1536) published a strangely paradoxical little book (also in Latin, the universal language for the educated of the day) entitled *Encomium moriae,* punning on two possible meanings, Praise of Folly and Praise of More. Erasmus was in the process of establishing himself as the leading intellectual of his day. An expert on the texts both of pagan Greece and Rome and of the early church, he was the foremost humanist of the early years of the century. A "humanist" was simply someone with the technical skills required to study classical literature (known at the time as "humane letters" in contrast to "sacred letters"), but most humanists were also committed to the view that the acquisition of these skills through the study of grammar, rhetoric, ethics, history, and poetry was a better preparation for life than the traditional education of the medieval schools (called scholasticism), with its emphasis on logic, natural philosophy, and metaphysics. Pride of place in scholastic education was given to the works of Aristotle, while humanists turned first to the writings (philosophical dialogues, speeches, and letters) of a practical statesman and lawyer, Cicero.[5]

With works such as *Praise of Folly* Erasmus established himself as the first modern author capable of writing best-sellers. The triple inventions

---

in More's *Utopia*" (1968), in R.S. Sylvester and G.P. Marc'hadour, eds. *Essential Articles for the Study of Thomas More* (Hamden, Conn.: Archon Books, 1977), pp. 290–301; Thomas I. White, *"Festivitas, utilitas, et opes:* The Concluding Irony and Philosophical Purpose of Thomas More's *Utopia,"* in *Quincentennial Papers on St. Thomas More,* Michael J. Moore, ed. (Boone, N.C.: Albion, 1978), pp. 134–50; Alistair Fox, *"Utopia": An Elusive Vision* (New York: Twayne Publishers, 1993).

5. For a good introduction to Renaissance humanism, see Paul O. Kristeller, *Renaissance Thought and Its Sources* (New York: Columbia University Press, 1979).

of the printing press, movable type and paper half a century before had made possible for the first time the mass production of books, but most of the first best-sellers had been either religious texts or long-established classics such as (inevitably) Aristotle and Cicero.[6] Unlike many of his contemporary humanists, Erasmus placed his classical learning at the service of Christianity (producing the first scholarly edition of the Greek New Testament in 1516) and wrote a Latin that was not slavishly Ciceronian but contained new words capable of describing the world of Renaissance Europe, the world of compass, gunpowder, and printing press, of Columbus and Luther.

Erasmus much admired "copiousness" or "abundance"—he wrote a textbook on eloquence entitled *De copia*—with the result that, though the core argument of many of his works can be crudely presented in a sentence or two, Erasmus took pride in reworking his argument with so many subtle and skillful variations that no one version of it can be described as an adequate epitome of the whole and the rest be dismissed as redundant.[7] The core argument of *Praise of Folly* is that anyone who adopts Christian values (turning the other cheek, taking no thought for the morrow) will look like a fool in the eyes of the world, while anyone who is wise in the eyes of the world is truly foolish in the sight of God. The *Encomium moriae* was written in the household of Erasmus's close friend Thomas More (b. 1478), a successful young lawyer who, by the time it was published, was undersheriff of London, and it is dedicated to him "because you always take such delight in jokes of this kind, that is, if I don't flatter myself, jokes which aren't lacking in learning and wit . . . Your intelligence is too penetrating and original for you not to hold opinions very different from those of the ordinary man, but your manners are so friendly and pleasant that you have the rare gift of getting on well with all men at any time, and enjoying it."[8] And indeed More was peculiarly taken with jokes (he employed his own jester or buffoon) and supremely good-tempered: his son-in-law William Roper later said that in sixteen years of living in his household he never once saw him in a "fume."[9]

A few years before, in 1508, Erasmus had published a large volume en-

---

6. On the impact of printing see Elizabeth Eisenstein, *The Printing Revolution in Early Modern Europe* (Cambridge: Cambridge University Press, 1983).

7. Lisa Jardine, *Erasmus, Man of Letters* (Princeton: Princeton University Press, 1993), pp. 131–32.

8. Erasmus, *Praise of Folly*, trans. B. Radice, ed. A.H.T. Levi (Harmondsworth: Penguin Books, 1971, rev. ed. 1993), p. 4.

9. William Roper, *The Lyfe of Sir Thomas Moore, Knighte*, Elsie Vaughan Hitchcock, ed. (Oxford: Oxford University Press, 1935), p. 36.

titled *Adagiorum chiliades*, or *Thousands of Adages*, a collection of 3,260 sayings from ancient Greece whose meaning and origin might puzzle a modern reader. Among them (no. 286) is *Omnium horarum homo*, "a man for all hours," or, in the words of an English translation of 1520 (where it is applied to More), "a man for all seasons," a Latin phrase echoed in the passage above, where it is translated as "getting on well with all men at any time": "The man who suits himself to seriousness and jesting alike, and whose company is always delightful—that is the man the ancients called 'a man for all hours'." Such a man, we are given to understand, represents the perfect friend.[10]

In 1529 More became Lord Chancellor, and in 1535 he was beheaded for refusing to accept the legitimacy of Henry VIII's divorce from Catherine of Aragon. Then he proved himself indeed "a man for all seasons," cracking jokes with extraordinary sang-froid as he climbed the scaffold to his execution.[11] The More who died in 1535 had long been a persecutor of Protestants and a faithful Catholic. But the Reformation did not begin until 1517, when Luther (allegedly) nailed his ninety-five theses to a church door in Wittenberg, and the More who wrote Utopia was no Counter-Reformation saint but Erasmus's ideal friend, a lover of wit and learning, and someone who held opinions "very different from those of the ordinary man."

THE COMPOSITION AND PUBLICATION OF *Utopia*

According to a letter Erasmus wrote in 1519, More wrote "the second book [of *Utopia*] . . . earlier, when at leisure; at a later opportunity he added the first in the heat of the moment."[12] Book Two, we can be confident, was written between July and October of 1515. More was in the Netherlands, where he had been sent in May as an ambassador to represent the King of England in commercial negotiations. But the negotiations stalled, and for months More hung around with little to do. This was when he wrote the description of the island of Utopia, and presumably the opening pages of Book One, which serve as a prelude to that description.

---

10. Erasmus, *Praise of Folly*, p. 4; in Erasmus, *Collected Works*, vol. 31, trans. Margaret Mann Phillips, ed. R.A.B. Mynors (Toronto: University of Toronto Press, 1982), pp. 304–5.

11. Roper, *Lyfe*, p. 103.

12. Erasmus, *Collected Works*, vol. 7, trans. R.A.B. Mynors, ed. Peter G. Bietenholz (Toronto: University of Toronto Press, 1987), p. 24. (The whole letter, pp. 15–25, is an extended portrait of "the friend I love best.") For a summary of the received view of the composition of *Utopia*, see C :xx–xxii.

It is generally agreed that More wrote the rest of Book One after his return to England in late October of 1515, and it seems that he had written much of it by early February 1516, though the book was not ready to be sent to the publisher until September.[13] But it was only at the last moment, it seems, that the island acquired its Greek name and the book its title. In correspondence prior to November 15 it is always referred to as *Nusquama*—"Nowheria" in Latin, not Greek—and one must assume that all (or almost all) the other Utopian place names were changed at the same time.[14]

Utopia was thus written in at least two distinct stages, and since the two books are radically different in character they would appear to reflect a sharp change in More's concerns. It is this juxtaposition of two works reflecting different conceptions that explains much of *Utopia*'s puzzling and ambiguous character. The preoccupations that shaped Book One are fairly transparent. Sometime between November 1515 and January 1516 Henry VIII offered More a full-time job in the royal service. By August 1517 he had accepted the king's offer, but he seems for months to have been of two minds as to whether to accept or reject it.[15] It is this uncertainty that provides much of the energy and anxiety of Book One, which focuses on the question of whether a philosopher should enter royal service.

As a youngster, More "worked on a dialogue in which he supported Plato's doctrine of communalism, extending it even to wives."[16] But at first sight nothing in More's immediate circumstances appears to explain why he should have returned, in the second half of 1515, to the praise of communism. *Utopia* is a curious text, yet it was published with a series of clues to its interpretation, and to these we must now turn.

---

13. The early February date comes from the reference to the King of Aragon, Ferdinand, as being alive. He died on January 23, 1516. News traveled slowly in the sixteenth century, but one can reasonably assume More would have heard within a fortnight. Hexter's "no later than mid-January" (More, *Complete Works*, vol. 4, Edward Surtz, S.J. and J.H. Hexter, eds. [New Haven: Yale University Press, 1965] [hereafter Y], p. xxxvi) is not logical. For September, see More, *Selected Letters*, Elizabeth F. Rogers, ed. (New Haven: Yale University Press, 1961), p. 73.

14. C:271. The single exception in the first edition is the city of Mentirano: a Latin name, which becomes the Greek "Amaurotico" in later editions.

15. Geoffrey Elton, "Thomas More, Councillor," in *St. Thomas More: Action and Contemplation*, R.S. Sylvester, ed. (New Haven: Yale University Press, 1972), p. 90.

16. Erasmus, *Collected Works*, vol. 7, p. 23.

READING/MISREADING *Utopia*

Utopia was seen through the press by More's friend Erasmus and their joint friend Peter Giles (who appears as a character in More's book). Perhaps it was they who changed the place names; certainly it was they who added a map of the island; a poem written in the Utopian alphabet; a poem written by the poet laureate of Utopia; a letter from Giles to the distinguished Burgundian statesman Jerome de Busleyden and a letter from Busleyden to More; a letter from a prominent humanist, Jean Desmarez, to Giles; poems about *Utopia* by Desmarez, Gerard Geldenhouwer (who had helped in the production of the first edition), and Cornelis de Schrijver (a friend of Peter Giles); and a series of marginal annotations. In a letter to Erasmus of late September 1515 More had asked that his book "be handsomely set off with the highest of recommendations, if possible from several people, both intellectuals and distinguished statesmen," and Erasmus and Giles had done their best to comply.[17]

More was an unknown author—all he had previously published were some translations of Lucian, and he was probably best known for the fact that in *De copia* (1512) Erasmus had demonstrated his skill in variation by offering one hundred and ninety-five variations on the simple sentence, "While Erasmus lives, he will remember More"[18]—and the prefatory materials were in part intended to serve the same purpose as the blurbs on a modern book. He may also have been concerned with protecting himself against official anger at Book One's account of English politics and society by laying claim to an international reputation.[19] But the prefatory materials were disastrous. They all treated Utopia as if it were a real place, and a significant proportion of the first readers seem to have failed to grasp that they were dealing with a fiction, for the simple reason that knowledge of Greek was extremely rare and so very few of them can have grasped the significance of Utopia's place names.[20] More must have been in despair of being understood (and convinced that the adoption of Greek roots for Utopian names was an error) when he added to the second edition (edited by Lupset and published in Paris in 1517) a postscript

---

17. More, *Selected Letters*, p. 76.
18. Erasmus, *Collected Works*, vol. 24, trans. Betty I. Knott (Toronto: University of Toronto Press, 1978), pp. 355–64.
19. More, *Selected Letters*, p. 76. It is clear that More believes there is opposition to the book. Rogers's note 4 is unhelpful. Is the opponent perhaps Wolsey?
20. See below, p. 54; Harpsfield in William Roper and Nicholas Harpsfield, *Lives of Saint Thomas More*, E.E. Reynolds, ed. (London: Dent, 1963), p. 110.

insisting that this was no fiction, for had it been he "would have needed only to give such names to the ruler, the river, the city, and the island as would alert the more expert reader to the fact that the island was nowhere, the city a chimera, the river without water, and the ruler without subjects" (p. 167)— which is precisely what the names were intended to indicate.

More's 1517 letter begins with ironic thanks to a critic who has actually bothered to read *Utopia* carefully, and it is hard not to suspect a covert dig at Busleyden, who seems either to have missed the point of *Utopia*, or to have wanted to convey his disagreement with its author. Busleyden had hoped to read a conventional humanist work on the education of a Christian prince ("for without good rulers, all laws, even the best—we are assured by Plato—are ineffectual" [p. 162]) and found himself faced not with a portrait of the ideal ruler—a model of probity, the perfect example of good conduct, the living embodiment of justice—but with an account of an ideal society that said almost nothing about education and concentrated on good laws. Busleyden wanted an account of how a society could make itself victorious in warfare, like Sparta, Athens, and Rome, and could acquire a far-flung empire. Instead he found himself confronted by a book that attacked militarism and had nothing to say about fame and glory. Such half-hearted patronage was not what More had been seeking, and in the 1517 edition Busleyden's letter is unceremoniously bundled into an appendix.

More's 1517 letter provides, one would think, invaluable advice on how to read *Utopia*, yet when Erasmus re-edited *Utopia* for the third edition in March of 1518 More's letter had disappeared. Clearly there was something about it Erasmus did not like, and we will shortly see what that was. But Erasmus held the presses in 1518 until a copy of the 1517 edition could reach him from Paris, not so that he could incorporate More's response to his readers, but so that he could install in pride of place a new prefatory letter by France's leading humanist Guillaume Budé.[21] Budé's letter has certain key advantages over Busleyden's. In the first place, it makes clear that Utopia is an imaginary place, invented by More, which is a crucial precondition for any sensible reading of the book. But Budé also said enough to show that he had solved the riddle of *Utopia:* he knew why More had written in praise of communism.

---

21. Erasmus, *Collected Works*, vol. 5, trans. R.A.B. Mynors and D.F.S. Thomson (Toronto: Toronto University Press, 1979), p. 326.

COMMUNISM

By the third edition of *Utopia* there were three clues to help the reader puzzled over More's decision to portray a communist society—clues, alas, so discrete as to have passed without notice. First, there were the marginal annotations, which contain a series of synonyms for "adage": *proverbium, paroemia, apophthegma.* Clearly Erasmus and Giles had adages in mind as they read the manuscript of *Utopia.* Second, there were the prefatory materials, which now contained a series of references to friendship, from Erasmus's reference to his *artissima amicitia* with More, which begins his own new prefatory letter (p. 40), through Budé's reference to Giles as the *amicus iuratissimus* of Erasmus (p. 47), to More's unambiguous *ego te amo,* which ends his "preface" addressed to Giles (p. 55). Above all, we have Budé's statement that *Utopia* portrays a Pythagorean community.

Erasmus's *Adagiorum chiliades* begins with a discussion of two adages: "Friends have everything in common" and "Friendship is equality." Erasmus attributes these adages to Pythagoras, and in the preface to the volume he argues that the whole of moral philosophy and the fundamental principles of Christianity are to be found in them. The main text begins with a discussion of Plato's arguments in favor of communism: "Plato is trying to show that the happiest condition of a society [*felicissimum reipublicae statum*] consists in the community of all possessions: So the best kind of city and polity and the finest laws [*Prima quidem igitur civitas est et reipublicae status ac leges optimae*] are found where the old saying is maintained as much as possible throughout the whole city; and the saying is that friends really have all things in common." In the revised and much expanded edition of the *Adages,* which appeared early in 1515, Erasmus added a sentence here: "Plato also says that a state would be happy and blessed in which these words 'mine' and 'not mine' were never to be heard,"and he also added the claim that Pythagoras had actually established communist communities. In the opening pages he also expresses the view that Pythagoras would have agreed with St. Paul, who said "If any will not work, neither shall he eat." Here we have the origins of Utopia's subtitle, *de optimo reipublicae statu;* of its name (for "Utopia" may as easily derive from "Eutopia" [or Happy Place] as from "Outopia" [or Nowhere]); and of its central characteristics: communism, equality, and (nearly) universal labor.[22]

---

22. Erasmus, *Collected Works,* vol. 31, pp. 14–15, 29–50; John C. Olin, "Erasmus's Adagia and More's *Utopia,*" in *Miscellanea Moreana: Essays for Germain Marc'hadour,* Clare M. Murphy, Henri Gibaud, Marto A. Di Cesare, eds. (Binghamton, N.Y.: Medieval and Renaissance Texts and Studies, 1989), pp. 127–36;

It is hard for us reading *Utopia* to imagine how strange its advocacy of communism, equality, and labor must have seemed to a sixteenth-century reader. Communism might be found in Plato, communism and labor in the New Testament, but the combination of communism, labor, and egalitarianism is scarcely paralleled before *Utopia* (unless it be in the monastic life), and later communists look back to More as marking the beginning of a new era in communist speculation. Or rather, these three key elements, in the context of a discussion of the best state, are to be found in only one other place: the opening pages of Erasmus's *Adages,* the new edition of which must have kept More amused during his idle months in the second half of 1515 (Erasmus had probably given him a copy when they met in May of 1515). Budé's reference to Pythagoras makes clear that he had traced *Utopia* to its source in Erasmus's discussion of the Pythagorean adages on friendship.

ABSURDITIES

But is *Utopia* an account of an ideal community? Several features of Utopia disconcert modern readers and lead them to suspect that More cannot agree with his character Raphael Hythloday, who praises it as an ideal society. There is "their pleasure ethic (with the euthanasia and marriage practices it appears to promote)." There is their religion, which is tolerant of everything but intolerance, and their imperfect conversion to Christianity (their converts have neither priests nor sacraments). There is the fact that neither their ethics nor their religion gives them "any understanding of the intrinsic value of suffering, a value which—under the symbol of the Cross—is central to the soteriological scheme presented in the New Testament"; and there are their "war practices, which involve bribery, assassination, the hiring of mercenaries, and the subversion of neighboring realms through covert fifth-columnist activities."[23] For these critics, *Utopia* is striking for its absurdities, and these absurdities are evidently deliberate and recognized by More to be incompatible with any account of an ideal society. They force us to acknowledge that we cannot

---

David Wootton, "Friendship Portrayed: A New Account of *Utopia,*" *History Workshop Journal* 45 (1998), 30–47.

23. The first and third quotations come from Fox, *Utopia,* p. 31; the second from Skinner, "More's *Utopia,*" p. 151. Fox is somewhat exceptional among those who emphasize negative elements in More's depiction of Utopia, in emphasizing the positive elements in his account of Utopian religion; in this respect Skinner's argument is the mirror image of Fox's, for he thinks More cannot have approved of Utopian religion, but did approve of Utopian society.

trust Hythloday's judgment and persuade us to side with the character called "More"—from now on I will call him "Morus," his name in the Latin text of *Utopia*, in order to avoid confusing the character "More" with the author who invented him—who refuses to be persuaded that the best society will be a communist one.

But what sort of absurdities are we dealing with here? In the 1515 edition of Erasmus's *Adages* there were a number of new, lengthy essays. Two of them ("The Sileni of Alcibiades" and "Sweet is war to those who do not know it") immediately became famous, and each acquired a life of its own, beginning with publication as independent pamphlets by Froben (the publisher of the two 1518 editions of *Utopia*) in 1517. "Sweet is war" mirrors the *Adages* as a whole in its praise both of friendship and of Pythagoras: "First of all, what is there, in the whole of existence, better and sweeter than friendship? Absolutely nothing. But what is peace, except friendship among many?" As for Pythagoras, he is nothing less than the "wisest of men."[24] "Sweet is war" lies near the end of the Adages, and we can imagine that by the time More came across it he had already begun to describe his ideal commonwealth, for it is only as his description progresses that absurdities creep into it, and some of those absurdities appear to come straight from "Sweet is war."

But first we must note how close is the spirit of "Sweet is war" to that of *Utopia*. Take the fundamental paradox of the whole book, the underlying puzzle of all Utopianism: One can imagine a society from which evil has been excluded (though to do so seems at odds with the Christian doctrine of original sin); but one cannot conceive of any way of transforming an existing society into such an ideal (which seems to vindicate the Christian doctrine). Here is Erasmus (who was deeply ambivalent on the question of original sin) formulating the same paradox for individuals rather than societies: "vice is like the sea: we have the power to shut it out altogether, but, once we have let it in, there is none of us who can impose a limit; both are forces which roll on by their own impulsion and are not controlled by our will."[25]

Take communism. Book One of *Utopia* ends with an exchange be-

24. As "Sweet is war" has yet to appear in either the Elzevier edition of Erasmus's *Opera omnia* or the Toronto edition of his *Collected Works* in translation, I quote from Margaret Mann Phillips, *Erasmus on His Times: A Shortened Version of "The Adages of Erasmus"* (Cambridge: Cambridge University Press, 1967) (hereafter E); since the text of this adage changed over time I cite, in the absence of a critical edition, the 1515 edition of the *Adagiorum chiliades* (Basel: Froben) [hereafter AC(1515)]. Here, E:117, 116; AC(1515):580, 579.
25. AC(1515):579; E:114 (translation revised).

tween Hythloday and Morus in which Morus reiterates Aristotle's objections to Plato's communism. Those who believe that Morus speaks for the author assume we should find these objections convincing. But for Erasmus in "Sweet is war" there is a straightforward choice to be made between Christian teaching and the teaching of Aristotle, and attitudes to communism represent a useful touchstone: "things have come to the point where the whole of Aristotle is accepted as an integral part of theology, and accepted in such a way that his authority is more sacred than that of Christ. For if Christ said anything which is not easily fitted to our way of life, it is permitted to distort its meaning through interpretation; but anyone who lightly dares to oppose the oracular pronouncements of Aristotle is immediately hooted off the stage. From him we have learnt that human felicity cannot be complete without worldly goods—both physical and financial. From him we have learnt that a state cannot flourish where all things are held in common. We try to glue together all his doctrines with the teaching of Christ, which is like mixing fire and water."[26]

Take capital punishment. Book One of *Utopia* contains what is probably the first systematic attack on capital punishment. But "Sweet is war," in the midst of its attack on the legitimacy of warfare, had raised the question of capital punishment: "'But,' they say, 'it is permissible to sentence a criminal to [capital] punishment; therefore it is permissible to take vengeance on a state by war.'" Erasmus, it is true, defends capital punishment on the grounds that "the reason for not sparing one is that all should be the safer" (precisely the argument that More attacks when it is used to justify capital punishment for theft), but nevertheless the issue has been raised.[27] Or take political authority. The Utopians are constantly on their guard against tyranny, while Hythloday regards the rulers of Europe as no better than tyrants. Here, as so often, Erasmus and Hythloday agree: "No one can have the same rights over men, free by nature, as over herds of cattle. This very right which you [kings] hold, was given you by popular consent. Unless I am mistaken, the hand which gave can take it away."[28]

"Sweet is war," with its idealization of peace and its contempt for actually existing society, is a Utopian text. Yet, precisely for that reason, it involves itself in the "absurdities" that Utopia lays bare. What then of Utopian warfare? Does it not show that Utopian principles are impractical? Are the Utopians not dependent on the "disgusting and evil" Zapo-

---

26. AC(1515):582; E:123–24 (translation revised) (see also 102).
27. E:130; AC(1515):584.
28. E:131; AC(1515):584.

letes (p. 140), mercenaries who delight in warfare? But Erasmus would
not have found this ridiculous, for not only do the Utopians share his
view that war is "a truly beastly activity" (p. 135), but the Utopian approach to war is entirely in accord with the argument of "Sweet is war":
"If there is no way of avoiding war, because of the general wickedness,
when you have left no way untried and no stone unturned in your efforts
for peace, then the thing to do will be to take care that only bad people are
involved in so bad a thing, and to bring it to conclusion with the minimum of bloodshed."[29]

Again and again we find that the supposed absurdities of Utopia are in
fact Erasmian principles. The Utopians permit, under certain circumstances, divorce. Surely More, who went to the scaffold rather than recognize Henry's divorce, must have disapproved? Perhaps. But Erasmus
(and More was surely aware of the fact, even though Erasmus had yet to
publish in defense of divorce) would have approved.[30] According to the
Utopians, the most important problem in moral philosophy is "the understanding of human happiness" (p. 115); according to Erasmus, Christ
taught "a philosophy which was worlds away from the teaching of the
philosophers and from the judgments of the world, but which is the only
philosophy to offer the one thing that all the others, each in its different
way, is after—happiness" (p. 172). The Utopians exhibit prospective
marriage partners to one another naked. One commentator observes that
this passage "seems placed in the narrative to provoke outrage . . . As if to
give a cue to his readers, More has Hythlodaeus observe that this custom
'seemed to us very foolish and extremely ridiculous.' The fact that More
included it at all betrays his awareness that the moral philosophy he had
given the Utopians might not stand the scrutiny of those who believed in
human dignity."[31] There are two problems here. In the first place, since
Hythloday disapproves of the practice, one has to wonder whether the
passage does not vindicate his good judgement. In the second, we have
the marginal comment of Erasmus or Giles, which is much more mea-
sured than that of either Hythloday or our modern commentator: *Et si
parum verecunde haud tamen incaute* ("Prudence will approve, though
modesty protests") (p. 129).

---

29. E:139; AC(1515):586.
30. *The Censure and Judgement of the Famous Clark Erasmus* [1550], facsimile
reprint (Amsterdam: Theatrum Orbis Terrarum, 1972); for the Latin see Erasmus, *Novum testamentum: Opera omnia*, J. Leclerc, ed., vol. 6 (Leyden, 1705),
pp. 692–703. The 1516 edition of the *Novum testamentum* does not contain this
discussion, but Erasmus states that his views were shaped by his experiences
while living in England.
31. Fox, *"Utopia,"* p. 61.

"Everything in *Utopia* can be matched from Erasmus's works," writes A.H.T. Levi.[32] This is the problem of the absurdities in *Utopia*. When More develops Erasmus's claim that pacifists may go to war as long as they employ evil men to fight on their behalf, he is certainly showing Erasmus's views to be problematic, but then Erasmus himself recognized that they were paradoxical and impractical, foolish in the eyes of the world. Erasmus, however, could scarcely have agreed that he was showing them to be absurd, and this, I think, is why More's 1517 letter, which acknowledges that there are absurdities (or at least "near-absurdities") in *Utopia* (and in which it is clearly More-the-author who speaks, not just Morus, who flatly says that many of the customs of Utopia are "simply absurd" [p. 159]), disappears from the 1518 editions edited by Erasmus.[33] More is sharper in his criticism of Utopia than Erasmus could be; we, for our part, may choose to read it in the uncritical spirit in which More began his account of an ideal communist society, the spirit in which Erasmus and Giles annotated More's text; or in the skeptical spirit in which More defends his work in 1517: "As if there were no absurdities to be found outside Utopia!" (p. 167); or in the critical spirit of Morus. For all three readings are grounded in the text.

PROSPERITY AND PLEASURE

In the Europe of More's day death rates rose in years of bad harvest, and peasants depended on the uncertainties of subsistence agriculture. Not so in Utopia, where there are always adequate supplies held in reserve (pp. 93, 104, 156). Throughout More's England one would have found "single-story dwellings, mere cottages and cabins, built haphazardly out of whatever lumber was at hand, and with walls plastered with mud" (p. 95). Not so in Utopia, where the houses are solidly built of brick and well maintained. Throughout England one could have found the unemployed and the sick begging, but not in Utopia, where there is employment for all able-bodied residents, and where the sick are well cared for in hospitals (pp. 104–5). In More's England the vast majority of the population labored from sunup to sundown; in Utopia no one need work for more than six hours a day (p. 98). In England the vast majority of the population could neither read nor write; yet education is available to all in Utopia (p. 98).

A considerable effort of imagination was required to conceive of such

---

32. In Erasmus, *Praise of Folly*, p. xliii.
33. Though More has earlier established a favorable connotation for *absurdus*, when Hythloday maintains that the teachings of Christ seem "ridiculous" to most people (p. 84).

prosperity: More's ideas on the working day were at the limit of John Locke's imaginative capacity some two hundred years later.[34] But More may well have been inspired by the sight of the prosperous cities of Flanders, where Book Two was composed. Thomas Starkey, who traveled abroad for the first time in 1521, records that he "thought when I came first into Flanders and France that I was translated as it had been into another world, the cities and towns appeared so goodly, so well builded and so clean kept," and here More might have seen, for example, hospitals for the poor.[35] Such prosperity—in Utopia or Flanders—represented progress. The Utopians had once been poor; now they were rich. When Starkey wrote about the lamentable state of the English economy he was well aware that the cities of England were shrunken and depopulated; they had been larger before the Black Death of 1348 killed one-third of the population. In Louvain, Paris, or Basel, where the first editions of *Utopia* were published, the world looked different. Erasmus could confidently declare: "we see towns ruled by secular monarchs thriving as day by day they increase their wealth, their buildings, and their population" (p. 189). When Erasmus thinks of the advantages of peace, "the construction of bridges, quays, embankments, and a thousand other amenities" immediately fills his mind with the sound of hammering.[36] In part, Utopia is an idealized picture of contemporary Europe, seen from the point of view of a visitor from a backward country.

More not only imagined universal prosperity, but also analyzed what would be required to bring it about: the rational investment of resources (buildings regularly maintained; forests grown near water transport); the elimination of conspicuous expenditure (on gold, jewelery, brocade, plate, and all the other trappings of nobility); the production of durable and simplified goods (clothing which is "not unattractive" [p. 97]); the elimination of obstacles to distribution occasioned by stockpiling and speculating. At times the details of More's argument now seem quaint: it would have surprised More's contemporaries, but does not surprise us, that glass windows are common in Utopia; our surprise, but not theirs, is evoked by the notion of windows made of oiled linen. It surprises us, not them, to be told that oxen are better for farm work than horses: It was not

---

34. John Locke, *Political Writings*, David Wootton, ed. (New York: Mentor, 1993), pp. 116, 440–42.
35. Thomas Starkey, *A Dialogue Between Pole and Lupset*, T.F. Mayer, ed. (London: Royal Historical Society, 1989), 62, 117.
36. E:127; AC(1515):583.

until the end of the century that horses were more frequently used than oxen as draft animals.[37]

Utopia's windows are indicative of another extraordinary aspiration that gleams through the pages of *Utopia:* the hope of seeing society transformed by technology. Twelve hundred years ago the Utopians acquired all the technology of ancient Egypt and Rome (p. 88); perhaps it was from Egypt that they learned how to incubate chickens' eggs, so that they are able to pioneer factory farming.[38] They can build temples comparable in size to medieval cathedrals, which means that their architects have skills the Romans never had. Presumably they acquire the use of the compass from Hythloday; certainly they learn from him how to produce the printing press, movable type, and paper. They do not passively take advantage of such technology, depending on the skills of others, but understand and master it. Perhaps they do not have gunpowder; or perhaps they do, for they are skillful in the invention of machines of war but conceal their discoveries from others, and the walls of their cities are thick, as if to withstand bombardment, as well as being high, so that they cannot be scaled (pp. 143, 94).

It is hard to find comparable confidence in technological change until we come to works such as Francis Bacon's *Advancement of Learning* in 1605. More's world, it is true, had been transformed by the compass and the printing press, and was in the process of being transformed by gunpowder—the key campaign that demonstrated the decisive capacity of cannon fire to demolish medieval city walls was the French invasion of Italy in 1494.[39] What More wants to foster is an attitude of mind that will make further transformations possible, an attitude of mind that was indeed to transform first England and then the world. In this important respect *Utopia* stands on the threshold of modernity.

Such an attitude of mind is inextricably linked to the notion of irreversible change. Whereas More's contemporary Machiavelli continued for another decade or so to believe that no change that had occurred since

---

37. John Langdon, *Horses, Oxen and Technological Innovation: The Use of Draught Animals in English Farming,* 1066–1500 (Cambridge: Cambridge University Press, 1986).

38. Franklin B. Williams, "Utopia's Chickens Come Home to Roost," *Moreana* 18, no. 69 (March 1981), 77–78.

39. Geoffrey Parker, *The Military Revolution: Military Innovation and the Rise of the West, 1500–1800* (Cambridge: Cambridge University Press, 1988), p. 10. See also Carlo M. Cipolla, *Guns and Sails* and *Clocks and Culture,* reprinted as *European Culture and Overseas Expansion* (Harmondsworth: Penguin Books, 1970) and Eisenstein, *Printing Revolution.*

the days of ancient Rome was irreversible, as if the printing press were unimportant and the cannon insignificant, More and Erasmus are conscious of living in a world in which the manuscript is being rendered obsolete, in which bombards, unknown to the Romans, demolish town walls.[40] Moreover, Erasmus had given careful thought to the irreversible character of technological progress as he puzzled over the skill with which men kill each other, tracing the development of military capacity from the time "long ago . . . when rude primitive men lived in the woods, naked, without ramparts, roofless," when men had first begun to make war upon the beasts and become carnivorous; outlining their progress from hunting to single combat and from single combat to warfare; from the use of stones and burned stakes to the invention of swords and arrows; "and so, little by little, military science developed with civilization, and city began to declare war on city."[41]

Civilization is something acquired by technological progress over time, and the Utopians can survive only because they have the military science of the civilized. Yet they try to shape their civilization so that war has only a secondary place within it. They follow the recommendation of Pythagoras as interpreted by Erasmus in insisting that citizens may not slaughter animals, as this destroys the sense of compassion.[42] In Utopian eyes the favorite activity of the warlike nobility of Renaissance Europe, the peaceful activity by which they prepared for war, that sport of kings, the hunt, is fit only for slaves; while in More's England wherever one went, one found hunting reserves, monopolized, of course, by the rich (pp. 120, 66).[43] In Utopia war, agriculture, and legal argument are the three activities in which every citizen—male and female—engages, in order to ensure that there is, on the one hand, no exploited class of agricultural laborers, and on the other, no military or bureaucratic ruling caste. Feudalism has been torn up by the roots, and much of the book is an attack on the values and culture of the nobility (which takes pride in "honors for fools," in "empty nobility" in the words of the marginal annotator [pp. 118–9]). Translating *Utopia* into English for the first time in 1556, Ralph Robinson could not bring himself to repeat More's comparison between a nobleman and a usurer, both equally useless to the commonwealth: this

---

40. Parker, *Military Revolution*, pp. 164–65. On printing, see E:9–10, 14–15; on military technology, see below, pp. 181, 187; E:112, 125 [AC(1515):578, 583].
41. E:113–6; AC(1515):578.
42. E:114, 116; AC(1515):578–89; below, pp. 104, 120.
43. Edward Berry's forthcoming book on "Shakespeare and the Hunt" will shed new light on attitudes to hunting in the Renaissance.

had to be censored.[44] But the nobility have not been replaced by a new ruling class of merchants, lawyers, or bureaucrats.

The Utopians have to do without certain pleasures—gambling, drinking, fornicating, hunting, perhaps the theater, and certainly all the competitive pleasures of conspicuous consumption; instead they enjoy reading, conversation, and music, and, even more fundamentally, leisure (in which they delight) and health. But by concentrating on utility (*utilis* and *utilitas* recur frequently in the Latin), on necessity, not luxury, they make it possible for self-interest, convenience (*commodum*), or prosperity (*commoditas*) to be attained, and for pleasure (*felicitas, iucunditas, voluptas*) to be maximized. It is important to see how More's argument at this point goes against the grain of his language. We might want to say that Utopia is a society dedicated to satisfying legitimate interests and maximizing happiness. More does not have, in Latin or in English, the word "society" in this sense (in English it dates to 1639); "interest" exists in English but has no Latin equivalent (and "self-interest" and "selfish" do not appear until much later, 1649 and 1640 respectively); and "maximize" is not invented until 1802.[45] There is no point now in trying to translate More's sixteenth-century Latin into sixteenth-century English; but it should surprise us that More's arguments seem so easily to find twentieth-century equivalents. One way of explaining this is to point out that the Utopians not only have no interest in feudal luxuries ("nobility, magnificence, splendor, and majesty" [p. 159]), but they also do not believe in sin, sacrifice, or suffering. In constructing the values appropriate to a society of rational, pleasure-seeking pagans, More ends up, predictably, with a set of values more reminiscent of those of Enlightenment deists than of the Protestant and Catholic Reformations.

---

44. "For what justice is this, that a rich [nobleman or a] goldsmith or an usurer or, to be short, any of them which either do nothing at all, or else that which they do is such that it is not very necessary to the commonwealth, should have a pleasant and a wealthy living..." More, *Utopia*, trans. Ralph Robinson (1556), facsimile reprint (Menston,Yorks: Scolar Press, 1970), p. 127v [spelling and punctuation modernized]; below, p. 156. Note also that Robinson makes the construction of Utopia seem impossible by omitting the word *facile* (easily) from a key sentence: pride "is so deeply rooted in men's breasts, that she cannot be [easily] plucked out." (p. 130v; below, p. 159) And that, living in a world of Protestant and Catholic conflict, he simply omits the sentence, "There is no principle they [the Utopians] observe more carefully than the principle that it is not easy to sit in judgment on someone else's religion" (below, p. 150; Robinson, p. 119v)

45. For the history of these and other words discussed here, see *The Oxford English Dictionary*.

MARKETS AND MECHANISMS

In Book One of *Utopia* More turned from a description of his ideal society to an analysis of the difficulties faced by anyone who held Utopian
values (or Christian values as understood by Erasmus) when faced with
the society of contemporary Europe. In portraying Utopia, More had
given an account of a society in which a number of different institutions
and conventions—communism, universal labor, contempt for gold—in-
terlocked to eliminate conspicuous consumption and competitiveness,
and eradicate pride. Giles comments in his letter to Busleyden "Goodness me, despite the five years he lived there, I can easily believe that
Raphael himself saw less while he was on that island than one is able to
see from More's description of it" (pp. 49–50). At one level this is ridiculous, as Morus knows nothing except what Hythloday has told him; we
must conclude that what More has seen, and Hythloday perhaps has not,
is the logic underlying the Utopian way of life.

Such an analysis opens up two possibilities. First, one may look at the
logic of a particular aspect of society—for example, having explored the
economic organization of Utopia one can explore the economic organization of England. Second, one may look at the way in which, in different societies, different institutions and practices interlock and interact. We can
see More exploring both possibilities in Book One. Thus, alongside accounts of the criminal justice systems of England and Utopia, one real and
the other imaginary, he places a third "scheme," the imaginary criminal
justice system of the Polylerites (pp. 70–73), and then suggests that alternative schemes could be tested to see which is most effective. After analyz-
ing this and other comparable passages (on the Acorians and Macarians),
George Logan concludes, "More's emphasis on carefully controlled experiment and on theoretical models as a way of evaluating proposed solu-
tions to social problems is, as far as I know, unprecedented."[46]

Logan's conclusion is both half-true and somewhat alarming, for the
language and concepts commentators use when discussing More as a social analyst are language and concepts More never uses himself. The idea
of a "carefully controlled experiment" can scarcely be traced back before
the founding of the Royal Society in 1660, and in any case the word More
uses is *periculum,* meaning a trial or test, not *experimentum.*[47] "Model,"

---

46. George M. Logan, *The Meaning of More's "Utopia"* (Princeton: Princeton
University Press, 1983), p. 104.
47. The Yale edition uses the word "experiment" twice to translate More's *periculum* (Y:81); the Cambridge edition avoids the term the first time, but not the
second (C:75–77); this translation avoids "experiment" on both occasions (p. 73).

which has no Latin equivalent, first appears in English in 1575 ("blue-print," another word commentators find hard to avoid, is even later, dat-ing to 1887; even "plan," yet another word without a Latin equivalent, does not appear until 1678); "scheme," which is used in the Cambridge translation of the key passage, appears in English in 1550; its Latin equivalent, *schema*, is never used in *Utopia*.[48] The Latin word More uses here is simply *res*, meaning "thing" or "matter." The evidence is cer-tainly insufficient to justify attributing a fully fledged experimental method to More, but it is clear that he does think in terms of schemes or models, and this implies a familiarity with objects like the planisphere, a type of astrolabe that "models" the heavens in two dimensions; indeed, such objects were entirely familiar to an educated man of More's day and were evidently to be found in Utopia (p. 114).

If we concentrate on the idea of a scientific model, however, we may be misled. At the heart of humanist education was the idea that one should learn to imitate models of good practice drawn from the classics—to learn to write a letter, for example, in the manner of Cicero—and the whole point of studying history was to learn how to model oneself on ex-amples of successful statesmanship—to learn to command an army, for example, in the manner of Manlius. So when Busleyden wishes to de-scribe how a political theorist should offer examples of how to rule he has a rich vocabulary to draw on, based on the perennial activity of copying engaged in both by authors and visual artists in the Renaissance: *simu-lacrum* [representation], *specimen, exemplar, imago* [imitation] (p. 162). Budé too knows the words to use: *exemplar, praescriptum* (both words for the original to be imitated), *argumentum* (the subject of a written compo-sition or artistic representation), *norma,* and *regula* (both words for a ruler or straightedge, but also for a pattern or example); but even he stretches his vocabulary when he uses a very rare verb, *architector,* to de-scribe Hythloday as having designed, devised, or constructed the Utopian community—constructed it, that is, according to a plan or model (p. 46). Yet it is Morus who has (supposedly) turned the model into words, as a builder turns the architect's plan into bricks. If Hythlo-day is the architect, Budé says, then Morus is the *structor* or mason.

Budé's use of *architector* signals the gap between the apprenticeship of the medieval craftsman or Renaissance poet, who works from an example to imitate, and the professional activity of a modern engineer or social sci-entist, who moves back and forth between his model, plan, or blueprint

---

48. *A Concordance to the "Utopia" of St. Thomas More*, Ladislaus J. Bolchazy, ed. (Hildesheim: Georg Olms Verlag, 1978).

on the one hand and the real world on the other. The craftsman and the poet are engaged in an activity that is self-consciously mimetic or traditional; but the architect or model-builder must understand the logic of what he is doing and be free to come up with a scheme that is entirely original, as original as the literary genre of Utopia or the institutions of the Utopians. More, both architect and craftsman, stands firmly on our side of this particular threshold of modernity.

In reading *Utopia* we must not only bear in mind the words that we automatically use in describing More's meaning and even in translating his Latin but which he lacks, words such as "model"; we also need to be aware that a number of words with which More is familiar (we have already come across the example of "society") do not bear their familiar meanings. A striking example of this occurs when we are told that the Utopians take delight in studying the *machina mundi*. Modern translators do not hesitate to translate this as "the mechanism of the world," but again we need to be extremely cautious.[49] The word "machine" first appears in English in 1549, but it originally means, like the Latin *machina*, merely a structure or fabrication. For Robinson, in 1556, the word *machina* does not convey any implication of a machine—he translates *machina mundi* straightforwardly as "the marvellous and gorgeous frame of the world."[50] Only in 1693 is "machine" used to mean "an apparatus for applying mechanical power," though words like "mechanism" and "mechanics" (1662, 1648) better mark the emergence of machine-oriented ways of thinking.

But just as it is helpful to think of More as constructing models, though he never uses the word, it is important to realize that he sees society as a system of causal interactions, comparable to those in a machine, even if we cannot rely on his reference to the *machina mundi* to prove that he thought in mechanistic terms. Thus demobilization of troops, the transformation of arable into pasture, and the rising cost of feeding servants all cause unemployment; unemployment, in the absence of charity or welfare, leads directly to crime; and criminals, when caught, are executed. More argues that capital punishment will not deter crime because he has placed it within a causal chain that capital punishment does not break. Much later, Sir Thomas Smith, in his *Discourse of the Commonweal of this Realm of England* (1581) uses a clock as an analogy for the workings of the economy: "as in a clock there may be many wheels, yet the first wheel being stirred it drives the next, and that the third, and so forth until the last, that moves the instrument that strikes the clock." The laden

---

49. Y:183; C:183.
50. Robinson, p. 90.

gallows of England are for More the result of just such a clockwork mechanism, and it is perhaps no coincidence that a clock is proudly on display in Holbein's drawing of More and his family.[51]

More's originality as a social theorist does not lie simply in the fact that he sees society as an interlocking and interacting mechanism. One of his most important contributions is his inquiry into the workings of one particular mechanism, that of the market. Something of More's importance was apparent to Joseph Schumpeter when he wrote his universally respected *History of Economic Analysis*. Unfortunately, the work was published from Schumpeter's posthumous papers, and by some peculiar editorial quirk the discussion of *Utopia* was placed long after that of other sixteenth-century texts. As far as More scholarship has been concerned, it might as well never have been published.[52]

What Schumpeter noticed was that More invented the word *oligopolium* or "oligopoly." It first appears in English in Lupton's edition of *Utopia* (1895), and soon after it begins to appear in the writings of economists. To come up with the concept of oligopoly you need to think quite hard about markets, yet More has no significant tradition of political economy to look back on, and it is almost a century—some would say longer—before one develops. How do we explain this? One might argue that there are four intellectual preconditions for economic analysis: the idea of a law of nature (or, broadly speaking, a mechanistic worldview); a preoccupation with progress; a respect for statistics; and an economic system in which the price of labor is set by market forces, for only in such a system can all the costs of production be accessible to analysis. These preconditions began to be met in seventeenth-century England and could not be met in any slave or serf economy; hence the impossibility of economic theory in classical Greece or Renaissance Europe.[53]

Hythloday stresses that the price of labor in England was set by legislation, not free bargaining (p. 157). This alone might seem to place a developed market theory outside More's grasp. But More's economic thought did not begin with his account of England, but with his account

---

51. Neal Wood, *Foundations of Political Economy: Some Early Tudor Views on State and Society* (Berkeley: University of California Press, 1994), pp. 213–14, 298.

52. Joseph A. Schumpeter, *History of Economic Analysis* (New York: Oxford University Press, 1954), pp. 207–8, 305, 979.

53. For these preconditions, see Moses Finley, "Aristotle and Economic Analysis" (1970), in Finley, ed., *Studies in Ancient Society* (London: Routledge and Kegan Paul, 1974), pp. 26–52, 46–47, 48–49, 50–52; and Finley, *The Ancient Economy* (Berkeley: University of California Press, 1973), pp. 23–26.

of Utopia. There all costs of production are in the end labor costs. And, since labor is an obligation of all, economizing on labor has the same pervasive significance that economising on costs of production has within a capitalist economy. Labor is not, as in slave and serf societies, primarily a mark of low status; rather, it is an investment of effort. When he turns to England, then, More is keen to identify factors that distort the rational operation of the economy, and (even if his conception of a rational economy is very different from that of a modern economist, since his primary concern is not profitability but the welfare of the population in general) oligopoly quickly emerges as a distorting factor, second only (from More's viewpoint) to the profit motive itself. More's originality as an economic theorist needs explanation, and the explanation offered here is that it is a result, not of the proto-capitalist character of the English economy of his day (which was, after all, relatively backward by European standards), but of his Utopian model making. More was able to analyze the working of markets because he could think in mechanistic terms and because he had first imagined a society that had no markets, but that economized on labor.

More's analysis of contemporary England, as voiced by Hythloday, results in a conservative program of reform: ban gambling, pull down enclosures for livestock, abolish oligopolies, train the young in hard work (p. 68). It doesn't take much to see that even such reforms are likely to prove impractical if contemporary society is, as Hythloday claims, a conspiracy of the rich against the poor (p. 157). Even when Hythloday presents himself as a practical reformer, his good judgment seems, to anyone familiar with the full range of his theories, suspect. Thus he recommends that capital punishment for theft be replaced by hard labor; and he is surely right to argue that to have identical punishments for theft and murder is "absurd" because this eliminates any disincentive to commit murder in the course of robbery (p. 70). But isn't it absurd also to introduce hard labor as a punishment in a society where wage laborers already undergo a form of wage slavery (p. 98), where "a laborer, a carter, a carpenter, or a plowman works so hard and unremittingly that a beast of burden could hardly support it" (pp. 156–7), and where unemployment carries with it the prospect of starvation? The Polylerite penal code has hidden preconditions—full employment and an abbreviated working day—yet Hythloday seems oblivious to the impracticality of transplanting it to England. Budé makes the same mistake: he describes *Utopia* as "a nursery garden of fine and useful institutions" (p. 47), as if practices that work in one society can easily be transferred to another.

In Book One of *Utopia* Hythloday offers two contrasting responses to the problem of political reform. First, he complains that reform is impossible because no ruler would take his ideas seriously. Then, he complains that piecemeal reform is in itself pointless: "there is not the slightest prospect of curing the disease or restoring society to true health so long as private property survives. For while you work on eliminating one symptom, you aggravate others" (p. 87). To see society as a causal mechanism is to see that reform does not simply require good intentions. It is not enough to aim at the right objectives; one has to face the fact that resources are scarce and that every intervention has unintended consequences, that the parts of society interlock in such a way that there is no privileged point at which systemic change can begin. Morus and Hythloday have two contrasting responses to this: Morus wants to do what good he can, insignificant and uncertain though it may be; Hythloday wants to preserve his principles and therefore resolves not to engage in practical reform but to stick to theory. Commentators on *Utopia* assume that this debate represents More's dilemma. The options are limited: impractical idealism (Utopianism); practical reformism (imitate the Polylerites, the Achorians, or the Macarians); practical conservatism (tear down the enclosures); hard-headed realism (employ the Zapoletes). More must intend either to recommend one of these options, or, to convey his ambivalence, to dramatize the difficulty of choosing among at least two and perhaps even all four of them. But there is evidence that as he read through what he had written he became persuaded that there was something profoundly unsatisfactory about this way of looking at the problem.

"THE SILENI OF ALCIBIADES"

Erasmus's essay "The Sileni of Alcibiades" is one of the most important of the additions to the 1515 edition of the *Adages*. It was quickly republished because it represents probably the best short introduction to Erasmian Christian philosophy. Its importance for anyone studying *Utopia* lies not in particular ideas that are replicated in *Utopia*, in the way in which Utopian communism and the Zapolete warriors have specific antecedents in the 1515 *Adages;* rather, the importance of "The Sileni of Alcibiades" lies in the fact that it offers a way of thinking about the world and, by implication, a model for how to read and write a text. From it we learn how to read *Utopia*.[54] For it is Erasmus's commentary on this adage that enables us to decipher what one scholar calls the "sphinx-like

---

54. Dominic Baker-Smith, *More's "Utopia"* (London: HarperCollins, 1991), pp. 66–67; Fox, *"Utopia"*, pp. 51, 81 (referring to the discussion of the Silenus statue in *Praise of Folly*, pp. 43–44, itself a passage markedly reminiscent of below, pp. 83–4).

ambiguity [of *Utopia*] . . . which compels the reader to shoulder the burden of interpretation."[55]

A Silenus as described by Alcibiades is a little statue of an ugly figure; open it up and inside one finds a contrastingly beautiful figure. It is therefore two opposite things in one; external and internal viewpoints are completely at odds with each other. Yet both are valid. For Erasmus, Socrates and Christ are Silenus statues: from the outside, or from a worldly viewpoint, they are insignificant, even ugly; but morally and spiritually they are beautiful. But there are also what we may term inverted Sileni. A wealthy and powerful man may be beautiful and glamorous on the outside; but morally and spiritually he may be corrupt and ugly, a Herod or a Pontius Pilate. In Erasmus's view the Church ought to be a Christlike Silenus, but as it has accumulated wealth and power it has become an inverted Silenus statue, with beautiful buildings and cloth of gold concealing a spiritual barrenness.

The image of the Silenus statue implies a conflict over values. The Roman emperor Augustus was worshiped as a deity in his lifetime; yet he is inferior to the publicans and fishermen who followed Christ. To argue that the Church should embrace poverty appears to attack its status, power, dignity, and glory, as well as its riches; only when one has realized that moral status and worldly authority are quite different can one grasp that to deprive the Church of its wealth might be to enrich it spiritually, and that the Church as a result might gain far more than it lost. In later life More turned his own body into a Silenus figure, embodying just such a conflict of values. To the outward eye he appeared as a noble statesman, but beneath his courtier's garb he wore the hair shirt of a hermit.

The Silenus statue also implies that such a conflict entails a radical uncertainty regarding the meaning of words. As Erasmus says, what one person calls bitter another calls sweet; what is life to one is death to another (p. 178). Once one grasps that "all human affairs are like the figures of Silenus described by Alcibiades and have two completely opposite faces,"[56] one realizes there can be no neutral description. From Erasmus's point of view, the wars of Pope Julius II are a disgrace, while the shipwrecks and sufferings of St. Paul are more glorious than the triumphs of Alexander, but there is an alternative description that sees Alexander and even Julius as great statesmen, and St. Paul as the leader of an obscure cult. The Silenus statue implies that every text participates in a debate about how to interpret the world, and that the language in which texts are written is slippery, with the meanings of words (such as "glorious" or

---

55. Baker-Smith, *More's "Utopia,"* p. 243.
56. Erasmus, *Praise of Folly*, p. 43.

"wealthy") constantly liable to turn into their opposites. Descriptions are not only partisan; they are unstable.

Utopia might almost have been written to illustrate this view of language. Two fundamental tensions run through the work. First, Hythloday claims that the test of the validity of his views lies in his direct experience of Utopian institutions (p. 88). But of course, as we know, Utopia doesn't exist. At the heart of *Utopia* lies the problem that it is fiction masquerading as fact.[57] Second, More puts himself into the text as Morus, presents himself as engaged in a discussion with Hythloday, and allows himself to sharply disagree with Hythloday at the ends of both Book One and Book Two (pp. 69, 159). Fundamental to *Utopia*, therefore, is the fact that it is a dialogue in which no one voice establishes itself as reliable and authoritative.[58] Commentators have found the clash of views at the end particularly problematic. Hythloday argues that if people realized where their true interest [*commodum*] lies they would adopt the institutions of Utopia; it is only pride that prevents them from doing so. Morus replies that Utopian institutions are absurd, and that Utopian communism takes away all the nobility, magnificence, splendor, and majesty that (in the popular view) are considered the true ornaments of any nation. Here contemporary society is turned into a Silenus statue: from one point of view it is corrupted by pride; from another it embodies nobility, magnificence, splendor, and majesty. Faced with this Silenus figure, some insist that we are intended to agree with Hythloday; others maintain that we are expected to agree with Morus.[59] It is surely relevant that Erasmus shares Hythloday's contempt for nobility, magnificence, splendor, and majesty and believes that whenever we encounter them we should reverse the values, open the Silenus, expose the alternative. In *Utopia*, it would seem, we are presented with two perspectives on secular power, just as in "The Sileni of Alcibiades" Erasmus had presented two perspectives on spiritual authority.

Fiction and dialogue are not the only sources of ambiguity in *Utopia*. There are a whole series of small-scale disruptive elements, such as the names More chooses to give to Utopian places and institutions, all of

---

57. Elizabeth McCutcheon, *My Dear Peter: The Ars Poetica and Hermeneutics for More's "Utopia"* (Angers, France: Moreanum, 1983).
58. R.S. Sylvester, *"Si Hythlodaeus credimus"*; R.J. Schoeck, "'A Nursery of Correct and Useful Institutions': On Reading More's *Utopia* as Dialogue" [1969], in *Essential Articles*, pp. 281–89.
59. Thomas I. White, *"Festivitas, utilitas, et opes."*

which seem to imply a critical or hostile viewpoint.[60] Another disruptive element is the use of litotes as a recurring rhetorical figure in Utopia.[61] Through litotes one affirms something by denying its contrary, but in the process one creates a field of ambiguity and uncertainty. Imagine, for example, visiting a house where the doormat, instead of saying WELCOME, said NOT UNWELCOME. Such inversions are frequent in *Utopia;* we have already come across the example of the clothing of the Utopians, which is "not unattractive."

Litotes presents difficulties for any translator. The opening words of Book One, where Morus says he was sent to Flanders to negotiate matters *non exigui momenti,* are a good example. Robinson, in the sixteenth century, steps back from the modest and ambiguous formulation of the original, stating that these are "weighty matters and of great importance." For Burnet in the seventeenth they are "some differences of no small consequence." Unlike Robinson, Burnet has preserved the litotes in the original, and with it the ambiguity. Is More saying that as ambassador he was dealing with matters of great importance? Or implying that he was a minor civil servant, dealing with matters that weren't completely insignificant? In *Utopia* the recurring use of litotes serves to figure in rhetorical terms the interpretive ambiguity that Erasmus embodies in the Silenus statue. Through litotes More constantly invites us to question whether Hythloday and Morus are reliable narrators, and to ask ourselves which of their points of view is the one we should adopt.

A similar sort of double coding occurs when we look at specific aspects of Utopian society. This is most obvious in the characterization of the Utopians as both warlike and peaceable. To some readers, what is striking is how they try to minimize bloodshed and to fight only when it is just to do so; to others it seems impossible to have sympathy with bribery, assassination, the use of mercenaries, and the subversion of established governments. Again, we are faced with a Silenus figure. On the one hand we have the values of chivalry, of international law, of the military code of honor; on the other we have the values expressed by Erasmus in "Sweet is war to those who do not know it." The figure would not be interesting if it was not possible to sympathize with both points of view; but at the same time, as soon as we place *Utopia* alongside "Sweet is war" and "The Sileni of Alcibiades" we can see that Erasmus and his close associates, including More, would have preferred bribery to bloodshed. Indeed,

---

60. Alan F. Nagel, "Lies and the Limitable Inane: Contradiction in More's *Utopia,*" *Renaissance Quarterly* 26 (1973), 173–80.
61. Elizabeth McCutcheon, "Denying the Contrary: More's Use of Litotes in *Utopia*" (1971), in *Essential Articles,* pp. 263–74.

Utopia's annotator shows no hesitation over approving of bribery as a way of minimizing bloodshed (p. 109). Only if we read *Utopia* without interrogating our language and values will we conclude (as Fox does) that Utopian methods of warfare are an indictment of Utopian society.[62]

Thus More marshals a whole series of devices—fictionality, dialogue, paradox (peaceable warriors), irony (the reference to public opinion in Morus's final speech),[63] litotes—to construct a text that is riddled with ambiguity whether one looks at it macroscopically or microscopically. In Erasmus's discussion of Silenus statues such double coding always resolves itself in the end into a "right" and a "wrong" viewpoint, and many read *Utopia* assuming that either Hythloday or Morus must be right. Such readers have a stable reference point, which enables them to find their way through the twists and turns of the text. But the Silenus figure also holds out the possibility that our ways of thinking about the world are fundamentally unstable; that even the "right" viewpoint may be parasitic upon the "wrong" viewpoint; that there are some intractable questions that will always be disputed. In such a slippery world a sense of balance may be more important than a sense of direction. Erasmus was confident that where disputes over religion are concerned Christ provides us with a reliable guide; but there is no guarantee that there is a single reference point that enables us to resolve disputes over politics. This is the fundamental problem that More explores in *Utopia*.

TABLETALK

There remains a key to the interpretation of *Utopia* that has been curiously overlooked. Since 1952, when J.H. Hexter published *"Utopia": The Biography of an Idea*, there has been general agreement that More wrote Book Two first; and that Book One is therefore in some sense a commentary on questions raised in Book Two.[64] But in 1965 Hexter announced

---

62. Fox, *"Utopia,"* pp. 61–65. Fox's argument patently breaks down when he compares European and Utopian attitude to diplomatic treaties. He forgets that Utopia is a country, not a region. There is no reason to think the countries neighboring Utopia are better than those of Europe.

63. Baker-Smith, *More's "Utopia,"* p. 208.

64. The first sustained critique of Hexter's approach (which I follow here) will be a forthcoming study by Cathy Curtis. I trust that, despite the strength of her arguments, it will continue to be appropriate to read *Utopia* in the same way that one reads Erasmus's *Adages* and Montaigne's *Essais*, that is, as a text with identifiable layers in which we can trace the author's own response to previous versions of the work.

another important textual discovery, which later commentators have chosen to ignore. He pointed out that the debate in Book One that takes place
in the household of John Morton, Cardinal, Archbishop of Canterbury
and Lord Chancellor, and which takes up almost half that book, appears
to be a later interpolation in the text.[65]

The evidence for this is purely internal, but it is convincing. This is
not just that a discussion between Morus and Hythloday is displaced by a
report of another discussion at another time. Hythloday is right in the
middle of giving a list of reasons why he would not be listened to in the
counsels of princes when he interrupts himself. "First of all, very nearly
all princes are more concerned to deal with military affairs . . . than with
the beneficent arts of peace" (p. 61). Many pages later, he begins to illustrate this point: "Come on, imagine I'm at the court of the King of
France . . ." (p. 77). And then he goes on from war to taxation: "So let's
go on . . . Consider some councillors who have met with their king to discuss novel schemes for accumulating money" (p. 79). Only to conclude,
"Kings have no time for philosophy" (p. 83). It seems clear that More
first wrote a coherent and seamless discussion of the false values that
shape the policies of contemporary governments; then, at the point
where Hythloday is about to embark on his first illustration, he introduced a long digression on a quite different subject: whether councillors
(rather than kings) will listen to good advice.

Most commentators have recognized that something strange happens
at Morton's dinner table, for Hythloday insists his example proves he
won't be listened to, when in fact Morton clearly listens to him with care.
As we shall see, repeatedly in the course of his digression he shows himself to be an unreliable narrator. Most have recognized too that there is
something exceptional about Morton: he is admired by both Morus and
Hythloday, and their respect for him is perhaps the only thing on which
they agree. For Hexter the importance of this lengthy interpolation is
that it is a discussion of England's economic problems, and it looks forward to More's own future career, following in the footsteps of Morton,
as a counselor to kings. But it is worth considering that, while the rest of
Book One was written by early February 1516, this section may well have
been written shortly after Erasmus was More's house guest in August
1516. Certainly we know that More must have written part of *Utopia* after this visit, as the manuscript was not ready for Erasmus to take away

---

65. Y:xxxvii–xxxviii. The Cambridge edition makes no reference to this aspect of
Hexter's account, which has been criticized by Clarence H. Miller, in his review
of the Yale edition, *English Language Notes* 3 (1965–66), 303–9, and by Logan,
Meaning of More's "Utopia," pp. 13–14.

with him.[66] Thus, we should ask if the interpolation not only looks towards More's future, but also represents a response to the first draft of *Utopia*, which grew out of More's conversations with Erasmus and their discussion of More's nearly completed manuscript.

Hythloday's long account of the discussions at Morton's dinner table ends with a dialogue that angered Counter-Reformation readers. It was omitted from Catholic editions, and one might almost form the impression that it is these editions which have been used by twentieth-century commentators, so rare are their references to it. It takes the form of an argument between a "parasite" and a friar. Hythloday introduces it by saying he doesn't know why he is going to tell the story he is about to tell; he ends it both by demonstrating that he has not understood a word the parasite has said (for the parasite has been offering, as Morton realizes, a perfectly sensible development of Hythloday's own views on how to eliminate the causes of crime, while Hythloday thinks he has merely been cracking jokes), and by claiming that his story shows that if he offers good advice he will be banished or treated with scorn, when in fact the only person who has been banished and treated with scorn is the parasite. If there is a single moment in *Utopia* when Hythloday's reliability as a narrator is in doubt it must be here, and our suspicions must be intensified when we note that this is very nearly the only point in *Utopia* where the Bible is quoted, and that the parasite is also a *morio* (an unusual word in Latin, where it appears as an import from Greek), a fool or jester. At once we should be reminded of Erasmus's *Encomium moriae* and should expect to find in the fool a third alter ego for More, alongside the characters of Hythloday and Morus. We should expect to find ourselves in the world of praiseworthy folly, the world of "The Sileni of Alcibiades."

What is the point of the dispute between the friar and the fool? The fool has no time for charity; but he knows how to eliminate poverty. He attacks the friar, but quotes the Gospel on being patient—indeed, these are his last words. He stands his ground with the friar, but leaves at a mere nod from the cardinal. He speaks sense, but Hythloday thinks he speaks nonsense. His fate illustrates what were probably the last words More wrote in writing the main text of *Utopia*, at a moment when he was considering the offer of a place at court: "Don't you think that if I proposed wise laws to any living ruler, and tried to pull out of his soul the pernicious weeds of evil views, I wouldn't be thrown out on the spot, or else turned into a laughingstock?" (p. 77)

---

66. More himself tells us that his introductory letter to Giles is a late addition (*Selected Letters*, 73), but this, one might think, could have been sent on after a completed text, if one had existed.

The fool, I would suggest, is a test of our ability to engage in the trans-
valuation of values More and Erasmus demand of their readers. Morus is
an ambassador, and proud of it, engaged in business *non exigui momenti*.
Hythloday is a philosopher, and proud of it, prepared to place himself on
a par with Plato. The fool merely makes jokes, and jokes that invite people to laugh at him rather than with him; no one gives him credit for the
clever remarks he does make. The fool is even a *furcifer*, a "gallows-bird,"
caught up in a discussion of capital punishment, someone worthy of cru-
cifixion (for the *furca* is a fork-shaped gallows, comparable to the cross).
Thus the friar and the fool are a Silenus statue, offering two contrasting
readings of the Bible. The one claims to be a follower of Christ, but is in
fact irascible, ill-educated, and quick to appeal to papal authority. The
other presents himself as a mere jester, but quoting Scripture is "just the
sort of thing he was good at" (p. 75).

Most readings of *Utopia* see More as offering us a choice between
Hythloday and Morus; some believe we are supposed to choose one,
some the other, but nearly all agree that this is the choice we are offered.
This is not a choice of which Erasmus would have approved. Reading
Utopia in August 1516, before More had made his final revisions, he
would surely have protested that Morus embodies worldly wisdom, and
Hythloday philosophical wisdom, but neither embody Christian folly.
The passage our *morio* quotes from Luke, by contrast, falls in the middle
of a discussion of how Christ's kingdom is not of this world and Christians must bear persecution—"And ye shall be hated of all men for my
name's sake. But there shall not an hair of your head perish. In your patience possess ye your souls."—and shortly before a passage that much
preoccupied Erasmus around this time, in which Christ tells his followers
"he that hath no sword, let him sell his garment, and buy one," a passage
that Erasmus took to be about spiritual warfare.[67] By bringing us to this
text in the Bible More intends to remind us that, if Plato's Republic and
Hythloday's Utopia are nowhere, the kingdom of heaven is by contrast a
reality, and our citizenship of that kingdom is more important than anything else. Only if we remember this can we be patient when facing the
corruption and exploitation of this world. More's final act in writing
Utopia was to turn from politics to theology, from political reform to spiritual salvation, from wisdom to folly, from Hythloday to Erasmus.

The text Erasmus received in September must have seemed to him a
great improvement on the text that had been waiting for him in August.
The attack on enclosures, which has impressed generations of later read-

---

67. Erasmus, *Praise of Folly*, 121–22; below, p. 181; E:128.

ers, would have interested him, but the "merry dialogue" between the friar and the fool, which has seemed curiously beside the point to later readers (as it did to Hythloday), would have fascinated him.[68] Our mistake lies in assuming that More had a higher opinion of ambassadors and philosophers than he had of jesters and fools; and we make this assumption because we have failed to open the Silenus and discover that political authority and intellectual status are of no account. Our mistake is to rely on our sense of direction, to idealize the forward-looking narrative of a developing career, rather than on our sense of balance, on our ability to possess our souls in patience.

TOLERATION

Hythloday's description of Utopia ends with an account of Utopia's religions, and like More I have left religion until last. More must have felt that no account of a new-found land would be complete without a discussion of the indigenous people's response to Christianity. But if Utopia embodies Erasmian and Christian ideals, there is no way in which More can make the Utopians Christian. He therefore invents for Utopia a rational religion, which, if it is without the Bible and the sacraments, nevertheless contains no trace of idolatry. And, as in the rest of their lives, so in their religions the progressive character of the Utopians is apparent; for "slowly over time they are abandoning the present variety of superstitions, and uniting in one religion, which seems more rational than all the others" (p. 145). They even welcome Christianity, perhaps because "Christianity seemed to them very similar to the religion that is most popular among them" (p. 145).

In constructing a religion for Utopia More had to step away from the Erasmian texts, which had anchored so much of what he had to say about his ideal society. Above all, there was nothing Erasmus had written prior to 1516 that required him to make Utopia a society in which "every individual should be free to follow the religion of his or her choice" (pp. 146–7). But at the same time, in doing so he stayed faithful to Erasmian principles. Just how successful he was in this is apparent from a remarkable passage Erasmus silently added to "Sweet is war" in 1523, while Europe was dividing into supporters and opponents of the Lutheran Reformation, and it was apparent that religious divisions were liable to become a major cause of military conflict. Valiantly, Erasmus continued to

---

68. He seems to have wanted to imitate More's dialogue. The next edition of the *Adages* contained a number of comparable passages, which he specifically drew to More's attention (*Collected Works*, vol. 5, p. 402).

seek to bring peace between the warring religious camps, as Utopus had brought peace to his island.[69]

"It will be easier to reach agreement on a few things," he writes, "and concord will be more easily maintained if on most questions each is free to understand things in his own way, so long as it is without contention." It is tolerance (beginning with St. Paul's conversion of the Gentiles) that made the spread of Christianity possible: "If the early messengers of the Gospel had been of the same mind towards us [Gentiles] as we are to the Turks, where should we be now—we who are Christians because of their forbearance?" His religion is not a religion of sacraments but of moral conduct: "The end and aim of the faith of the Gospel is conduct worthy of Christ." But this is precisely what is not to be found in the contemporary Church, with its wealth, its secular power, its pervasive corruption, and, worst of all, its persecuting spirit.

Erasmus is prepared to pursue this line of thought to a remarkable conclusion: "Those whom we call Turks are to a great extent half-Christian, and probably nearer true Christianity than most of our own people."[70] Utopians, Protestants, and Turks are, as far as Erasmus is concerned, closer to true Christianity than most Catholics because they are less corrupt. Unlike many Catholics (Erasmus is thinking of Pomponazzi's *On the Immortality of the Soul* of 1516), they genuinely believe in the immortality of the soul. They are untainted by idolatry and do not imagine they can buy an exemption from God's justice, as Catholics purchase indulgences. One can easily imagine Erasmus concurring with Budé's view that the heathen Utopians "have adopted genuine Christian customs, and an authentic wisdom in both public and private life" (p. 45), and with the view that the Utopians, "far more than the nominal Christians of Europe, have succeeded in establishing a truly Christian commonwealth."[71]

Thus in calling for toleration for Turks and Protestants, Erasmus re-

---

69. On Erasmus's position in 1523 see Henry Kamen, *The Rise of Toleration* (London: Weidenfeld and Nicolson, 1967), pp. 24–28; Joseph Lecler, *Toleration and the Reformation*, 2 vols. (New York: Association Press, 1960), vol. 1, pp. 127–29.

70. E:136, 134, 135. The interpolated passage runs from "In the same way" to "Up and at the Turks!" and then from "There are so many mendicant Orders" (E:134) to "without contention." (E:136). It first appears in *Adagia* (Basel: Froben, 1523), pp. 734–35.

71. This was Quentin Skinner's view in 1978, but not in 1987; see "Sir Thomas More's *Utopia,*" p. 151.

stated the principles of toleration propounded in *Utopia*.[72] If much of *Utopia* reflected views Erasmus had expressed in 1515, when it came to toleration More foreshadowed the views Erasmus would come to hold, while More himself, by contrast, was to play a major and enthusiastic part in the persecution of the nascent Protestant Church in England.[73] Even when it addressed questions Erasmus himself had not yet had occasion to address, *Utopia* was a book written in the spirit of Erasmus.

In many respects, indeed, *Utopia* was a prescient text, but one which looked towards a more distant future: a future of economic analysis and material prosperity, of democracy and social equality, of toleration and multiculturalism. The genre More had invented enabled him to place at the center of his text themes that were marginal to the culture of his day but have come to be foundational for us. But, apart from writing *Utopia*, More did nothing to bring this future into being, while Erasmus inspired a generation, and continued to be widely influential as long as Latin was the common language of the educated. If *Utopia* is now far more widely read than anything Erasmus wrote, his name still deserves to be linked to More's, for his commitment to the views expressed by Hythloday went far deeper than More's. Indeed, as we listen to Hythloday, it is Erasmus's voice we hear, for *Utopia* is best read as a dialogue between two friends who were soon to go separate ways.[74]

THE COURT

In the spring of 1516, More, who was writing Book One of *Utopia* in his spare time, went out of his way each morning to greet Thomas Wolsey, cardinal and chancellor, at Westminster Hall.[75] He was unashamedly seeking preferment and was described as "haunting" the court.[76] In 1517 he became a member of the king's council.[77] In the spring of 1518 Eras-

---

72. "It is impossible to read these words without thinking of the *Utopia*," writes Margaret Mann Phillips (E:136). She appears not to have realized that they date to 1523, not 1515.

73. J.A. Guy, *The Public Career of Sir Thomas More* (New Haven: Yale University Press, 1980), esp. pp. 103–11, 164–74.

74. On *Utopia* as an implicit critique of Erasmianism, see Dermot Fenlon, "England and Europe: *Utopia* and Its Aftermath," *Transactions of the Royal Historical Society*, 5th series, 25 (1975), 115–36.

75. Peter Ackroyd, *The Life of Thomas More* (London: Chatto and Windus, 1998), pp. 176–77.

76. Erasmus, *Collected Works*, vol. 5, p. 239.

77. Here, as with Erasmus's movements in 1516, scholars do not agree on exact

mus described him as "entirely absorbed by the court" and regretted that "meanwhile there is no news out of Utopia to make us laugh."[78] In June 1521 he described More wryly as so successful at court "that I am sorry for him."[79] For Erasmus had never aspired to be a Morton or a Wolsey, but this was now, it would seem, More's ambition. More had become Morus, and his friendship with Erasmus could not survive the transformation. He had introduced a fool into *Utopia* so that it would faithfully portray the values of the Erasmian adages from which he had taken his inspiration, but he was turning away from those values himself. In "Sweet is war" Erasmus explained that this saying could be used to warn against other dangerous undertakings:

> There are some things in the affairs of men, fraught with dangers and evils of which one can have no idea until one has put them to the test.
> How sweet, untried, the favour of the great!
> But he who knows it, fears it. [Horace]
> It seems a fine and splendid thing to walk among the nobles at court, to be occupied with the business of kings, but old men who know all about the matter from experience are glad enough to deny them-selves this pleasure. It seems delightful to be in love with girls, but only to those who have not yet felt what bitter there is in the sweet. In the same way this idea can be applied to any enterprise carrying with it great risks and many evils, such as no one would undertake unless he were young and without experience.[80]

More would soon discover that the service of Henry VIII involved great risks and many evils, but at the end it provided him with an opportunity to rediscover his identity as a fool, prepared to die for a principle that meant nothing to most of his contemporaries. If the statesman, the phi-losopher, and the fool all represented disparate parts of his divided self, he seems to have found at last in the final part he played, that of Christian martyr, an ideal to which he could commit the whole of his being.[81]

---

dates, but their differences do not affect the main picture. I follow Guy, *The Public Career*, p. 8.

78. Erasmus, *Collected Works*, vol. 5, pp. 389, 410.

79. Erasmus, *Opus epistolarum*, ed. P.S. Allen, vol. 4 (Oxford: Clarendon Press, 1922), p. 506

80. E:107; AC(1515):576.

81. See Stephen Greenblatt, *Renaissance Self-Fashioning from More to Shake-speare* (Chicago: University of Chicago Press, 1980), pp. 11-73.

FURTHER READING

The best Latin and English edition of *Utopia* is now that edited by George M. Logan, Robert M. Adams, and Clarence H. Miller (Cambridge: Cambridge University Press, 1995). The outstanding modern critical accounts of *Utopia* are (in chronological order): J. H. Hexter, *More's "Utopia": The Biography of an Idea* (Princeton: Princeton University Press, 1952); Stephen Greenblatt, *Renaissance Self-Fashioning from More to Shakespeare* (Chicago: Chicago University Press, 1980), pp. 11-73; George M. Logan, *The Meaning of More's "Utopia"* (Princeton: Princeton University Press, 1983); Quentin Skinner, "Sir Thomas More's *Utopia* and the Language of Renaissance Humanism," in *The Languages of Political Theory in Early-Modern Europe*, ed. Anthony Pagden (Cambridge: Cambridge University Press, 1987), pp. 123-57.

Particularly helpful are also *Essential Articles for the Study of Thomas More*, R. S. Sylvester and G. P. Marc'hadour, eds. (Hamden, Conn.: Archon Books, 1977); Dominic Baker-Smith, *More's "Utopia"* (London: Harper Collins, 1991); and Alistair Fox, *"Utopia": An Elusive Vision* (New York: Twayne Publishers, 1993). On *Utopia* and the *Adages* there is my own "Friendship Portrayed: A New Account of *Utopia*," *History Workshop* 45 (1998), 25-47. The earliest and most influential biography of More is that by his son-in-law, William Roper, of which there are many editions; the modernized text in *Two Early Tudor Lives*, Richard S. Sylvester and Davis P. Harding, eds. (New Haven: Yale University Press, 1962) may be particularly recommended. The most recent is that by Peter Ackroyd (London: Chatto and Windus, 1998).

Three key texts by Erasmus in translation are *The Education of a Christian Prince*, Lisa Jardine, ed. (Cambridge: Cambridge University Press, 1997); *Praise of Folly*, A. H. T. Levi, ed. (Harmondsworth: Penguin Books, 1993); and a selection of the *Adages* in Margaret Mann Philips, *The "Adages" of Erasmus* (Cambridge: Cambridge University Press, 1964), abbreviated by the same author in *Erasmus on His Times* (Cambridge: Cambridge University Press, 1967). Of general studies of Erasmus one may note in particular Richard J. Schoeck, *Erasmus of Europe* (Edinburgh: Edinburgh University Press, 1993) and Lisa Jardine, *Erasmus, Man of Letters* (Princeton: Princeton University Press, 1993).

A Note on the Text

Utopia was first published in Louvain in 1516 (under the supervision of Erasmus and Giles), quickly followed by editions in Paris (1517; supervised by Lupset) and Basel (March and November 1518; supervised by Erasmus). The first of the Basel editions, by the great scholar-printer Johann Froben, appears to have been based on corrections made by More himself. The standard modern editions (both of which provide facing page translations of the Latin) are *The Complete Works of St. Thomas More*, vol. 4, E. Surtz, S.J. and J. H. Hexter, eds. (New Haven: Yale University Press, 1965) and *Utopia*, G. M. Logan, R. M. Adams, and C. H. Miller, eds. (Cambridge: Cambridge University Press, 1995). Because I am following the authoritative edition of March 1518, I omit a letter and poem by Desmarez that appeared in the editions of 1516 and 1517 but were dropped in 1518. But, in view of its importance, I have added the letter from More to Giles, which appeared in the 1517 edition but not in later editions. To these I have added one of Erasmus's most important adages, which I have translated from the text of the edition of 1515. Here, the standard modern edition is in the *Opera omnia* (Amsterdam: Elzevier, 1969–). A complete English translation of the *Adages* is in progress in *The Collected Works of Erasmus* (Toronto: University of Toronto Press, 1974–).

As far as corrections to the Latin text of *Utopia* are concerned, I have accepted the proposals of the editors of the Cambridge edition, with the following exceptions (page references to that text): p. 146, n. 20 (I believe *vilis* makes better sense); p. 268, n. 4 (*Exsicentur* should surely be emended to *Exsiccentur*); on p. 172 *setius* is a misprint for *secius*.

A number of Latin poems accompanied *Utopia;* Alison Mark has translated these for me.

A Note on Gendered Language

Latin is a language full of ambiguity where questions of gender are concerned. Pronouns are rare, so one often cannot tell whether the subject of a verb is intended to be male, female, or either. Key words such as *homo* and *puer* have both an exclusive sense in which they refer to males only, and an inclusive sense in which they refer to both males and females. The ambiguities are particularly problematic in *Utopia*, where More advocates what to a contemporary would have seemed an extraordinary degree of equality between the sexes, while at the same time taking it for granted that certain positions of authority are confined to men: we see him catching himself making assumptions that on second thought he felt could not be defended on p. 151. I have therefore opted for gender-neutral language wherever it seems reasonable in the account of Utopia (though it is clear that the language of the Utopians themselves, at least as translated by Hythloday, is not gender-neutral, see p. 137); and I have also (following the best recent authorities) occasionally employed "they" as a third-person singular pronoun of common gender, in order to avoid "he or she."

ON HOW BEST TO ORGANIZE A STATE
AND ON
THE NEWLY DISCOVERED ISLAND OF
UTOPIA

a true jewel of a book,
which is as instructive as it is entertaining

by the famous and eloquent
THOMAS MORE
Citizen and Undersheriff of the
glorious City of London

ERASMUS TO FROBEN

From Erasmus of Rotterdam to his dearest friend Johann Froben, with whom he is united in fatherhood,[1] greetings.

I have always taken great delight in everything written by my friend More, but, until now, I have always somewhat mistrusted my own judgment on account of the extraordinarily close friendship between us. But when I see that learned men are unanimous in agreeing with my own judgment, and find that they admire the superhuman genius of this man even more enthusiastically than I do, not because they love him better but because they understand him better, then I have to take my own assessment seriously, and in the future I will not be afraid to express my own views in public. One can only imagine the extent to which his natural genius would outshine others' if he had received the benefit of an Italian education. Or if he had devoted himself entirely to a life of letters, so that his abilities could mature, as grain ripens and is ready in autumn for harvest. When he was a young man he amused himself writing epigrams—indeed many of them were written when he was still a boy. He was brought up in Britain and has never been abroad, except on two occasions when he was sent by his ruler as an ambassador to Flanders. He has the usual distractions in that he is married and the head of a household. Moreover, he has public duties to perform and is swamped by the demand for his services as a lawyer. On top of all that he is constantly distracted by important affairs of state. One's bound to marvel that he has time to catch his breath, let alone the energy to write books.

This is why I am sending you his *Exercises*[2] and his *Utopia* so that, if you agree, their publication by your press will make them known throughout the world and ensure that they continue to be read by future generations. For the reputation of your company is

---

1. Erasmus was the godfather of Froben's son.
2. Translations of Greek epigrams, which appeared after *Utopia* in the Froben editions.

such that if a book is known to be published by the house of Froben then it is automatically well received by the learned.

Farewell to you, and to your excellent father-in-law, your delightful wife, and your sweet children. Please ensure that Erasmus, the young son we share in common, who was born surrounded by books, is educated through the study of the best of them.

Louvain, 25 August 1517

BUDÉ TO LUPSET

Guillaume Budé to Thomas Lupset of England, greetings.

Dear Lupset, you are the most extraordinarily learned of young men, and have given me reason to be immensely grateful to you by giving me a copy of Thomas More's *Utopia* and thereby diverting my attention towards reading a book that is wonderfully amusing but will also prove useful. For only recently you were begging me to do something that I was in any case more than eager to do, that is, to read the six books *On Keeping Oneself Healthy*, which the physician Thomas Linacre, who is equally outstanding in his knowledge of both Greek and Latin, recently translated out of Galen's works into Latin: such excellent Latin indeed that if all the works of Galen (which I believe embody the whole science of medicine) were so well translated there would cease to be any real need for those training as doctors to learn Greek. I read Linacre's manuscript copy too quickly—I am immensely grateful to you for permitting me to keep it for such a long time—but I believe I profited greatly from this first reading. From the published edition, which you are now carefully seeing through the presses of this city, I am sure that I will gain even greater benefits. So I thought that I was already more than sufficiently obliged to you, when you proceed to give me, as a sort of appendix or supplement to your previous gift, the *Utopia* of More, who is a man of the sharpest intellect with a delightfully original way of expressing himself, and who is a profound judge of human affairs.

I was in the country bustling about, without a moment to catch my breath, supervising my workmen (for from your own experience and the reports of others, you must know that for the last two years I have devoted much of my time to business associated with my country house), but I had More's book with me and kept opening it. And as I read it I was so caught up in it, so excited to learn about the customs and institutions of the Utopians, which certainly set one thinking, that I broke off from taking care of my household responsibilities; indeed I almost abandoned them completely, for I realized that all the skill and effort that goes into one's business is completely worthless, as is all the striving that goes into accumulating more and more wealth.

And yet there is not a single person who does not see and understand that the whole human race is tormented by this quest for wealth: it is as if there were some physical drive that is born with us. One is almost forced to admit that the whole point of the training and skills of both politics and the law is this: to enable people to use a malicious but effective cunning against each other, despite the fact that we are obligated to each other by ties of citizenship, and sometimes of kinship. We are always grabbing, grasping, and gouging, chiseling and cheating, extracting and extorting, fleecing and filching, pinching, purloining, and pilfering, snatching and snitching, shaking down and beating up. We make off with and claim a right to the property of others, sometimes because there is a loophole in the law, and sometimes because the law requires us to.

This is particularly the case in those countries where the two codes of law that are called secular and ecclesiastical have extensively overlapping jurisdictions. It's evident that both codes, whether written or customary, have given credibility to the view that only men skilled in drafting contracts (which are really licenses to take advantage of others, traps laid for unwary fellow citizens), who know how to turn out a well-crafted clause, studded with exemptions and restrictions; only men with remarkable expertise in legal intricacies, always on the lookout for an excuse to litigate, authorities on a disputatious, distorted, and perverse body of law; only men such as these are to be thought worthy of being licensed to practice the craft of justice and equity. Theirs are the only opinions worth having on how to distinguish right from wrong. Moreover—and this is far more important—it is they who have the power and authority to decide what each individual should have, and what they should not have, how much they may have, and how long they may have it. This is the common-sense view, but common sense has taken leave of its senses. Most men see the world through the bleary eyes of ignorance; they might as well be blind. We think people have been treated with perfect fairness if they have received everything the law says is unquestionably theirs, and everything on which it says they have a claim.

But if we chose to demand rights that are in accord with the truth and with the principle of evangelical simplicity, then there is no one so stupid that they do not understand, no one so dumb that they will not admit, at least if pressed, that justice and the spiritual law (as embodied in papal decrees, both nowadays and as far back as one cares to go), and justice and the principle of equity (as embodied in secular law and the decrees of rulers) are as much at odds as the decrees of Christ, who created humankind and society, and the practices of his disciples on the one hand, and on the other the decrees and rulings of those who think that the height of human happiness and the good that exceeds all others is to be found in the treasure chests of Croesus and Midas. If you intend the term "justice" to mean what it meant for classical authors, that is, the authoritative principle that gives each person what they are entitled to have, then you will find no remnant of justice in our public life, or (if I may be permitted to put it bluntly) the only place you will find equity is in the kitchen when the meal is being dished up. There's no choice but to admit this is true, whether you look at the behavior of those who are in authority, or at the attitude that citizens and subjects show towards each other.

It is true that it is generally held that our contemporary legal system derives from a form of justice that is closely related to it but is as old as the world, which is called the law of nature. According to this law, the more successful people are at getting their own way the more they should own, and the more they own the more they should be deferred to by their fellow citizens. The result is that there is a consensus among nations that people who are incapable of helping their fellow citizens and subjects by exercising any exceptional skill or effort should (providing they are expert in those contractual knots and binding clauses by which they establish a claim to the rightful inheritance of others) have incomes equal to thousands of citizens', often equal to or exceeding the incomes of whole cities, and should be addressed with respect as trustworthy, as prudent, and as remarkable accumulators. This happens in every age, in every type of society, no matter what its customs, among peoples of all sorts, once they have agreed on the basic principle that someone should have supreme authority and the highest reputation if they have accumulated the greatest wealth for themselves and their heirs. And the situation steadily deteriorates as each generation of heirs struggles to increase the inheritance they have received from their ancestors by amassing further wealth, while at the same time going to any lengths to exclude not only distant relatives and relations by marriage but also kindred and close relations from any share in the family's wealth.

But Christ, the founder and governor of all property, left a Pythagorean community of property and mutual respect in existence among his followers, and he confirmed his position by an unambiguous warning, when Ananias was sentenced to death for breaking the law of communal property.[3] By this ordinance Christ seems to me to have repealed, at least as far as Christians are concerned, the whole body of secular law, which is collected into so many wordy volumes, and the more recent mass of ecclesiastical law. Yet it is this law which at present claims to be the embodiment of wisdom and which determines our destinies.

But the island of Utopia, which I hear is also called Udepotia,[4] by some marvelous stroke of luck, is reported (if we believe what we are told) to have adopted genuine Christian customs and an authentic wisdom in both public and private life, and to have preserved them undefiled until the present day. It has achieved this by strenuously defending three divine principles: equal distribution of both good and evil things among her citizens (or, if you prefer, unconditional citizenship for all); a constant and steadfast love of peace and tranquillity; and contempt for gold and silver. One might say these are three fishing nets, which catch every fraud, swindle, cheat, imposture, and deception. If only the gods would employ their powers to ensure that these three principles of the Utopian legal system were attached by screws of firm and settled conviction in the minds of all human beings. Immediately you would see pride, greed, and inane competition struck down and dying, along with almost all the other deadly weapons employed by our sulfurous enemy. The immense mass of all those law books, which captivate so many brilliant and reliable minds throughout their lives, would be left as meaningless rubbish for the worms to gnaw on, or else used as wrapping paper by shopkeepers.

In heaven's name, in what way were the Utopians exceptionally holy, so that they deserved such a divine blessing, that the one place avarice and greed were neither able to force their way in nor insinuate themselves was that island, even though centuries went by? Why were they unable to drive out and expel justice and modesty with their shameless impudence? If only the supreme deity had been as kind in his treatment of those parts of the world which have taken his sacred name as their own and are devoted to him! Then avarice, which depraves and destroys so many minds that would otherwise have been eminent and admirable, would leave for ever, and the golden age of Saturn would return. One might even feel

---

3. Acts 5:1–5.
4. Or "Neverland."

forced to conclude that perhaps Aratus and the first poets were mistaken when they said justice had abandoned the earth and claimed she had taken up residence in the Zodiac.[5] If we are to believe Hythloday[6] she must have stayed behind on the island of Utopia and cannot yet have reached the heavens.

I have discovered as a result of my own investigations that Utopia lies beyond the limits of the known world. It is surely one of the Fortunate Isles, which may lie close to the Elysian Fields[7]— Hythloday, as More himself says, has not yet told us exactly where it is located. It is divided into numerous different cities, but they all unite or cooperate in one community called Hagnopolis,[8] a community comfortable with its own customs and possessions, blessed with innocence and leading what we might call a heavenly life— Utopia is not in heaven, it is true, but it is certainly far superior to the muck that pervades the known world, which, while its inhabitants bustle about, as vigorous and agitated as they are futile and ineffectual, is being violently and impetuously swept away into the abyss.

We owe our knowledge of this island to Thomas More, for it was he who let our generation know about this illustration of a happy way of life, this example of how to live, although he reports that it was found by Hythloday, to whom he attributes all the credit. So if Hythloday designed the society of Utopia, and constructed its customs and institutions, borrowing from Utopia and bringing home to us the essence of a happy life, More has certainly made that island and its holy institutions famous through his impeccable style and his astonishing eloquence. It is he who perfected the city of the Hagnopolitans so that it serves as a standard or measure. He added all those details which give beauty, grace, and authority to this superb book, even if he claims that his own role in carrying out this project was merely that of a craftsman. It would seem that he scrupled to claim a more important role for himself in case Hythloday might have grounds to sue him, claiming he had been deprived of the glory that would have been his had he decided to give his own

---

5. Aratus was a poet of the third century B.C.E., according to whom the goddess of justice had fled the earth and become the constellation we know as Virgo.
6. "Peddler of Nonsense."
7. Both are places the ancients believed to be inhabited by the virtuous dead.
8. "City of the Pure."

account of his labors, because More had plucked glory's buds before they had flowered and harvested fame before it was ripe. *It was his fear that Hythloday, who was voluntarily living on the island of Udepotia, would return one day and be angered and irritated by More's having unfairly left him only the rind of the reputation he should have had for his discovery. Such an anxiety is typical of wise and virtuous men.*[9]

More is a man of reputation, who can be confident of his own considerable authority, but it is the testimony of Peter Giles of Antwerp that makes me accept his story without question. Though I have never met him and will leave aside any commendation of his learning and his character, I love him because he is the most intimate friend of Erasmus, that most distinguished of men, who has contributed so much to the study of every sort of literature, including both the sacred and the secular, for I number Erasmus among my own friends as a result of the correspondence there has been between us.

Farewell, my dearest Lupset. Take the first opportunity you can find to convey my greetings to Linacre, either in person or by letter. He is an outstanding representative for Britain in everything which concerns scholarship, though I hope we can now think of him as no more yours than ours. Indeed, he is one of the select few whose approval I would like to have if I possibly could. When he was here both I and my friend and intellectual collaborator Jean du Ruel were very impressed with him, and I will always have a very high opinion of his excellent learning and painstaking hard work.

Please also give my regards to More, either, as I said before, in person or by letter. I have long thought and often said that he is someone whose name is recorded in a position of honor in Minerva's[10] ledger, but now I particularly love and admire him for his account of Utopia, an island in the New World. For our own time and in times to come his account will serve as a nursery garden of fine and useful institutions. From it we will be able to import tried and tested practices and adapt them for use in our own societies. Farewell.

Paris, 31 July [1517]

---

9. This passage is in Greek in the original.
10. The Roman goddess of wisdom.

POEMS OF UTOPIA

A poem of six lines on the Island of Utopia, written by
Anemolius,[11] Poet Laureate, and Hythloday's nephew by
his sister:

"No-Place" I once was named, by reason of my solitude;
But now I rival Plato's state, perhaps exceed her, for
What he sketched out in words, that I alone exemplify
In men and skills, and the most excellent laws:
By the name of "Happy-Place"
I do deserve to be called.

A quatrain in the language of Utopia:

Utopus ha Boccas peu la chama polta chamaan.
Bargol he maglomi baccan soma gymnosophaon.
Agrama gymnosophon labarem bacha bodamilomin.
Volvala barchin heman la lavolvala dramme pagloni.

This is a literal translation of these lines:

General Utopus made me, from no island, an island.
I alone of all lands, in the absence of philosophy
Have represented for mortals the philosophical city.
Willingly I will share what is mine, without reluctance accept
    something better.

[1516]

---

11. From the Greek for "windy."

GILES TO BUSLEYDEN

To that most distinguished gentleman, Jerome de Busleyden, Provost of Aire and Councillor to the Catholic King Charles, from Peter Giles of Antwerp.

Most eminent Busleyden, a few days ago Thomas More (who is, as you will certainly agree, for you know him extremely well, the most remarkable ornament of our times), sent me his *Island of Utopia*. Utopia is a place that very few people have known about until now, but it more than anywhere is a country about which everyone ought to know, for it far excels Plato's ideal society. And it is all the more interesting because it has been described by someone so extraordinarily eloquent that it is as if we had a painting rather than a description, as if we could see it with our own eyes. Every time I read it I seem to see Utopia more vividly than I did when I listened to Raphael Hythloday himself speak about it—for I was just as present during his narration as More himself.

Indeed Hythloday's own account proved him to be a man endowed with a quite unusual capacity for self-expression, for it was quite obvious that he was not simply repeating things that he had learned from the accounts of others, but describing what he had seen close up with his own eyes and experienced as a result of living there for a considerable period of time. In my judgment Raphael is someone with more experience of different parts of the world, of different peoples, and of different ways of doing things even than Ulysses himself. I don't believe there has been a single person comparable to him born in the course of the last eight hundred years. In comparison to him Vespucci might be thought to have seen nothing at all. Leaving aside the fact that we can give a better description of things we have seen ourselves than of things we know only at second hand, Raphael had a particular talent for describing things.

But when I look at the very same things as More has painted them I am so moved that I sometimes imagine I am living in Utopia myself. Goodness me, despite the five years he lived there, I can easily believe that Raphael himself saw less while he was on that is-

land than one is able to see from More's description of it. One
comes across so many remarkable things in the course of his description that I am left in doubt as to what I should find most remarkable or should single out for mention. Perhaps I should stress
the reliability of his superb memory, which enables him to repeat
almost word for word so many things that he had heard only once;
or his intellectual grasp, which enables him to understand the origins (completely concealed from ordinary observers) of all the evils
that occur within societies, and of all the good that might occur; or
else the vigor and forcefulness of his language, which combines
such purity of Latin style, such liveliness of manner, and such
abundance of information. These qualities are all the more remarkable in someone who is constantly distracted by official commitments and private business. But of course you will find all this
somewhat less astonishing, my learned Busleyden, since you already know him to be, as a result of your close relationship to him,
a man of more than human, indeed almost divine, intelligence.

Obviously he has left nothing out that I could usefully add to
what he has written. I have merely taken the trouble to add four
lines of poetry written in the language of Utopia, which Raphael
happened to show me after More had parted from us. It follows a
transcription of the Utopian alphabet, and I have also added some
brief annotations in the margins.

More seems embarrassed not to be able to report the location of
the island. Raphael made no attempt to conceal it, but he did mention it only briefly and incidentally, as if he was saving it for another time. And then unfortunately neither of us took in what he
did say. For while Raphael was talking about it one of More's servants came over and whispered something or other in his ear. Of
course I listened all the more carefully, but one of the people present, who had, I think, caught a chill while at sea, coughed so
loudly that he prevented me from hearing some of what Raphael
was saying. But I will never be satisfied until I am fully informed
about its location, so that I'll not only be able to tell you roughly
where it is, but even be able to tell you its exact latitude—assuming
our friend Hythloday is still alive to tell me. For there are differing
accounts as to what has happened to him, and all are unreliable.
Some say that he died in the course of his travels. Others say he returned safely to his homeland, but both because he could not stand
the way of life there and because he was unable to settle because he
missed Utopia, he left and set out to return there.

You may be puzzled why the name of this island can't be found anywhere in the works of the geographers, but Hythloday had an entirely satisfactory explanation for this. It's perfectly possible, he said, that it was known to the ancients by a name that was later changed. Alternatively, they never did learn about the existence of this island. For during the last few years we seem to have been constantly bumping into new lands that were unknown to the cartographers of the past. In any case, there seems no point in constructing additional arguments to make this story credible: More's word should be good enough for anyone.

It is true he was uncertain whether to publish his account, but I attribute this hesitation to his modesty and regard it as praiseworthy. I have taken the view that it is a book which for all sorts of reasons doesn't deserve to be hidden away any longer; if any book deserves to be made available to the public this one does; and it is particularly appropriate that your name should serve to recommend it to a wider world. You are especially well placed to judge of More's fine qualities, and there is no one better qualified than you to give advice on how to govern. For you have devoted many years to advising your ruler and have acquired a remarkable reputation for great wisdom and unblemished integrity. Farewell, you who are a true patron of learning and an ornament of our age.

Antwerp, 1 November 1516

MORE TO GILES

Thomas More to Peter Giles

I am almost ashamed, dear Peter Giles, to be sending you this little book about the state of Utopia, now that nearly a year has gone by. I'm sure you thought it would take me six weeks at the outside. After all, you knew there were no painstaking researches involved, and I did not even have to work out how to arrange my materials. All I had to do was repeat what you and I both heard Raphael Hythloday report. There was no point in polishing the prose, for it would have been unrealistic if I had made him speak elegantly. In the first place he spoke without preparation or notes, and in addition he is, as you know, someone who knows more Greek than Latin. So the nearer my own prose came to his casual simplicity, the more accurate it would be. Accuracy is the only thing I ought to be concerned about, and the only thing that concerns me.

I confess, dear Peter, that so much of the work was already done that there was scarcely anything left for me to do. Of course if I had been obliged to think for myself, or to decide how to organize the material, I might have had to invest a good deal of time and effort, even assuming I had the necessary intelligence and learning. And if I had been obliged to produce something that was not merely accurate but eloquent, then I know I couldn't have done it, no matter how hard and long I tried. But I didn't have to worry about any of these problems, over which I might have sweated. All I had to do was straightforwardly report what I had heard: nothing could have been simpler.

Yet it was almost impossible for me to complete even this straightforward task because my other occupations left me without a moment to myself. The law takes up almost all my time. Sometimes I'm acting on behalf of a client, sometimes settling a dispute, either because I've been appointed to arbitrate or because the case has come before me in court. I have to call on some people out of politeness and visit others on business. I'm out almost all day long dealing with other people's concerns, and in the time that's left I get on with my own. There's no time at all left for myself, that is to say for reading and writing.

Even when I return home, I must chat with my wife, amuse my children, and talk to my employees. All these I think of as chores that have to be done. At least they have to be done unless you're prepared to discover that you're a stranger in your own home. In any case, we are all under an obligation to be as pleasant as possible to those with whom we share our lives, no matter whether we are linked to them by blood, by choice, or by chance, provided of course we don't spoil them with kindness, or give our employees so much freedom that they believe they're the ones in charge. So, caught up in my occupations, I've watched days, months, a whole year slip by.

When do I find time to write? I haven't said anything yet about sleeping, which takes up almost half of our lives, or about eating, to which many people devote as much time as they do to sleeping. This is the only time I have to myself, the time I steal from sleeping and eating. There isn't much of it, so it takes me ages to get anything done, but it's enough to enable me to make painful progress.

So at last I'm sending you, dear Peter, my *Utopia*, so that you can read it and correct me if I have left anything out. I'm reasonably confident that you won't find much to criticize: I may not be particularly intelligent or learned, but I'm quite good at remembering things. But I'm not so sure of myself that I'm not prepared to admit that I may have made the occasional mistake. Indeed John Clement, my trainee, who was there with us, as you'll remember (for I wouldn't want him to miss any conversation that might be instructive)—I believe this young man, who has begun to make great progress in Greek as well as Latin, will one day prove that the time I spent on his education was time well spent—anyway, he has made me very concerned that I may not be able to trust my own memory. As I remember it, Hythloday told us that the bridge which spans the river Anydrus at Amaurotum is five hundred yards long. But my John says it's two hundred less than this, and that the river is only three hundred yards wide at that point. I'd be grateful if you would tell me what you remember. For if you agree with him, I'll give way and conclude that I've made a mistake. If you don't remember, I won't change it, but will report what I believe I remember. For I'm prepared to go to great lengths to ensure that nothing in this book is untrue. And if anything is doubtful, I'd rather make an honest mistake than tell what I believe to be a lie: I'd rather be frank than cautious.

Note the theological distinction between a lie and a misrepresentation.

In any case, it should be easy for you to set my doubts at rest, for you only have to ask Raphael himself, either by going to see him or by writing to him. Indeed, it's essential you do so because of another problem that I haven't been able to resolve. I don't know whether to blame myself, or you, or Raphael himself. We forgot to ask, and he forgot to tell us, just where in the New World Utopia is to be found. I'd be prepared to spend a fair amount to make good this omission. In the first place I'm somewhat ashamed not to know even the name of the ocean in which one can find this island about which I've written so much, and secondly there are several people here in England who desperately want to sail to Utopia. The most eager is a devout man, a theologian by profession. He isn't driven by a foolish curiosity to see new things but wants to foster the growth and development of our religion, which has already made a promising start there. To go about this properly, he has decided to ensure that he receives a commission from the pope. Indeed, he wants to be appointed bishop of the Utopians. He isn't embarrassed at the idea of asking for such an appointment, for he believes *Selfless* his motives are religious, and that it is neither ambition nor greed *careerism!* but missionary zeal that drives him.

So I beg you, dear Peter, to get in touch with Hythloday, either in person, if you conveniently can, or by letter if he's left town, and check that my book contains no errors and leaves out nothing important. Perhaps it would be best to show him the book. For nobody else is as well qualified as he to correct any mistakes, and even he can't help me unless he reads through what I have written. Moreover, that way you will be able to find out whether he is pleased that I have written this book, or resents it. If he has decided to write his own book about his adventures, he may not want me to publish. Although I want people to know about this Utopian society, I do not want to rob his own story of the charm and delight that derive from originality.

Indeed, to be frank, I still haven't yet decided whether I am committed to publishing. For people have such varied tastes, and many *Hypercriti-* of them have such twisted characters, such cantankerous intellects, *cal critics* such wrongheaded opinions that it seems foolish to wear oneself out in the attempt to publish something that might in theory be instructive or entertaining, but that in practice will provoke only scorn and ingratitude. It would seem much more sensible to be cheerful and jolly, and to take life as it comes. Most people know nothing about writing; many despise it. The ignoramus rejects as impossibly difficult anything that isn't elementary and commonplace; the pedant dismisses as trivial anything that isn't teeming with obsolete words. Some men enjoy reading only the classics; many only enjoy reading themselves. Here's one so solemn that he can't stand a joke; there's one who likes everything so bland that he can't stand anything that is spiced with wit. Some have a positively *Satiro-* phobic response to satire, just as someone who has been bitten by a *phobia* rabid dog becomes terrified of water. Then there are those who just can't make up their minds. They like one thing when they are sitting down, something quite different when they are standing up.

These people hang out in bars, and, half-drunk, they decide who the real authors are. They condemn any author they feel like by finding fault with his publications. They speak with authority, like bullies mocking weaklings. Meanwhile they take care not to endanger themselves by publishing: since they plan to throw stones, they *Proverb* avoid living in glass houses. These good men are so slick and smooth all over there's not so much as a hair to grab hold of.

Some people are so ungrateful that even if they love a book, it doesn't mean that they are any fonder of the author. They are like *An apt* rude guests who have been entertained at a lavish and sumptuous *comparison* dinner and go home stuffed, without a word of thanks to their host. I'm sure you would love to entertain, at your own expense, people like this: people who have such refined tastes and are such picky eaters; people who always remember a favor and never forget to say thanks!

Anyway, dear Peter, sound out Hythloday as I have asked you to. It still won't be too late for me to change my mind when I know his response. However if he does approve publication it will be a bit late for me suddenly to see sense, since I will already have done all the hard work of writing. So when it comes to deciding the other matters involved in publication I will follow the advice of my friends, and especially yours. Good-bye, Peter Giles, my dearest friend. Give my regards to your excellent wife. Love me as much as you always have done; for my part I am fonder of you than ever.

[1516]

ON HOW BEST TO ORGANIZE A STATE:
A DISCOURSE BY A REMARKABLE MAN,
RAPHAEL HYTHLODAY,
AS REPORTED BY THE HONORABLE THOMAS MORE,
CITIZEN AND UNDERSHERIFF OF LONDON,
BRITAIN'S MOST FAMOUS CITY.

BOOK ONE

Henry VIII, most invincible King of England, who, above all others, is a ruler adorned with all the qualities of a great monarch, recently found himself involved in a dispute with his serene highness, Charles, Prince of Castile, over certain matters of not inconsiderable significance. He sent me to Flanders to negotiate on his behalf in the hope of resolving the conflict. I was to serve as companion and associate to the incomparable Cuthbert Tunstall, whom the king has just created Master of the Rolls, to everyone's immense satisfaction. I will say nothing in praise of Tunstall, not because I fear the opinion of a friend is likely to be dismissed as biased, but because his integrity and learning exceed my powers of description. Moreover, they are too well known wherever one goes for it to *Proverb* be wise to attempt to describe them; I would only be accused of trying to light up the sun with a lantern, as the saying is.

Those selected by the prince to negotiate with us, all distinguished men, met us at Bruges, as had been agreed. Their nominal leader was the mayor of Bruges, a most distinguished man. But the real negotiations were handled by Georges de Themsecke, the provost of Cassel, who is persuasive by nature as well as by training, and completely familiar with the legal issues. He is an exceptional diplomat, because of both his sharp intellect and his extensive experience. After several meetings we had not yet agreed on acceptable terms. So they adjourned the discussions for some days and went to Brussels to obtain further instructions from their ruler.

Meanwhile, I went to Antwerp, still on the same business. While I was staying there one of the people who visited me often—and no visitor was more welcome—was Peter Giles. He is a native of the city, has a fine reputation and a good position, and deserves to go on to even greater things. I hardly know whether to single out his character or his learning for the highest praise. In any event, he is both a fine and a learned man. He is frank with everyone, and in his dealings with his friends he is open-hearted, affectionate, loyal, and sincere. It would be far from easy to find anyone who deserves to be considered his equal in all those characteristics that make a true friend. His modesty is exceptional, and he is quite incapable of hypocrisy. He alone manages to combine frankness with worldly wisdom. Indeed, he is such a charming associate, so innocently entertaining, that the pleasure of his company and the delights of his conversation went a good way towards easing my longing for my country and my home, and even my longing for my wife and children, from whom, by then, I had been separated for more than four months.

One day—I had just attended a service at Notre Dame, a beautiful church crowded with worshippers, and, mass being over, I was on the point of returning to my lodgings—I happened to see him engrossed in conversation with a stranger. His companion was in late middle age, with a sunburned face, a long beard, and with a cloak hung carelessly over his shoulder. Judging by his appearance and the way he was dressed, I guessed he was a ship's captain. Peter, when he caught sight of me, came over and greeted me. I was about to say something, but he drew me to one side and said, "You see that man?" (As he said this he pointed to the man with whom I had seen him talking.) "I was just about to bring him straight over to your place."

"Bring him along," I said. "He'll be very welcome if he comes with you."

"If you knew the man," he replied, "you'd welcome him warmly if he came on his own. For there is not a single person alive today who can tell you as much about unknown peoples and unexplored lands. And I know that you can't hear enough about that sort of thing."

"So," I said, "I wasn't far wrong, for the moment I set eyes on him I guessed he was a ship's captain!"

"Oh no," he said, "you're completely wrong. It's true he's been to sea, but he's more like Ulysses than Palinurus,[12] and even more

---

12. Aeneas's pilot in Virgil's *Aeneid*.

like Plato. Raphael, for that's his name, Raphael Hythloday, knows a good deal of Latin and a great deal of Greek. He's studied Greek more than Latin because his only interest has been philosophy, and he knew that no Roman philosophy of any consequence survives, except for certain essays by Cicero and Seneca. He's Portuguese, but he handed over to his brothers the right to the inheritance that would have been his had he remained at home, and, eager to see the world, signed up with Amerigo Vespucci. He went everywhere with him throughout the last three of his four voyages—the ones that everyone is now reading about.[13] Except, on the last voyage, he did not come home with him. He begged and even threatened Amerigo until he agreed to let him stay behind as one of the twenty-four who were to be left garrisoning a fort at the furthest point to which their journey had taken them. And so he was left behind, which suited him fine, since he was keener to travel than anx-

Apothegm   ious to die at home. There are two sayings he loves: 'The dead are as content to lie under the sky as under the earth,' and 'No matter where you are, you're always the same distance from heaven.' He would have paid a high price for this way of thinking, if God had not looked after him. For after Vespucci had sailed away he traveled through many countries accompanied by five others from the fort. By remarkable good luck he was on a ship that was driven by a storm to Ceylon, and from there he made his way to Calcutta. There it was easy to find a berth on a Portuguese ship, and so he finally returned to his homeland, which he had expected never to see again."

When Peter had told me all this, I thanked him for his kindness towards me, for he was quite right to think I would enjoy talking to such a man. Eagerly I turned to Raphael. When we had been introduced and had said to each other those polite phrases that strangers usually exchange on first meeting, we set out for my house. There in the garden we sat down on a grassy bank and began to talk.

He told us how, after Vespucci had left them behind in the fort as agreed, he and his companions met the local inhabitants and did their best to ingratiate themselves with them. Little by little they won their confidence, until they were not only in no danger living among them but were on friendly terms. The local ruler (I have forgotten his name and that of his country) was well intentioned

---

13. Two accounts of Vespucci's voyages had been published in 1504.

and helpful. Raphael described how he supplied him and his five companions not only with ample provisions for a journey but also with a trusty guide. They traveled by raft along the rivers and by wagon along the roads, bearing with them letters of recommendation to the neighboring rulers. After many days' journey, he said, they found towns and cities, linked together in states, with many inhabitants and decent institutions.

To be sure, south of the equator, and indeed on either side of it for almost as far as the sun is distant from the earth, there lie vast empty deserts, scorched by the perpetual heat. In every direction the view is gloomy and dismal. Nature is wild and uncultivated. There are savage beasts and dangerous serpents, and a few men who are no less savage and dangerous than the creatures they live among. But if you keep traveling, slowly nature becomes more friendly. The climate is less harsh, the sun less scorching, the creatures less predatory. At length you reach civilization again. There are towns and cities that not only trade among themselves and their neighbors by land and sea, but even do business with distant lands.

Once they had traveled far enough south it was easy for them to voyage in any direction and visit innumerable lands, for there was no ship ready to set sail, no matter where it was bound, that did not willingly welcome Raphael and his companions on board. He reported that the first vessels they came upon were flat bottomed. They were propelled by sails stitched together out of papyrus or sometimes of hides, or made of reeds lashed together. Further south they found ships with keels and canvas sails, just like our own. Their sailors could handle wind and wave, but they were immensely grateful to him, Raphael said, for showing them how to make a compass. This was something they had never seen before, so they had never felt at home on the open sea and did not dare travel fearlessly except in summer. Now, because they trust their compasses, even winter weather does not scare them, though one would call them more confident rather than safer. For there is a danger that this device, which it was thought would be of great benefit to them, may, thanks to their inexperience, cost many lives.

It would take many pages to tell you everything Raphael said he saw in each place he visited, and such an account would be out of place in this book. Perhaps I will devote another book to his journeys and report especially on those things he noticed that it would be sensible for us to imitate: I'm thinking particularly of the institutions of nations that share a civilized way of life, and whose intel-

ligent and wise practices might be of use to us. We asked him many
eager questions about such matters, and he answered willingly. But
we didn't ask him about monsters, for they are commonplace. You
can go almost anywhere and find Scyllas, or rapacious Celaenos, or
man-eating Laestrygonians, or other monsters just as remarkable.[14]
But you can travel vast distances without coming across citizens
who have been well and wisely educated. Naturally he told us about
many ill-conceived practices that he had noticed among these new-
found peoples, but he also noticed quite a few that could be copied
in order to solve the problems of our own cities, nations, peoples,
and kingdoms. I will discuss these elsewhere, as I said. Here I plan
to report only what he told us about the customs and institutions of
the Utopians.[15] But first let me relate the conversation that drew
him into a description of that state.

Raphael had been incisively discussing failings in the societies of
both this hemisphere and that (and there are plenty of faults to be
found in both), and had also talked about some of the wise and sensible policies pursued among us and among them. He described the
customs and institutions of each of the peoples he had visited as if
he had lived his whole life among them, and hadn't just been passing through. Peter was astonished. "Dear Raphael," he said, "I
don't understand why you don't attach yourself to some king. I'm
sure there isn't a single ruler who wouldn't welcome you with open
arms. Your learning and your experience of places and of peoples
would surely entertain; but in addition you are well equipped to
provide instructive examples and helpful advice. Do as I suggest,
and you will not only find that your own interests flourish, but you
will be able to be of tremendous assistance in advancing all your
friends and family."

"I don't fret much about the fate of my friends and family," he
replied, "for I believe I have already fulfilled my various obligations
to them reasonably well. Most people don't give away their possessions until they are old and sick; and even then they only hand
them over grudgingly because they can no longer hang on to them.
But I, when I was in the best of health and still young, distributed
my possessions among those close to me. In my view they ought to
be satisfied by this proof of my generosity; they certainly shouldn't

14. Monsters from the *Odyssey* and the *Aeneid*.
15. There has been general agreement since J.H. Hexter's *More's
"Utopia": The Biography of An Idea* (1952) that the rest of Book One is a
later addition to More's original text.

demand, or even expect, that I should sell myself into the service of some king so that they may benefit."

"Fair enough," said Peter, "but I didn't mean you to become a king's servant, merely to be at his service."

"You're playing with words," he replied. "Those who serve are servants."

"But in my view," Peter said, "it's you who's being literal-minded. What I'm recommending is the one policy that will enable you not only to help others—both your friends, and the general public—but also to put yourself in a situation that will make you happier."

"But why would this policy make me happier," protested Raphael, "when I find the thought of it loathsome? As things are, I do as I please. I can't believe there are many king's ministers who could say as much. There's a plentiful supply of people keen to ingratiate themselves with those in power. You needn't think it a great loss if I and a few others like me choose not to compete."

"Well," I said, "it's plain enough, dear Raphael, that you aren't after either wealth or power, and I certainly admire and revere someone who thinks like you every bit as much as I respect those who wield the greatest power. But you must admit that it would be a worthy undertaking for someone as public-spirited as yourself, a true philosopher, to resolve to redirect your intelligence and your energy to public service, even if it did involve some personal sacrifice. And the very best way of doing this would be to become a councillor to some great prince, so that you could urge him to act justly and honestly (for I've no doubt that this is what you'd do). For everything that happens to a people is the result of the actions of their ruler: good and bad flow from top to bottom like water in an uninterrupted stream. Your theoretical understanding is so remarkable that, even if you had no practical experience, you would prove a superb counselor for any ruler; and your practical experience is so extensive that this would still be true even if you had no theoretical understanding."

"Dear More," he replied, "you've made two mistakes. You've misunderstood both me and the nature of political activity. I don't have the skill you attribute to me; and even if I had it in the highest degree, the public would be no better off if I should turn from theory to practice. First of all, very nearly all princes are more concerned to deal with military affairs (of which I have no experience, and no desire to acquire any) than with the beneficent arts of peace. They are much more interested in working out how they can acquire new territories, by fair means or foul, than in learning how to administer well the lands they already own.[16]

"Moreover, those who advise kings, without exception, are either so wise that they don't stand to benefit from anyone else's advice, or else believe themselves so wise that they don't want to listen. Nevertheless, they give their admiring approval to the most ridiculous statements, provided they are made by the ruler's special favorites, hoping their uncritical praise will win them favor. And of course it's in the natural way of things that each person has a good opinion of his own contribution, just as the crow finds his fledgling handsome, and the monkey is charmed by his whelp.

"Imagine a gathering of people, each of whom either envies everyone else or else genuinely believes in his own superiority. A newcomer proposes a policy, which he has perhaps discovered through his reading was successfully employed in the past, or perhaps has seen successfully employed during his travels. Those who heard him would respond as if their entire reputation for wisdom was endangered, as if in future everyone would think they had been exposed as dunderheads unless they could think up something that would demonstrate his proposal to be defective. If they can't think of anything else, then they'll take refuge in saying this: 'Our present policies seemed good enough to our ancestors, and we can only wish that we were as wise as they.' And having delivered this little speech, they'll sit down as if they had advanced an unanswerable argument. As if it would be dangerous indeed were anyone to be discovered to have improved on the thinking of our ancestors on any question! Although of course we don't feel a moment's hesitation in abandoning those of their policies that really worked well. But if it is a question of a problem that they failed to resolve satisfactorily, then we insist on repeating their mistakes, no matter what the consequences. I have often come across such proud, ridiculous and stubborn reasoning; once even in England."

"Goodness," I said, "have you been to my country?"

"I have," he replied, "and I spent several months there. It wasn't long after a dreadful event: the westcountrymen had been engaged in a civil war with their king, and when their revolt was crushed there was a horrific massacre.[17] During my visit I received much kindness from the Reverend Father John Morton, Cardinal Arch-

---

16. This argument is completed below on p. 77. It would seem that at this point More made a late addition to the text (see p. 28).
17. In 1497.

bishop of Canterbury, and at that time also Chancellor of England.[18] He was a man, dear Peter—for More will already know what I am about to say—who not only held high office, but also was truly admirable for his prudence and virtue. He was of medium height and stood up straight, although he was advanced in years. His appearance commanded respect but did not instill fear. He was not difficult to talk to, though his manner was serious and grave. When petitioners appeared before him he liked to speak sharply to them in order to discover whether they were quick-witted and resilient, but he never pressed them too hard. He loved these qualities, perhaps because he himself had them in abundance, providing they were not combined with impudence, and he thought well of those who have them, believing them to be good at getting things done. He spoke eloquently and effectively. He was learned in the law. He was very clever, and his memory was exceptional, even astonishing. He had admirable natural abilities, which he had improved through study and practice. When I was there it seemed evident that the king put considerable store by his advice, and that public policy was shaped by his recommendations. He was still little more than a boy when he was taken straight from school and plunged into the life of the court. He had spent his whole life dealing with affairs of state. The variations of fortune had tossed him perpetually to and fro. He had learned practical wisdom in the conduct of affairs by surviving many and grave dangers, and such wisdom once acquired the hard way is rarely lost.

"One day when I was dining with him, there happened to be present a layman who was an expert in your legal system. I can't remember what set him off, but he began to express well-informed approval for the tough sentences that were currently being imposed on English thieves. He reported that they were being executed all over the place, with as many as twenty being strung up at a time. And yet, he said, he was frankly astonished that when so few escaped the gallows, still for some inexplicable reason, new ones appeared all over the place as fast as the old ones were killed. I spoke up, for I dared to speak freely in front of the cardinal. 'There's nothing to be surprised at,' I said. 'For capital punishment of thieves is contrary to justice and of no benefit to the public. The penalty is too harsh to avenge the crime, and it isn't an effective deterrent. Simple theft is not so dreadful a crime that the criminal

On unfair laws

18. More had served as a page in the household of Morton (1420–1500).

ought to pay with his life; yet there is no punishment severe enough to discourage those who have no other way of putting food on the table. When it comes to punishing crime, you English, along with much of the rest of the world, remind me of bad schoolteachers, who flog their pupils with more enthusiasm than they teach them. Dreadful and terrible punishments are decreed against theft, when it would be much better to ensure that everyone has enough to eat. Otherwise people will face the dreadful prospect of knowing they must steal now and die for it later.'

How to lower the crime rate

"'But we've already seen to that,' he replied. 'They can work as craftsmen or farmers, and thus ensure their own livelihood. If they steal it is because they have freely chosen to be evil.'

"'No,' I said, 'I won't let you get away with that. First, let's put to one side all those who return to their homes crippled as a result of foreign or civil wars, those, for example, who were injured in the battle with the men of Cornwall, and those not long before that who came back from the wars in France. They gave their limbs in the service of king or of country. Now their injuries leave them incapable of following their former trades, but they are too old to start again. I concede we should regard them as exceptions, for wars occur unpredictably and irregularly. Let's concentrate on things that happen every single day. There are great numbers of noblemen who lead a life of leisure, or rather live off the labor of others, like drones. For instance, they raise their tenants' rents until they have reduced them to the barest necessities and no more can be extracted from them. They know how to make other people pinch and save, while they're happy to spend money themselves until they go bust. Wherever they go they are accompanied by a crowd of idle retainers who have never learned any craft by which they could feed themselves. As soon as they fall ill or their master dies they are let go, for those who support the idle refuse to succor the sick, and often the heir is unable to support all his father's employees straightaway. Those let go quickly start starving, unless they start stealing. What else would you have them do? For a life on the road soon wears out their clothes and wears down their health. Before long they are dressed in rags and repulsive with diseases. Noblemen won't stoop so low as to employ them, and the peasants are frightened of them. Rightly too, for they realize that people brought up in idleness and luxury, used to swaggering about wearing a sword and buckler, scowling at everyone they meet and thinking of themselves as a cut above the rest, won't prove good employees for a poor man who needs to put them to work with a pick and shovel, to feed them little and pay them less.'

"'But,' he replied, 'we need to ensure we have a plentiful supply of men of this type. If war breaks out it is they who will be the backbone of the army, for they are bolder and nobler than laborers or farmers.'

"'Actually,' I said, 'you might as well argue that we need to ensure we have a plentiful supply of thieves, for you can be sure that you'll never be short of thieves if you have plenty of these men. Just as thieves make decent soldiers, so soldiers make capable thieves; these two occupations go well together. But this problem, which afflicts England severely, is not yours alone; it is common to almost every nation. In France they suffer from their own, even more dreadful, plague. Even in peace (if you can call it peace) their whole country is overrun with mercenary soldiers, imported for precisely the same reason as that which makes you want to defend the maintenance of idle retainers. Know-it-alls believe the public safety depends on having a strong and reliable army always ready, preferably one made up of veteran soldiers. They don't dare rely on unblooded troops. So they look for excuses to make war in order to harden their soldiers, and men have their throats cut for no reason, for fear that otherwise (to quote Sallust's[19] aphorism) the brain will become slow or the hand clumsy for lack of practice. France has discovered to her cost just how pernicious it is to nurture such creatures, though she could have learned as much from the history of the Romans, the Carthaginians, the Syrians, and that of many other nations. In every case you will find that not only was their system of government destroyed, but their fields were laid waste and even their cities were sacked by their standing armies, not once but again and again. *The evils of standing armies*

"'Moreover, in this case this policy isn't even particularly necessary, for the French soldiers, who have been trained in arms almost since childhood, when matched against your militia, cannot claim that they have regularly emerged victorious. I won't put it more strongly than that, lest you suspect me of flattering you. Nor does anyone really think that either your urban craftsmen or your uncouth peasants (leaving aside those whose physique is unsuited to tests of strength and courage, and those whose spirits have been broken by their own poverty and that of their families) are scared of the idle retainers of the great. So there's no danger that young men who are healthy and strong (the sort of young men the nobility now

---

19. A Roman historian of the first century B.C.E.

corrupt, for only the best are good enough for them), who now become feeble through inaction or soft through doing what is virtually women's work, would become effeminate if they acquired the
skills required to earn their own living and were put to manly labor.

"'In any case, whether I am right or not on this question, you'll
never persuade me that it is in the public interest to support a vast
multitude of this sort, who disturb the peace, merely as a precaution against the possibility of war. For you'll never find yourself at
war except by your own choice, and peace, not war, ought always to
be your first priority. But this isn't the only factor that makes for
thieving. There is another, which I think is probably more important, and which is peculiar to England.'

"'What's that?' asked the cardinal.

"'Your sheep,' I said. 'Normally sheep are placid and eat very little, but now I hear reports that they have become so voracious and
fierce that they have even started eating men. They are laying waste
and depopulating fields, houses, towns. For, anywhere in the land
where the sheep produce fine, and consequently valuable, wool,
there the nobles, the gentry, and even some of the abbots (though
they're holy men!) are no longer content with the old rents and
profits that their ancestors used to obtain from the land. It's no
longer enough for them to live a life of idleness and luxury, which
contributes nothing to the public good. Now they want to do positive harm. They convert arable land to pasture and enclose the
fields for sheep. They demolish houses and pull down villages.
They leave churches standing, but only so they can pen sheep in
them. And, as if they were afraid that too small a proportion of
England was given over to hunting reserves and parklands, these
good men eliminate houses and crops and restore the waste. In order that one insatiable glutton, a menace to society, can enclose
thousands of acres into one vast field, the peasants are ejected.
Some are tricked out of possession of their lands; others are driven
off by force; yet others, worn down by harassment, are reduced to
selling their rights. One way or another, these poor people are driven out. Men and women, husbands and wives, widows and orphans, parents with little children and many servants—which
doesn't mean that they are wealthy, but only that agricultural labor
requires many hands—are forced to move out, I tell you, from the
homes they know and love; and there's nowhere for them to go.
Their furniture and fittings wouldn't be worth much, even if they
could sell them at leisure; since they're being thrown out, they virtually have to give them away. They won't be on the road long be-

fore they've spent that bit of cash. Then what choice do they have but to steal and so be hanged (as they deserve, of course), unless they become wandering beggars? But then, since they are unemployed vagrants on the loose, they will be seized and thrown into jail. No one will give them work, though there is nothing they want more. For they are trained as agricultural laborers, but there is no labor to be done if no crops are sown. A single shepherd or herdsman is enough to manage the sheep on land that once, when cereals were cultivated, required numerous hands.

'"The consequence of the reduction of arable land is that in many places bread has become much more expensive. But the price of wool has also shot up, so that the common people, who in England used to buy wool in order to make cloth for resale, can no longer afford it, with the result that many of them have become unemployed. The explanation is that, after the land under pasture had expanded, rot killed off vast numbers of sheep, as if a vengeful God were punishing their owners' greed by inflicting a plague on their sheep, when it would have been fairer to inflict it on the owners themselves. But even if the number of sheep increases greatly, still the price does not fall. It's true that where there is more than one seller you cannot talk of a monopoly, but you can still have an oligopoly. Virtually all the sheep are now owned by a few wealthy landlords. They will never be forced to sell unless they feel like it, and they won't feel like it unless they can get a price that suits them.

'"Moreover, other types of livestock have risen in price as much, and for the same reason; in addition, with farmhouses demolished and agriculture in decay, there is no one around to care for the calves. Nor will the wealthy landlords breed cattle as they do sheep. Instead they will buy them lean and cheap; then they will fatten them on their pastureland; and finally they will sell them dear. In my view we have yet to see all the evil consequences of this system. We already know that the landlords drive up prices when they bring the cattle to market. But suppose they buy up calves slightly faster than they can be bred; then little by little the available stock will fall, and eventually there will be a serious shortage. England used to seem exceptionally prosperous; now the unchecked greed of a few is destroying that prosperity. The high price of bread explains why everyone who can is laying off servants and hired hands. And what, tell me, can they turn to except to begging, or—and this seems less humiliating if you have any pride—to theft?

'"Alongside this miserable poverty and scarcity there flourishes gross extravagance. The retainers of the nobility, plus craftsmen,

even some farmers—people of every social rank—spend vast sums
on luxurious clothes and far too much on fancy foods. There are
brothels, whorehouses, and escort agencies; taverns, wine bars, and
beer halls also pander to the appetites. Then there's gambling: on
the throw of dice, on cards and backgammon, on throwing the
javelin, putting the shot, and tossing the caber. If you're addicted to
these, your money soon goes. Before you know it you'll be turning
to robbery.

"'You must eliminate these evils. You should decree that either
those who have torn down farmhouses and villages should restore
them themselves, or else they should hand over the property to
people who are willing to build and restore. You must prevent the
rich from engrossing the supply of commodities and exercising a
quasi-monopoly control of prices. Fewer people would be brought
up without a trade. Agriculture would be restored. Clothmaking
would recover. Then there would be honest work to which the
army of unemployed could usefully be put—I mean those whom
poverty has already made into thieves, along with those who are
now beggars and those who are now idle retainers (but in both
cases they are thieves in the making).

"'For sure, unless you cure these evils, your boasts about enforc-
ing the law against theft will be unjustified, and your law may look
like justice but will be neither fair nor effective. If you allow the
young to be dreadfully brought up and their characters to be corrupted little by little from childhood, and then punish them when
they finally perpetrate, as adults, those crimes which from their
earliest youth they seemed destined to perform, what are you doing, I ask, if not manufacturing thieves and then blaming them for
being thieves?'

"Even while I was speaking, the lawyer was preparing his response. He had decided to adopt the usual method employed by
disputants who are better at declaiming a prepared speech than at
replying to an argument. Such people think the ability to memo-
rize is the key to speaking well. 'Bravo!', he said, 'you have spoken
very well. But you are a stranger who may have picked up a good
deal of information about our affairs, but who has not been able
fully to understand what's at issue. It will take me only a minute or
two to make that perfectly clear. I will start by recapitulating what
you said; then I will explain in what respects your ignorance of our
affairs has led you astray; finally I will refute and destroy each one
of your arguments. Thus let me begin my speech where I promised
I would. As I understood you, there are four . . .'"

"'Oh do shut up!' said the cardinal. 'For it hardly seems likely *An example* that you'll be finished in a minute or two if you start like that. We *of the* will spare you the task of replying for the moment; but we will re- *cardinal's* quire a complete reply from you at our next meeting, which I trust *informal* will be tomorrow (unless either you or Raphael has a previous en- *way of* gagement). But meanwhile, dear Raphael, I would very much like *with a bore* to hear why you think thieves should not face the death penalty, or what other punishment you think would be more effective in re- ducing crime. For surely even you do not think that theft should be legalized! If people now start stealing without compunction when they face the prospect of death, what force or fear will there be ca- pable of restraining criminals if we suppose they are sure they will not be executed? They will interpret a reduction in the punishment as being virtually an incentive encouraging them to commit crimes.'

"'Most reverend father, it seems to me,' I said, 'that to take a man's life because he has taken some money is simply unjust. For I do not think that there is anything which fortune can give or take away that is the equivalent of a human life. If they say this punish- ment is inflicted not because money has been taken, but because the law has been broken and justice violated, then what distin- guishes the highest justice from extreme injustice? Surely we *On* should not approve of laws that amount to Manlian edicts[20] and *Manlian* require that whenever the law is infringed, even slightly, the of- *edicts,* fender must immediately be executed. Nor should we adopt the *see Livy.* Stoic doctrine that all crimes are equally dreadful. They deny there's any relevant difference between killing someone and pick- ing their pocket. Yet, if the concept of equity means anything at all, there's no comparison between these two crimes, for they cannot be classed together. God has forbidden us to kill anybody. Can we be justified in killing someone so readily for stealing small change? Perhaps you interpret God's commandment as denying us a right to kill except where man–made law says one may kill. But then what would prevent men from deciding among themselves that there are circumstances in which rape, or adultery, or perjury are to be permitted? God has denied us the right, not only to kill others, but also to take our own lives. Suppose all that is required to ex- empt our agents from God's command is that human beings, by

---

20. The Roman general Manlius was notorious for the severity of the punishments he inflicted on those who disobeyed him (Livy, VIII.vii. 1–22).

agreement among themselves, should adopt particular laws regarding killing one another, with the result that, without any precedent
set by God, they can eliminate those whom man-made laws have
condemned to death. Then isn't the consequence of this agreement
that this particular command of God's is to be regarded as valid
only insofar as it is confirmed by man-made law? Of course, by the
same logic human beings can decide in each and every situation
how far they feel like observing God's commands. Finally, the law
of Moses had to be harsh and severe because it was to govern a
stubborn people accustomed to slavery; even so, it did not decree
that theft of money should be punished with death.[21] It would
surely be mistaken to think that God, in his new law of mercy,
through which he governs us as a father governs his children, has
given us more extensive permission to be cruel to each other.

"'These are my reasons for thinking capital punishment for theft
is wrong. In addition, I would think that everyone can see that it is
ridiculous for society to have the same punishment for theft and
homicide, and that the consequences of this must be pernicious.
For if a thief knows that he will receive just as great a punishment
if he is convicted of theft as if he is convicted of murder as well,
this knowledge is an incentive to him to go and kill victims whom
otherwise he would only have robbed. It's not just that if he is
caught, his situation is none the worse; for murder is a better bet:
the prospects of being caught are less, since he removes the witness
to the crime. Thus while we make every effort to terrify thieves
with dreadful and excessive punishments, in fact we simply incite
them to eliminate the innocent.

"'Of course, the standard challenge put to opponents of capital
punishment for theft is that they should suggest a form of punishment that would be preferable. But in my view it's a good deal easier to suggest punishments that would be preferable than it would
be to suggest a worse form of punishment. Why should we doubt
the utility of the form of punishment that was for centuries employed by the Romans? After all, their skill in government has
never been equaled. They condemned those who had been convicted of major crimes to labor in shackles for the rest of their lives,
putting them to work in quarries and mines. Yet on this particular
question, I know of no policy preferable to the one I observed during my travels in Persia, when I visited the people commonly called

---

21. Exodus 22.

the Polylerites.[22] They are a people one might describe as strong and well governed, except for the fact that they pay an annual trib- ute to the King of Persia. Otherwise they are free and independent. But since they live far from the sea and are almost surrounded by mountains, and since they are content with what they produce lo- cally (their land is by no means unfertile), they do not often travel abroad, and few people visit them. By long-established custom they make no attempt to extend their frontiers; and the territory they do possess is securely protected from attack, both by their mountainous borders and by the pension that they pay to the re- gional power. So they live out their lives without being called up for military service. Their lives are comfortable rather than glorious, happy rather than valorous or distinguished. Indeed, their very name is almost unknown, I believe, except to their immediate neighbors.

The land of the Polylerites, near Persia

"'Now in their country, anyone who steals has to return the stolen property to the owner, not (as usually happens elsewhere) forfeit it to the ruler. They see no reason for thinking that the ruler has any more right to benefit at the owner's expense than the thief. If the stolen property has been consumed, then its value is made up out of the thief's other possessions and handed over; ownership of everything else that is his is transferred to his wife and children, while he himself is sentenced to hard labor.

N.B.: Not what we do

"'Unless the theft has been aggravated by violence, the con- demned are neither imprisoned nor shackled, but are put to work on public projects and left free to come and go. If they refuse to work, or do not put their backs into it, they are not chained down, but are flogged into action. If they work with a will, then they re- ceive no ill treatment, except that at night they must answer to roll call and then are locked in their cells. There is nothing unpleasant about their lives, except for their unremitting labors. Since their work benefits society, society ensures they are reasonably well fed. The form of funding varies. In some places what is spent on them even comes from charitable donations. The revenue raised by this method might seem unreliable, but the Polylerites are a charitable people, so that as much is raised this way as would be by any other means. In other places some of the general government revenue is set aside for this purpose. Sometimes a special tax is levied on every resident to support them. There are places where they do not work

---

22. "The People of Much Nonsense."

on public projects, but whenever a private individual wants a hired hand he can go to the marketplace and hire one of these men for the day at a fixed rate, which is set a little lower than the rate a free man would be paid. Moreover, if the convict is lazy, his employer is permitted to whip him. Consequently there is never a shortage of work for them, and each one of them earns a little more each day than the cost of his keep, the surplus going into the public treasury.

And now the servants of noblemen think a haircut like this makes them handsome!

"'All of them wear clothes of a particular color, one that no one else wears. Their heads are not shaved, but their hair is cut short so that their ears show. The tip of one of their ears is cut off. They are allowed to receive gifts of food, drink, and clothing (providing it is of the regulation color) from their friends. But if they are given money, both the giver and the receiver are executed. The penalty is just as severe for any free man who receives money from a convict, no matter what the reason; and for any slave (for this is what they call the convicts) who lays his hand on a weapon. The slaves of each district wear a distinguishing badge. It is a capital offense to discard it, or to be found outside the district's territory, or to be seen talking to a slave from another district. Plotting escape carries the same penalty as actually escaping. If a slave knows of a plot and fails to declare it to the authorities he dies; a freeman guilty of the same crime becomes a slave. Informers, on the other hand, are guaranteed a reward: freemen receive money, while slaves are granted their liberty, and of course both slave and free are given pardon and immunity from the crime of knowing of a planned escape. Consequently every conspirator knows it is in his interest to betray his fellow conspirators.

"'These are their laws and policies where theft is concerned. It should be evident that they are both humane and socially beneficial. Punishment is directed at eliminating crime, not criminals. Convicted criminals have no choice but to behave well, and they spend the rest of their lives making up for the harm they have done. The risk of their reverting to their old habits is negligible, so anyone setting out on a journey thinks himself safest if he hires these slaves as guides, arranging for the slaves of one district to hand him over to those of the next at each frontier. Even if they wanted to, they'd lack the means to succeed as muggers. They are unarmed; for them merely to possess money is proof of guilt; if they are captured, their punishment is preordained; they may run, but they can't hide. How could anyone hope to conceal the fact that he is a fugitive, when every item of his clothing distinguishes him from a law-abiding citizen, unless he goes on the run naked? And even then his ear would betray him. You may think there is at least a danger that the slaves would band together and conspire to overthrow the government. As if the slaves of one district could have any hope of succeeding unless they first sounded out and offered inducements to the slaves of many other districts! But the slaves of different districts have no opportunity to conspire together, since they never even encounter each other, let alone have the freedom to talk together. And why would anyone risk entrusting his fellow slaves with information regarding a conspiracy of this sort, when he knows they endanger themselves through silence but stand to obtain their heart's desire through betrayal? Moreover, every slave retains some hope that if he endures his punishment and does as he is bid, and gives grounds to believe that he is a reformed character, then one day he will regain his liberty. Every year, in fact, some of them are released as a reward for good behavior.'

"When I had said all this, and had added that I couldn't see any reason why these procedures couldn't also be adopted in England, where they would prove much more beneficial than the judicial system that my learned opponent had praised so unreservedly, his reply was characteristic of a lawyer: 'These methods could never be employed in England without endangering the very fabric of society.' And having said this he shook his head, grimaced, and fell silent. And everyone present rushed to declare their agreement with him.

"Then the cardinal said: 'It is not easy to predict whether this untried policy would work well or not, unless one runs the risk of testing it out. Supposing the king were to order that the execution of some criminals who had been sentenced to death should be deferred, while steps were taken to ensure they could not claim sanctuary. Then we could try out this system, and, if it proved beneficial in practice, then it would be right to put it into general use. But if it proved unsatisfactory, then the criminals, since they had already been condemned to death, could be executed. The end result would be no worse for society, and no more unjust, than if the execution had not been deferred, nor would the trial itself involve any risks. Indeed, I'm of the view that it might not be a bad idea to treat vagabonds in the same way, for although we've tried out many different laws against them, so far none of our measures have been successful.'

"Once the cardinal had spoken, those ideas which they had all received with scorn when I suggested them, they now competed to praise; but they especially admired the idea that vagabonds be enslaved, as this was the cardinal's own suggestion.

An amusing   "I don't know; perhaps it would be better not to mention what
dialogue   happened next. For it was pretty ridiculous. Nevertheless, I will tell
between a   you the story. There's no harm in it, and it has some relevance to
friar and   the subject we're discussing. There was a certain hanger-on present
a fool   who liked to behave as if he were a self-appointed jester. By acting
                  the fool he proved that he really was one. He was always cracking
                  jokes in the hope of raising a laugh, but the jokes usually fell flat, so
                  that people laughed at him, not his wit. Still, occasionally he said
                  something that wasn't stupid, thereby demonstrating the truth of
A common   the old proverb, 'If you throw the dice often enough, you're bound
saying,   to win in the end.' One of the people present happened to say that
especially   my little speech had taken care of the problem of theft; and the car-
among   dinal had dealt with beggars; all that was left now was that they
beggars[23]   should devise a government policy to look after the old and the
                  sick, who often found themselves reduced to poverty and were un-
                  able to work for a living.
                      "'Let me have a go!' said the fool, 'I can handle this. I'm desper-
                  ate to have these people put out of sight. They're always getting on
                  my nerves, with their wailing and whining as they beg for money;
                  though there's never been a beggar yet who could tell a tale sad
                  enough to get a penny off me. Sometimes I don't feel like giving to
                  them; sometimes I just haven't any spare change. The end result is
                  the same. By now they've begun to figure it out. When they see me
                  go by they save their breath, for they know they'd be wasting their
                  effort. They no longer hope for anything from me—I might as well
                  be a clergyman, as far as they're concerned. But I hereby decree
                  that all the beggars should be parceled out among the Benedictine
                  monasteries and be turned into what they call "lay brothers." As
                  for the women, I order that they become nuns.'
                      "The cardinal smiled. He evidently thought it was a good joke.
                  But everyone else took it seriously. Still, a certain friar, a theolo-
                  gian, was so excited by this attack on the clergy and the monks that
                  he thought he would join in the fun, though he was normally so se-
                  rious as to be positively solemn. 'Oh no!' he said. 'You won't have
                  eliminated begging until you've gotten rid of us friars.'
                      'But,' said the hanger-on, 'we've already dealt with you. For the
                  cardinal took excellent care of you when he decreed that vagabonds

---

23. In all previous editions this annotation appears opposite the next para-
graph; but it is clearly out of place there, and would seem to have been displaced from here.

should be arrested and forced to work; for you're always on the road.'

"Everyone glanced at the cardinal; but when they saw he wasn't going to object to this attack any more than he had to the others, they all began to join in with a certain amount of enthusiasm—except for the friar. For it's scarcely surprising that the acid burned, and he naturally got angry, even furious. He couldn't stop himself from hurling abuse. He called his opponent a rascal, a slanderer, a tattletale, and a 'son of perdition.'[24] He quoted terrible threats to him out of the Bible. Now the fool began to set seriously about the task of making fun of his opponent, for this was just the sort of thing he was good at.

An allusion to a line from Horace: "Drenched with Italian vinegar"

" 'Don't get angry, good friar,' he replied. 'For the Bible says, "In your patience you will possess your souls." '[25]

"Back shot the friar (I remember his very words): 'I am not angry, though I'd like to see you strung up.[26] Or if I am I don't have to apologize for it. For the Psalmist says, "Be angry and sin not." '[27]

Note how he tells a story which is true to life!

"At this point the cardinal gently advised the friar to calm down. 'No, sir,' he replied, 'for I'm speaking from righteous anger and doing my duty. For holy men are often moved to righteous anger, which is why the Bible says, "The anger of your house has eaten me up,"[28] and we sing in church, "Those who mocked Elisha as he went up to the house of God felt the anger of the baldhead."[29] Maybe that's what this mocker, this buffoon, this creep should feel.'

The friar's Latin isn't good enough for him to know how to decline zelus *[anger].*

" 'Perhaps you're entitled to your strong feelings, but I rather think your behavior would certainly be wiser—I hesitate to say more Christian—if you didn't lower yourself to the level of this foolish idiot and get involved in a silly shouting match.'

" 'No, sir,' he replied, 'my behavior wouldn't be wiser. For Solomon, the wisest man there has ever been, said, "Answer a fool according to his folly,"[30] which is what I'm doing now. I am showing him the pit into which he will tumble if he doesn't pay attention. For if the many mockers of Elisha, who was only one bald

---

24 John 17:12; II Thessalonians 2:3.
25. Luke 21:19.
26. *Non irascor, inquit, furcifer . . .* On *furcifer,* see above, p. 30.
27. Psalms 4:4 in the Vulgate translation.
28. Psalms 69:9.
29. A medieval hymn based on II Kings 2.
30. Proverbs 26:5.

man, felt the anger of a baldhead, then someone who mocks all the friars in the world—which is to say innumerable baldheads[31]—has a good deal more to be afraid of. After all, we have a papal bull which decrees that anyone who mocks us is automatically excommunicated.'

"The cardinal, when he realized the argument would go on and on, gestured to the hanger-on to leave, and turned the conversation to a more suitable subject. Shortly afterwards he rose from table, and, since he had to meet with his staff to discuss matters of business, he dismissed us.

"Oh! dear More, what a long story I have made you listen to! I'd really be ashamed of myself if you hadn't eagerly begged me to tell it, and if you hadn't seemed to be listening so attentively as to suggest that you didn't want me to omit a single detail. Perhaps I should have cut it short, but I did need to tell you the story because I needed to illustrate how people form judgments. The cardinal's associates had contempt for my views when I advanced them; but when they discovered that the cardinal had no objection to them, then they approved of them. Their approval became so uncritical that they were sympathetic to the suggestions of his hanger-on and almost took them seriously, although the only reason the cardinal didn't reject them was because he took them as a joke. This episode will enable you to judge just how far courtiers are likely to approve of me or agree with my proposals."

"Indeed, dear Raphael," I said, "you've given me great pleasure, for everything you've said has been both instructive and amusing. While you were speaking I felt as though I were back in my mother country; I even felt as though I were a child again, so much did I enjoy remembering the cardinal, in whose household I received my education. I was already very fond of you, Raphael; but you wouldn't believe how much fonder of you I am now that I have discovered you revere his memory. But I still can't see any good reason to change my mind. For I really believe that your recommendations on matters of policy could be immensely beneficial to society, if only you could persuade yourself not to loathe life at court. You're under no greater obligation than this one, for no honest man can escape public service. Especially since your favorite author, Plato, says there will never be a happy society until philosophers rule or rulers become philosophers. We're going to have to wait a long time

---

31. A reference to the shaven heads of friars.

for happiness if philosophers won't even condescend to give rulers good advice!"

"The problem isn't that philosophers are standoffish," replied Raphael. "They'd gladly help, and indeed they've offered their advice in book after book. If only governments were prepared to follow good advice! But Plato was unquestionably right when he predicted that unless kings learn to philosophize themselves, they'll never be impressed with the advice of philosophers. Instead, they are deeply tainted and thoroughly infected with dangerous views from childhood. Plato had personal experience of this in his dealings with Dionysius.[32] Don't you think that if I proposed wise laws to any living ruler, and tried to pull out of his soul the pernicious weeds of evil views, I wouldn't be thrown out on the spot, or else turned into a laughingstock?[33]

"Come on, imagine I'm at the court of the King of France, sitting at the council table. We are meeting in secret session, with the king himself in the chair, surrounded by his wisest advisers. They are racking their brains to devise stratagems and tactics that will enable them to hold on to Milan and recover control of Naples, which has slipped from their grasp.[34] That's the first step. Afterwards they want to destroy the power of the Venetians and bring all Italy under their control. Next Flanders and Brabant, and then the whole of Burgundy would be added to France's territories. Then there would be other countries that the king has long had marked down for invasion. One of his councillors advises him to enter into an alliance with the Venetians, but only for so long as it suits France's convenience. He should develop a common strategy with them, and even permit them to seize some new territory, which he can in due course recover from them, if things go according to plan. Someone else proposes hiring German mercenaries; a third argues in favor of bribing the Swiss to ensure their support. They in turn are opposed by someone who wants to make a sacrificial offering of gold on the altar of his imperial majesty. Yet another proposal is that priority should be given to reaching an accommodation with the King of Aragon, and, to guarantee good relations with him, he should be permitted to seize the kingdom of

Our author's hidden purpose is to discourage the French from aggression in Italy.

Swiss mercenaries

---

32. Plato is supposed to have given advice to both Dionysius the Elder and his son Dionysius the Younger, tyrants of Syracuse.
33. Here the interpolation that began on p. 62 ends.
34. This suggests that the conversation is taking place in 1499–1501. France gained Milan in 1499, lost Naples in 1496, and regained it in 1501.

Navarre from its legitimate ruler. And then there is the suggestion that the ruler of Castile should be inveigled with vague promises of a marriage alliance and by purchasing the support of some of the nobles of his court.

"At this point they recognize that the most difficult problem of all is that of deciding what to do about England while they are busy elsewhere. They agree that they should enter into peace negotiations with the English and should establish as close relations with them as possible (though they are never likely to be very close). They should be caressed as friends, yet always be suspected of being enemies. The Scots are to be encouraged to arm themselves and stand guard, ready for any eventuality, so that if the English step out of line they can immediately intervene. Moreover, they should secretly support some exiled nobleman who could lay claim to the throne of England—of course it must be secret, or negotiations will break down. He can serve as an insurance policy should the King of England, whom they are bound to distrust, prove difficult to manage.

"Now, I ask you, when such an important undertaking is being planned, when so many distinguished men are competing to produce the best strategy to ensure success in war, what would happen if a mere nobody like myself were to stand up and advise steering in a quite different direction? Suppose I recommended that the king forget about Italy and stay home? Suppose I argued that the kingdom of France is already too big for one person to be able to govern it properly, and that consequently the king shouldn't give a moment's thought to acquiring new territories? Imagine my describing to them the laws of the Achorians,[35] a people who live to the southeast of Utopia. Many years ago they fought a war so that their king could acquire another kingdom. He claimed he had a legitimate claim on it by virtue of some distant marriage between the two ruling families. But when they won the war they realized that hanging on to their new territory would be every bit as difficult as conquering it had been. Their new subjects might have admitted defeat, but nevertheless there were constant threats, either of internal rebellion or external invasion, so that they were always fighting, either against them or in order to defend them. There was no prospect of their ever being able to disband their army. Meanwhile they were paying punitive taxes; money was flooding out of the country;

An example worth noting

---

35. "The People without a Country."

they were shedding their own blood for the sake of their ruler's vanity; and they were making no progress towards peace. War was corrupting the morals of their citizens at home. Soldiers returning from the front brought back with them a taste for robbery, a willingness to kill in cold blood. Nobody enforced the law because their ruler, overwhelmed with the problems of two kingdoms, could not give either enough attention.

"When they realized that there was only one way of putting an end to these evils, they came to an agreement and very generously offered their king a choice as to which kingdom he wished to rule, explaining to him that keeping them both was not an option. There were too many of them, they said, to be ruled by half a king, pointing out that no one will willingly agree to share even his mule driver with someone else. So that fine ruler had no choice but to make do with his original kingdom, handing over the new one to one of his friends (who was kicked out before long).

"Supposing I went on to point out that all these wars he was planning, which would see so many nations torn apart so that he might benefit, would exhaust his treasury and kill off his people. And in the end one could be sure that something or other would go wrong, and he would end up no better off than before. Consequently he should concentrate on seeking the welfare of his ancestral kingdom. He should do everything he could to embellish it and ensure that it was as prosperous as it could be.[36] He should love his subjects, and they would love him. He should live at one with them and rule them gently. He should let other kingdoms grow strong, recognizing that the kingdom he already had was plenty big enough, perhaps too big. How do you think my audience would respond to this speech, dear More?"

"I don't imagine they'd be delighted," I said.

"So let's go on," he said. "Consider some councillors who have met with their king to discuss novel schemes for accumulating money. One man recommends driving up the value of money when the king has large expenditures to make; and then devaluing it below its natural rate when he has taxes to collect. That way he can pay off a substantial debt with a small amount of gold and collect a large amount of gold from a modest tax. Another councillor suggests he should pretend to be drawn into a war and use that as a

---

36. A reference to *Spartam nactus es, hanc orna*, an extensive discussion of which appears for the first time in the 1515 edition of Erasmus's *Adages* (II.v.i): "Your fate is to be a Spartan; make the best of it."

pretext for collecting taxes. Then when that is accomplished, he should make peace with a great show of religious ceremonies. The common people will be taken in and think their ruler is godly and reluctant to be the cause of bloodshed. Yet another councillor brings to his attention some ancient, moth-eaten laws that have been effectively annulled through long disuse. Since no-one re-members that they were ever passed, they have all been broken, which means the king has an opportunity to levy fines. There is no more profitable source of revenue, and none that serves as effec-tively to enhance the ruler's reputation, since it can be disguised as the expression of a concern for justice. Yet another proposal is that he should forbid all sorts of things under penalty of heavy fines, but especially things which are contrary to the interests of his sub-jects. Afterwards he should offer to sell dispensations to those indi-viduals who have lost out by the new regulations. This policy will not only win him popular approval, but it will generate two sorts of income, for on the one hand he will be able to fine those who, eager to enrich themselves, have risked breaking the law and been caught; on the other hand he can sell exemptions. Moreover, the more he charges the better a ruler he will be thought to be, as it will be thought that he is exceedingly unwilling to allow any individual to act against the nation's interest, and that is why he insists on such a high price.

"Yet another suggestion is that he should bring pressure to bear on the judges to ensure that they decide every case in the interests of the royal prerogative. From now on they should be summoned to hold court in the palace and invited to discuss their cases in his presence. There won't be a single case involving his interests, no matter how obviously it ought in justice to go against him, in which at least one of the judges, either eager to contradict the others, or ashamed of simply repeating their views, or keen to win royal favor (and knowing the king is present), will find some loophole to justify a perverse judgment. As long as the judges can be induced to dis-agree, then a case that is really open and shut becomes complicated, and the truth of the matter becomes doubtful. So the king is given a convenient excuse to step in and interpret the law to his own ad-vantage. The other judges will adopt his view, either out of defer-ence or fear. Afterwards the judgment can be boldly declared in open court. There's never going to be a shortage of pretexts for rul-ing in the prince's favor. For all he needs is that equity should be on his side, or the letter of the law, or a strained interpretation of a contract, or the one thing that scrupulous judges agree should take precedence over each and every law, the king's prerogative, which no one dares question.

"But nevertheless all these councillors speak with one voice, echoing the maxim of Crassus: There's no amount of gold that is sufficient for a king who has to raise an army.[37] They also agree that a king can do no wrong—not even if he tries to! Every individual's property belongs to him, and so do his subjects themselves. What someone owns is properly speaking only what the king in his generosity chooses not to take from them. And it's very much to the king's advantage that he should leave his subjects no more than the bare minimum, for his own safety depends on ensuring that they are not emboldened by wealth and freedom. Riches and liberty make a nation more willing to resist a harsh and unjust government, whereas poverty and want dull their spirits and make them long-suffering, crushing the noble spirit of rebellion. *A saying of Crassus the Rich*

"What if at this point I were to stand up again and declare that it would be both dishonorable and dangerous for the king to adopt any of these recommendations? What if I maintained that not only his honor but also his safety require that his subjects should be rich, not that he should be? What if I pointed out that the people choose a ruler to further their own interests, not his? It's obvious they want him to work and watch so that they may live comfortably and come to no harm. Consequently the prince should be more concerned with looking after the people's welfare than his own. In the same way, the duty of a shepherd, if he is to live up to his calling, is to fatten his sheep, not himself.

"Experience shows that such councillors are completely wrong to think that if the people are made destitute peace will be ensured. Where are you more likely to encounter a brawl than among beggars? Who is keener to turn the world upside-down than the man who is most discontented with his present way of life? Who is more recklessly determined to throw everything into disorder than he who has nothing to lose and everything to gain? If a ruler is so hated and loathed by his subjects that he can keep control of them only by strong-arm methods, by violence, plunder, and confiscation, so that he reduces them to beggary, then it would obviously be preferable for him to abdicate than to stay in power by using such methods. They may allow him to hang on to his title, but they deprive him of the respect that should accompany it. A king who

---

37. Cicero, *De officiis*, I.viii.25.

rules over beggars has nothing to be proud of, but one who rules over prosperous and happy subjects will be admired. That's certainly what Fabricius—a man of principle and of noble spirit—meant when he replied that he would rather rule over rich men than be rich himself.[38] A single individual who leads a life of pleasure and delight while all around him people are groaning and weeping isn't really a king; he's in charge of a prison. Finally, just as it's proof that a doctor is incompetent if every time he cures a patient he leaves him with some new ailment, so a ruler who does not know how to reform the lives of his citizens except by depriving them of all life's rewards might as well admit that he's incompetent to rule free men.

"What he should concentrate on reforming is either his own laziness or his own pride; for it is almost always one of these two vices that causes a people to despise or hate its ruler. He should live on his own income, without harming anyone else; and he should ensure that his expenditure does not exceed his revenue. He should be tough on crime, and by seeing that his subjects are raised with the right values he should ensure they do not turn to it, rather than allowing lawlessness to become widespread and then punishing it harshly. He should not rashly revive laws that have fallen into disuse, especially if they have been long forgotten and never missed. And he should never collect a fine because a law of this sort has been broken if a judge would think it unjust or underhand for a private person to benefit in such circumstances.

A fine law from Macaria

"At this point I might describe to them a law that exists among the Macarians,[39] a people who also live not far from Utopia. On the day their ruler is inaugurated into office, he is required to swear in the presence of the gods that he will never have at any one time more than the equivalent of a thousand pounds of gold in his treasury (valuing his silver at the current exchange rate). They claim this law was made by an excellent ruler of theirs who was more concerned with his country's welfare than with accumulating wealth for himself. He intended it to prevent any ruler from amassing money on such a scale that he was bound to impoverish his people. He thought that a thousand pounds of gold was enough to enable a king to put down a rebellion, or the kingdom as a whole to

---

38. Gaius Fabricius Luscinus, fl. 280–275 B.C.E.

39. "The Happy People." More does not make up this name—it is to be found in Erasmus's *Adages*—which is perhaps why it differs from his other names, which all have negative connotations.

resist an invasion; but it was not so much that a ruler would be tempted to use it to finance the invasion of his neighbors. Indeed, the primary purpose of the law was to discourage military aggression. His second objective was to ensure that there would be adequate supply of specie for the normal functioning of the economy. Lastly, he thought that a ruler who has to redistribute any money that accumulates in his treasury once a set limit has been reached won't be on the lookout for opportunities to acquire money unjustly. Such a king will instill fear in the wicked and inspire affection in the good. If I were to press arguments such as these on men who were strongly inclined to hold the opposite point of view, don't you think it would be like telling stories to amuse the deaf?"

"I'm sure they wouldn't listen to a word you had to say!" I replied. "And goodness me, that's not surprising. To tell you the truth, I can't see the point in pressing these sorts of views on people, or proposing these sorts of policies, if you know they're never going to meet with approval. What do you hope to gain? How could such eccentric views be expected to influence people who are already persuaded by and committed to an entirely different approach? This sort of academic theorizing may be an amusing occupation for close friends chattering among themselves. But in a king's council chamber, where important matters are debated by important people, there's no time for such matters."

"But," said Raphael, "that's exactly my point. Kings have no time for philosophy."

"Yes they do," I replied, "but not for this ivory-tower theorizing, which makes no allowances for time or place. There's another philosophy, better suited to politics, which recognizes the play that's being staged, adapts itself to playing a part in it, revises what it has to say as the drama unfolds, and speaks appropriately for the time and place. That's the philosophy you should adopt. Otherwise it's as if one of Plautus's comedies is being performed, and the household slaves are on stage cracking silly jokes. Then you step into the limelight dressed as a philosopher and recite from *Octavia* the speech in which Seneca criticizes Nero.[40] Wouldn't it be better not to have a speaking part than to speak lines from the wrong play and mix together comedy and tragedy? You will have made a complete mess of the play that's being performed when you mixed it up with

Ivory-tower theorizing

A fine comparison

A non-speaking part

---

40. In More's day Plautus was mistakenly thought to be the author of *Octavia*.

another, even if your speeches come from a better play than the one on stage. It doesn't matter what the story is. Play your part in it as best you can, and don't muck the whole thing up because you suddenly remember a speech from a different play, even if it's wittier than the one you've been given.

"The same applies if you're speaking in the senate or in a king's council. If evil views can't be pulled out by the roots, and if long-established vices can't be reformed just as you might like, that doesn't mean you should refuse to participate in government, any more than you should abandon a ship in a storm simply because you can't control the winds. Nor should you deliver eccentric and peculiar speeches to an audience that you know will not be persuaded by them because it has already made up its mind. Instead, you must attempt an indirect approach and must make every effort to handle matters tactfully. If you cannot transform things for the better, you can at least make sure that they are no worse than necessary. For you can't hope to make everything perfect unless you only have perfect people to deal with—which isn't likely to be the case for a few years yet!"

"The only thing I'd achieve by this approach," he responded, "is that, while I was trying to cure others of insanity, I'd be acting like a madman myself. For if I intend to speak the truth, then I'll have to make the speeches you've just heard. Whether it's appropriate for a philosopher to tell lies, I don't know; I do know that it's wrong for me to do so. Although they might not like what I have to say, and it might even make them uncomfortable, I don't see why it should be thought so peculiar as to be absurd. What if I should re-*The policies* peat to them the policies Plato describes in his imaginary republic; *of Utopia* or tell them about what the Utopians actually do? Such policies might be better than ours (indeed there's no doubt that they are), but they would be bound to seem strange, because here individuals own private property, while in Plato's republic and in Utopia everything is owned collectively.

"People who have decided to rush headlong in a particular direction are never pleased with someone who calls them back, points out the danger, and proposes an alternative. But even allowing for that, what was there about my speech that made it unsuitable and inappropriate for delivery anywhere, at any time? If we are to suppress as eccentric and ridiculous every proposal that the evil habits of human beings might make seem strange, then we will have to suppress, even among Christians, almost everything that Christ taught. Yet Christ forbade dissimulation, and he commanded those truths that he had whispered into the ears of his disciples should be preached openly on street corners.[41] Most of what he taught is much more at odds with the common customs of humankind than the policies I recommended in my speech. But preachers are cunning and seem to have followed your advice. As soon as it was apparent that people would have great difficulty changing their behavior to conform to Christ's commands, they adapted his commands to their behavior, as if his standards were flexible. That way, at least, they could be sure of eliminating the discrepancy. But I don't see what they really accomplish by doing this, except that people can be bad without their consciences being troubled.

"And that's the full extent of what I could hope to accomplish if I were an adviser to some prince. For either I would express different views from such advisors, in which case I might as well express no views at all, or I would agree with them, in which case, as Mitio says in Terence, I'd just be helping them to be more accomplished lunatics.[42] As for the 'indirect approach' that you recommend, I don't understand what you mean by it. You think I should struggle to ensure that, if everything can't be made perfect, then at least, with tactful handling, things will turn out no worse than absolutely necessary. But a royal council is no place to dissimulate, nor to close one's eyes to what's going on. You must openly support the worst policies and give your approval to vicious legislation. Someone who praised wicked advice half-heartedly would be suspected of being a spy, or even a traitor. Moreover, you'll never have any opportunities to do good, for you'll be surrounded by colleagues who are much more likely to corrupt the best of men than they are to reform themselves. Either you will be infected by their wicked ways, or they will exploit your integrity and honesty to camouflage their own knavery and folly. There's no chance of your making things better by adopting an 'indirect approach.'

"That's why Plato says that the wise are right to avoid being involved in government.[43] He has a fine metaphor, which illustrates the problem perfectly. The philosophers see all the people out in the streets, being soaked in a thunderstorm. They cannot persuade them to get out of the rain and take shelter. They realize that if they go out and join them they will achieve nothing, they will simply all get wet together. So they stay indoors and accept that if they

---

41. Matthew 10:27; Luke 12:3.
42. *Adelphoe*, I. 145–7.
43. *Republic*, VI.496d–e..

cannot cure others of their folly, then the best they can do is keep themselves dry.

"But actually, dear More, let me tell you what I really think. I believe that wherever you have private property, and money is the measure of all things, you will find society can scarcely ever be just or prosperous, unless you are prepared to call it justice when the worst people acquire possession of the best things, or to call it happiness when a tiny group monopolizes everything; when even the members of that group are never at ease, while the rest are utterly wretched.

"Consequently, I think that the institutions of the Utopians are the wisest and the most Christian that one can have. They have very few laws, but those laws govern them exceedingly well. In Utopia virtue has its reward, but at the same time everything is shared equally, and everyone is prosperous. You only have to contrast their society with all the other nations, which are constantly passing new laws, yet not a single one of them is ever in good order. In such nations, whatever you have managed to get hold of you call your private property. But for all the laws they have passed, and the new ones they add every day, they are unable to ensure that anyone gets what is rightly his, that is, his so-called private property, or is able to hang on to it, or is able properly to distinguish it from everyone else's. That this is true is evident from the innumerable lawsuits. New ones spring up every day, while the old ones drag on and on. When I think about all this, Plato goes up in my estimation, and I am less surprised that he refused to legislate for cities that rejected laws giving everyone an equal share in everything. Because he was the wisest of men, he easily recognized that there is one way and only one way to attain general well-being, and that is equality in the distribution of goods. I doubt if such equality can ever be achieved where there is private property. For wherever people amass together as much as they can, distinguishing their own property from that of everyone else, no matter how abundant the supply of goods was to begin with, a tiny number end up sharing the whole lot among themselves, while the vast majority are left in poverty. Moreover, the usual outcome is that the winners are the people who ought to have been losers, and vice versa. For the rich are generally rapacious, unscrupulous, and useless, while the poor are generally modest and unassuming, while their daily labors are of more benefit to society than to themselves.

"So I am completely convinced that there can be no fair and just distribution of goods (however justice is defined), nor can the business of human beings be conducted so as to ensure happiness, unless private property is utterly abolished. As long as it survives, by far the greatest and by far the best part of humankind will be oppressed by the inescapable and gnawing suffering associated with interminable penury and toil. I admit that this suffering can be alleviated to some limited extent; but I maintain that it cannot be completely eliminated. One could pass laws restricting the amount of land any individual could own and requiring everyone to declare their financial reserves. One could go on and make laws ensuring that no prince could be too powerful, and no people too disobedient. Then one could decree that no one can actively seek any government appointment, that such positions are not to be sold, nor may those that are appointed to them be obliged to spend their own money in conducting their official duties—otherwise officials are bound to seek opportunities to recover their costs, if necessary through fraud and extortion; moreover, the prerequisite for being appointed will be that you are rich, when it should be that you are wise.[44] Just as the sick may be kept alive by constant care and attention even though any hope of recovery has been abandoned, so too the evil consequences of inequality may be alleviated and its effects mitigated. But there is not the slightest prospect of curing the disease or restoring society to true health so long as private property survives. For while you work on eliminating one symptom, you aggravate others. Every treatment you try results in new symptoms requiring treatment, for you cannot transfer wealth to one person without taking it away from another."

"But I think the opposite is true," I said. "I believe there can never be prosperity where all things are held in common. For how can there be a plentiful supply of goods if everyone gives up working? The prospect of turning a profit will not act as an incentive, and everyone will work half-heartedly, trusting they will be fed by the labor of others. Then when need spurs them on, there will be no law enabling someone to keep what they have produced. Isn't the result bound to be perpetual conflict and bloodshed? Especially since respect for authority and deference towards superiors will have been destroyed, for I cannot even imagine how respect and deference could exist among men who are identical in every respect."[45]

---

44. It was commonplace in More's day for government offices to be sold, and some honorific positions (such as that of ambassador) often left their holders out of pocket.
45. This is the argument (against Plato) of Aristotle, *Politics,* II.i–v.

"I'm not surprised you think that," he said, "since either you have no mental image of such a society to help you, or if you have one, it's mistaken. But if you had traveled to Utopia with me, and you had seen their way of life with your own eyes, as I did—for I lived there for more than five years, and I would never have had any desire to leave, had I not wanted to publicize the existence of that new world—then you would not hesitate to admit that you have never seen any other society as well governed as theirs."

"Well now," said Peter Giles, "you will have difficulty persuading me that it is possible to find a better-governed society in your new world than in this world, which is known to us all. We're as clever as they are, and our political systems are, I suspect, older than theirs. When it comes to ruling, prolonged experience has enabled us to invent many institutions that make for a better life. I could add that we have also made a number of chance discoveries that no one would be clever enough to formulate, if they merely reasoned from first principles."

"As to our governments'being older than theirs," he replied, "you would have been in a better position to express an opinion if you had read the histories written about that world. If one can trust what they say, there were cities there before our own world was first settled. So any beneficial policy, whether it could be worked out by theorizing or only discovered by chance, would seem to be at least as likely to have been discovered there as here. But my own view is that we are cleverer than they are, but they are far in advance of us because they have applied much more effort and industry to resolving society's problems.

"According to their history books, they had no information whatever regarding our part of the world (they call us the Ultra-equatorials) before I made landfall there, with one exception. Twelve hundred years ago a ship, which had been blown off course by a storm, was wrecked on the island of Utopia. Some Romans and Egyptians were tossed onto the shore and remained on the island for the rest of their lives.

"Because the Utopians put their minds to it, they extracted the maximum benefit from this one opportunity. There wasn't a single technical skill in the whole Roman empire that could be of any use to them which they did not learn, either because it was explained to them by their guests, or because they worked out how to do it by building on the information they could glean from them. That's how much they benefited from the fact that a few of us, on a single occasion, landed there! Perhaps a similar chance event has brought someone from there here before now. If so, the event has been completely forgotten. So too in the future any knowledge of the fact that I have been there may be completely obliterated. On the basis of one encounter, they quickly acquired for themselves every useful technique of ours; but I believe it will be many years before we adopt any of their practices, which are superior to our own. Their willingness to learn from others is, I believe, the primary reason why, although we are as clever as they are, and have technical skills the equal of theirs, their society is much better administered than ours is, and they live much happier lives."

"Then, dear Raphael," I said, "for goodness's sake describe their island to us. And don't try to be brief. Give us an orderly account of their fields, rivers, towns, peoples, customs, institutions, laws, and of anything else you think we might like to know about. And you should assume we want to know everything that we don't yet know."

"There's nothing would give me more pleasure, for I know exactly what to say. But we will need a good deal of time, free of interruptions."

"Then let us now go in to lunch," I said. "Afterwards we can have as much free time as we want."

"Fine!" he said, and so we went in to eat. Afterwards we came back to the same spot and sat down on the same bank. I told my servants to ensure that no one interrupted us, and Peter Giles and I urged Raphael to make good his promise. When he saw that we were eagerly waiting for him to begin, he sat there for a moment in silence, thinking over what he wanted to say, and then he began as follows.

END OF BOOK ONE

THE DISCOURSE IN WHICH RAPHAEL HYTHLODAY
DISCUSSES THE BEST WAY OF ORGANIZING A STATE

BOOK TWO
BY THOMAS MORE,
CITIZEN AND UNDERSHERIFF OF LONDON

The position and shape of the new island of Utopia

The island on which the Utopians live is two hundred miles across at its central zone, which is where it is widest. The bulk of the island is not much narrower than this, but it gradually tapers towards each end. These ends curve around as if to complete a circle five hundred miles in circumference. As a result the island is shaped like a new moon. Between the horns of the crescent there is a gap about eleven miles wide through which the ocean flows, spreading out into a vast empty space. This sea is surrounded by land on all sides, and so it is protected from the winds. The waters are calm, not rough, as if it were a huge lake. Thus almost the whole of the inner coast offers safe mooring, and ships shuttle back and forth across the water, which benefits the island's residents greatly. With shoals on one side and reefs on the other, the strait that leads to the open ocean is perilous to shipping. Almost in the middle one large rock rises above the waves. Since it is visible, it presents no danger.

Its natural defenses mean there need be only one fort.

On it they have built a fort, which they keep garrisoned. But the reefs are underwater and therefore dangerous. Only the locals know the safe channels, and consequently it is difficult for any stranger to enter this enormous harbor unless he takes on board a Utopian pilot. Even they would find the passage dangerous, if they

Defense through misdirection

did not know how to take their bearings from certain artificial markings on the coast. The Utopians would only have to move these markings from their proper positions in order to ensure that an enemy fleet, no matter how large it might be, would be smashed upon the rocks.

On the outer coast of the island there are numerous sheltered

harbors. But everywhere one might plan to come ashore is protected either by natural obstacles or by fortifications, so that a small
number of defenders would be able to hold off a large invasion
force. It is said—and the appearance of this coastline seems to con-
firm the claim—that this country has not always been surrounded
by the sea. But Utopus, who gave his name to the island when he
conquered it (previously it had been called Abraxa),[46] and who
transformed its backward, uncouth, and disorderly inhabitants so
that now they are more civilized and sophisticated than those of almost any other nation, was not satisfied when he had decisively defeated the inhabitants in his first assault. He then ordered that a
fifteen-mile-wide stretch of land that linked the peninsula to the
continent should be cut away, turning it into an island. He did not
force only the native peoples to do the work, but, to ensure they realized there was no disgrace attached to physical labor, he ordered
all his own soldiers to lend a hand. With the work shared among
such a vast number of laborers, the job was completed with incredible speed, and the neighboring peoples, who at first had laughed at
such a foolish undertaking, were both amazed and terrified when
they realized it would succeed.

Utopia named after General Utopus

A bigger undertaking than cutting across the Isthmus![47]

Working together, you get more done.

The island has fifty-four cities. Each one has open spaces and
magnificent buildings. They all share a common language and culture, and they all have the same institutions and laws. Insofar as
their locations permit, they are all laid out on the same plan, and
their buildings resemble one another. The distance between the
two that are closest together is twenty-four miles, and none of them
is so cut off that you cannot walk to another city within a day. Each
city sends three old and experienced representatives to Amaurot
once a year to make decisions on matters of concern to the island as
a whole. The city of Amaurot[48] is the seat of government because,
being placed like the hub at the center of a wheel, it is the location
that involves least inconvenience for the representatives of all the
other cities.

Utopia's towns

Like cooperates with like

A moderate distance from city to city

The surrounding farmland is assigned to each city, so that each

Distribution of farmland

---

46. According to the second-century Greek Gnostic Basilides there are
many heavens, and "Abraxas" is the best.
47. On several occasions the ancient Greeks sought unsuccessfully to construct a canal across the Isthmus of Corinth.
48. "City of Darkness."

This is the curse of all societies in our world.[49] has a minimum of twelve miles of land at its disposal in every direction—much more in some directions, depending on how far it is to the next city. No city is preoccupied with expanding its frontiers, for they think of their territory as land to be worked, rather than as estates to be owned. Throughout the countryside, situated at convenient intervals from each other, they have built houses and *Agriculture takes precedence.* equipped them with agricultural implements. The citizens of the towns take turns spending periods of time in the country. No rural household has fewer than forty adults in it at a time, and each house has two slaves permanently attached to it. There is one man and one woman, both responsible and mature individuals, in charge of each household, and a phylarch[50] in charge of every group of thirty households. Each year twenty people move back to the city from each household, after they have completed a two-year stint on the land. They are replaced by the same number of people newly arrived from the city, so that these can be trained by those who have already been there a year and are consequently more experienced at farming, just as they themselves will train their successors in a year's time. For if they were all equally ignorant and inexperienced when it came to farming, the harvest would suffer as a result of their incompetence. This pattern of constantly renewing the agricultural labor force is the norm, in order to ensure that no one is compelled to endure a harsh way of life longer than necessary; but many individuals whose character is such that they positively enjoy working on a farm obtain leave to stay on year after year.

The farmers' tasks

An admirable method of hatching eggs!

The farm laborers plough the fields, feed the animals, and cut firewood, and deliver their produce to the city, either by sea or by land, whichever is convenient. They raise enormous numbers of chickens by making use of a remarkable technique. The chickens lay the eggs, but they do not incubate them; instead, large numbers of them are kept alive until they hatch out, by maintaining them at a constant warm temperature. The moment they emerge from their shells, the chicks mistake human beings for their mothers, and follow them everywhere.

The value of horses

They rear very few horses, and those that they do are all high-spirited. They have no use for them except to teach their young

---

49. The Latin text says "here and now"; but many later marginal comments refer to Utopia as if it were distant in time ("then") not space ("there").

50. From the Greek for "ruler of a tribe," but the spelling in 1518 (*philarch*) suggests another Greek word meaning "greedy for power."

people horsemanship. It is oxen who carry out all the work of plow- *The value* ing and hauling. They admit that oxen don't have the pulling *of oxen* power of horses, but they can keep going much longer, and the Utopians believe them to have better resistance to disease. More- over, the expenditure, both of effort and of money, involved in feeding them is less. Finally, when they are worn out with work, they can be slaughtered for their meat.

They use grain only to make bread [not beer]. For they drink *Food and* wine made from grapes, or cider made from apples or pears, or *drink* even sometimes plain water. Often they will have dissolved honey or soaked licorice (of which they have an ample supply) in the wa- ter. Although they know perfectly well (for they have studied the question closely) how much food each city and its surrounding ter- ritory will consume, they produce much more grain, and rear many *Extent of* more cattle, than they need for themselves. They export the sur- *arable land* plus to their neighbors. If the inhabitants of the countryside need anything that they do not produce themselves, they request that it be supplied by the city; and they get what they want from the city authorities without having to offer anything in exchange and with- out being put to any trouble, for almost everyone goes to town once a month in any case to observe the religious festival. When it is nearly time to bring in the harvest, the phylarchs in the country no- tify the authorities in the city how many extra hands they could *Cooperative* use. An army of harvesters arrives at just the right time, and, if the *work the* weather is fine, they can bring in the whole harvest in little more *most* than a day. *efficient*

The Cities, Especially Amaurot

To know one of their cities is to know them all, for they are indistin- guishable from each other, except insofar as their locations impose differences upon them. So I will describe one of them, and it makes *Amaurot,* no difference which I choose. Still, why would I not choose Amau- *the* rot? There is no city that is more distinguished, for the rest acknowl- *principal* edge the authority of the senate, which meets there; nor is there any *city of* that I know better, as I lived there for five years without a break. *Utopia,*
described

So, Amaurot is built on a gently sloping hillside and is laid out so that it nearly forms an exact square. In one direction it runs from a little below the ridge of the hill down to the river Anyder,[51] a dis- *The river*
Anyder
described

---

51. "The Waterless River."

tance of two miles. It extends a slightly greater distance along the bank of the river. The Anyder begins as an insignificant spring eighty miles above Amaurot, but other streams flow into it, and two of these are of a decent size, so that by the time it flows past Amaurot it has grown to be half a mile across. It soon becomes still larger, and then at last, sixty miles further on, it flows into the ocean.

Just like the river Thames in England
Along the whole of its course between the city and the sea, and even for some miles above the city, the river is tidal, flowing swiftly first in one direction and then the other for six hours at a time. When the tide rises it fills the whole channel of the Anyder with salt water for a distance of thirty miles, driving the fresh water back. Even for some miles above that it turns the water brackish; then little by little the water becomes fresh, and the river is pure as it flows through the city. Then when the tide falls the river runs sweet and unpolluted almost to the point where it meets the open sea.

Here again London is like Amaurot.
The city is connected to the opposite bank of the river by a bridge, not one constructed out of wooden piles and pillars, but one made of fine stone arches. The bridge stands upstream, at that part of the city furthest from the sea, so that ships can sail unhindered along the whole length of the city quays. There is also another river flowing through the city. This one is not particularly large, but it is quiet and delightful. It gushes from the hillside on which the city is built and flows downhill through the town center

The supply of drinking water
until it enters the Anyder. The source and spring of this river rises a little way above the town, but the inhabitants have extended the city's fortifications so that it lies within the defensive perimeter, so that if the city came under attack the enemy would not be able to dam and divert the stream, nor poison the water. Water from this river is carried through tiled pipes into the various neighborhoods of the lower town. Where buildings stand on higher ground they collect rainwater in large cisterns, which is equally satisfactory.

Defensive walls
The city is surrounded by a wall, which is both tall and thick. There are towers and battlements at frequent intervals. On three sides a ditch, which is dry but deep, broad, and filled with thorn

Character of the streets
hedges, runs alongside the ramparts; on the fourth side the river itself serves as a moat. The streets are laid out so that they are convenient for traffic and provide shelter against the weather. The

Buildings
buildings are well maintained. An unbroken row of houses stretches the length of each block, facing another row across the street. The

Gardens attached to the houses
street that runs between these terraces is twenty feet wide. The houses back onto a large garden, which runs the length of the block and is enclosed by buildings on all sides.

Thus, every house has a front door that opens on the street and a back door that opens on the garden. The doors are double swing doors, which open easily with a push and close automatically behind you, so that anyone can walk in—with the result that there is no private space. Every ten years they even swap houses among themselves, drawing lots to decide where they will live. The Utopians love their gardens. They grow vines, fruits, herbs, and flowers, and they are so well cared for and flourishing that I have never seen gardens anywhere that were more productive or more beautiful than theirs. They put such effort into gardening not just because they take pleasure in it, but also because each square regards itself as being in competition with all the other squares to have the best garden. It would certainly be hard to find anything else in the whole city that is better adapted both to be functional and to give pleasure. So it would seem that the founder of the city must have had the design and construction of gardens as his first priority. *Reminiscent of Plato's community*

Virgil also stressed the value of gardens.

In fact, they say that the whole layout of the city was designed by Utopus himself before construction began. But he realized that one person, even if they spent a lifetime on it, could not deal with all the details of design and decoration, so he left these to be perfected by later generations. They have a written record of the history of the island from its conquest 1,760 years ago.[52] This gives a detailed account and is carefully and conscientiously preserved. According to these records, the first houses were single-story dwellings, mere cottages and cabins, built haphazardly out of whatever lumber was at hand and with walls plastered with mud. The roofs were pitched and thatched with straw. But now all their houses are elegantly designed and three storys high. Their façades are made of flints, cobbles, or bricks, and the space within the walls is filled with gravel and cement. The roofs are flat and rendered with a material that is extremely cheap but whose composition is such that it is fire-retardant and more weatherproof even than lead. They keep out the drafts by fitting windowpanes (the Utopians use glass in great quantities). Instead of glass they sometimes use thin linen cloth, which they treat with a clear oil or with varnish. This has the double advantage of letting in more light and fewer drafts than glass. *Windows of glass or linen*

---

52. This takes us back (from 1516) to 244 B.C.E., when Agis IV became King of Sparta. He was put to death for upholding egalitarian principles.

THEIR ADMINISTRATION

Once a year every group of thirty households elects an administrator, who used to be known as a syphogrant,[53] but in modern times has been called a phylarch. There is another administrator in charge of every group of ten syphogrants with their households.

"Tranibor" in the language of Utopia means senior official. An admirable way of appointing officials

He used to be called a tranibor,[54] and is now called a senior phylarch. All the syphogrants—there are two hundred of them—elect the chief executive. They swear they will select the person they believe will do the best job, and then there is a secret ballot, in which they choose among four people nominated by the population as a whole.[55] The city is divided into four sections, and each section nominates a candidate to the senate. The chief executive is appointed for life, though he can be dismissed if he is suspected of trying to establish a tyranny. The tranibors are elected annually, but

Tyranny detested in a well-ordered state

the same people are reelected from year to year under normal circumstances. All the rest of the administrators serve for a one-year term.

Disputes are rapidly resolved, while we make every effort to prolong them indefinitely.

The tranibors meet as a committee, with the chief executive in the chair. They normally meet on one day in three, but they meet more often if necessary. They discuss affairs of state and act quickly to put an end to conflicts between private individuals (if there are any, for such conflicts are infrequent). Each tranibor invites two syphogrants to attend the senate with him and brings a different two to each meeting. They have a rule that no decision can be made on a matter of public business unless it has been discussed in the senate on three separate occasions prior to the decree

No hasty decisions

being issued. To engage in the discussion of matters of public policy outside the senate or the popular assembly is punishable by death. They say these rules have been introduced to ensure that it would be difficult for the chief executive and the tranibors to conspire to alter the system of government and subject the people to tyrannical rule. Moreover, anything that they think is of importance is referred to the assembly of all the syphogrants. The syphogrants discuss the question with their households and then debate it among themselves. Finally they forward their recommen-

---

53. "The Old Man of the Sty."
54. "The Chief Guzzler."
55. Secret ballots were unusual in sixteenth-century Europe. This, and other features of the Utopian constitution, would have reminded readers of the constitution of the Venetian Republic.

dation to the senate. Occasionally a difficult question is referred to the council of the whole island.

In addition the senate has an established practice whereby no proposal is ever discussed on the day on which it is first put forward, but instead it is always held over to the next meeting. The intent is to prevent people from blurting out the first thought that comes into their heads and then afterwards making their best efforts not to defend the policy that would be most advantageous to the community as a whole, but to vindicate their own hasty proposals. They realize that some people have such a depraved and pathetic sense of self-esteem that they would rather see the community suffer than have their own reputation diminished by an admission that their original proposals were shortsighted—although they were under an obligation at the start to think first and speak afterwards! *If only we did the same in our modern assemblies.*

This is the meaning of the old proverb, "to sleep on a decision."

THEIR OCCUPATIONS

Farming is the one occupation in which everyone is engaged, both men and women; no one is exempt. They are all trained in it from childhood. At school they learn the theory. Then they go out into fields near the town. There they don't just watch others at work but have a go themselves. This gives them healthy exercise, and the whole outing is fun as well as being instructional. *Agriculture involves everyone, whereas now a despised few do the work we evade.*

Apart from farm work (in which, as I have said, everyone engages), each individual specializes in a particular occupation. The common trades are spinning and weaving, both of wool and flax, masonry, blacksmithing, and joinery. There are no other crafts practiced by enough people there to be worth discussing. They do not, for example, have specialist dressmakers and tailors. Each household makes its own clothing, which is, except for those features which distinguish the sexes and the married from the unmarried, of the same pattern throughout the whole island, and the same for both young and old. Their clothes are not unattractive, they do not interfere with physical activity, and they are designed to be suitable in both hot and cold weather. *Trades taught so that needs may be met, not luxuries provided*

All dress alike.

But every individual (including women, and not just men) learns one of the other trades I have mentioned. It is true that the women, as they have less strength, learn the lighter crafts, usually spinning and weaving. The other crafts, which involve heavier work, are assigned to the men. In the majority of cases, boys are apprenticed to their fathers, for this is what most of them naturally prefer. But if a *No citizen without a craft*

Each learns the trade to which they are suited by nature. boy wants to learn a different trade, then he is adopted by a household that can train him in the craft of his choice. Both his father and the administrators take care to ensure that he is apprenticed to a reliable and responsible householder. Moreover, once you have mastered one trade, you can, if you want to learn another, obtain permission to begin a new apprenticeship. Once you've learned both, you can practice whichever you prefer, unless the city has a particular need for one rather than the other.

Idlers are expelled from society.   The primary, and almost the only, function of the syphogrants is to take care to ensure that nobody lounges around doing nothing. Everyone is required to work hard at his or her chosen trade. But they aren't expected to work non-stop from first light until it is pitch black, wearing themselves out like beasts of burden.[56] A life of such hardship is worse than that of a slave; yet almost everywhere—except in Utopia—this is the life that workingmen endure. The Utopians divide a day and a night into twenty-four hours of equal length. Of these they devote only six to work: three before noon, after which they go to lunch, then rest for two hours in the afternoon, after which they return to work for a further three hours. Dinner marks the end of the working day. Since they call the first hour after noon one o'clock, they go to bed about eight o'-clock, and sleep claims about eight hours of their day.

Laborers not to be overworked

     Whatever time they have left over when they are not working, eating, or sleeping they are free to spend as they choose, providing they do not waste it in debauchery or idleness. They are expected to make good use of their free time, applying themselves to some occupation that interests them. Most of them use these intervals to engage in intellectual activities. They have a routine whereby public lectures are delivered each day in the hours before daybreak.[57] Only those who have been specially selected to devote themselves to learning are required to attend, but a great many others, from all sorts of occupations, both men and women, crowd in to hear them. Depending on their interests, some go to lectures on one subject, some on another. But anyone who prefers to devote this time to his or her trade is free to do so. In fact many of them, who are temperamentally unsuited to the study of an academic subject, opt for

Scholarly study

---

56. Recent English legislation (the Act Concerning Artificers and Labourers of 1514–15) required laborers to work from daybreak to nightfall during the winter months and for more than fourteen hours a day during the summer months.

57. This would have seemed normal in the sixteenth century.

this. They receive as much praise as their more studious fellow citizens, for their labors benefit the community.

After supper they while away an hour in recreation: in summer they go into their gardens, while in winter they stay in the communal halls where they have eaten. There they either play musical instruments or entertain themselves in conversation. They don't even know about dice and other such pointless and corrupting games of chance, but they do play two board games, which are somewhat similar to chess. One is a game of counters, in which one counter captures another; the other a game in which the vices and the virtues are drawn up in order of battle and fight against each other. This game very cleverly illustrates how the vices are at odds with each other but united in their attack on the virtues. It also shows which vices seek to destroy which virtues; which vices attack head on, relying on brute force, and which creep up on you, hoping to deceive you; how the virtues can muster themselves to withstand a charge, and what stratagems they can use to foil the vices' tricks; and, finally, how one side or the other comes to gain a decisive victory. *Recreation at suppertime*

While nowadays princes love to gamble

Their games are also instructive.

At this point, in order to prevent a possible misunderstanding, there's something I must explain more carefully. Because the Utopians work for only six hours a day, you might think they were bound to suffer from a shortage of basic supplies. But this is far from being the case. The hours they work are not merely enough but actually more than enough to ensure that they have a plentiful supply, not only of basic necessities, but of whatever is needed to make life pleasurable. You will realize why if you consider what a large proportion of the population in other societies does no [productive] work at all. First, half the population consists of women, nearly all of whom produce nothing; or, if the women are hard at work, then usually the men are sleeping the day away. Then think what vast numbers there are of priests and of what are technically called "religious",[58] all of whom do nothing at all. Add to them all the rich, especially the landlords, who are usually (though inaccurately) called gentlemen and noblemen. And add too their numerous retainers, for their households are vast cesspools of worthless bruisers. Finally add on all the fit and healthy beggars who pretend to be far too sick to work. You will find that far fewer people than you would have thought do the work to produce the goods that people consume. *Different types of idler*

The bodyguards of the nobility

A very acute remark

---

58. Monks and nuns.

Now I ask you to estimate what proportion of these are engaged in producing basic necessities, for where everything has a price it is inevitable that there will be numerous occupations that are quite pointless and superfluous, and that exist only to satisfy a demand for luxury and licentiousness. Suppose the vast army of those who now produce goods were redistributed across only a few occupations, those few occupations required to satisfy our true needs and authentic pleasures. The inevitable result would be that goods would be produced in such abundance that prices would fall below the level at which the workers could support themselves. And if, in addition to all those who are now engaged in producing useless luxuries, we were also to redeploy the vast numbers of people who now idle their lives away producing nothing—every one of whom consumes twice as much as the workmen who produce what they consume—and assign them not merely work to do, but useful work, then you can easily realize how little time would be required to supply plenty and to spare all the things that either survival or a comfortable life require. There'd be ample to cater for the demands of pleasure too, providing it were true and natural pleasure.

This is perfectly clear from the practical experience of Utopia. For there, in the whole city of Amaurot and the countryside *Even the* around it, there are scarcely five hundred people—out of all the *adminis-* men and women whose age and physical condition make them fit *trators* for work—who are exempted from labor. Included in the five hun-*continue to* dred are the syphogrants, who are under no legal obligation to *do manual* work, but in practice do not exempt themselves, since they know *work.* that their own example provides the best encouragement to their fellow citizens. Also free not to work if they choose are those who the community has agreed (on the basis of a recommendation from the priests, confirmed by a secret ballot of the syphogrants) should be given the privilege of a perpetual sabbatical so that they can concentrate on intellectual inquiry. If any of these scholars fail to live up to the community's expectations, they are sent back to manual labor. On the other hand, it is fairly common for manual laborers to devote their spare hours so earnestly to study, and to *Only the* make such progress as a result of their hard work, that they are *learned* exempted from labor and promoted into the order of scholars. *serve in* From among those who are officially recognized as people of *positions of* learning are chosen ambassadors, priests, tranibors, and the head *authority.* of state himself. In their original language he was called

Barzanes,[59] but in more modern times he is known as the Ademus.[60] Since almost all the rest of the population is neither unemployed nor engaged in pointless occupations, it is easy to grasp why their society is so productive, even though the working day is so short.

There is another important factor that reduces their workload, in addition to those I have already mentioned. In most of the essential occupations there is less for them to do than there is for workers in other societies. Everywhere else, for example, large numbers of laborers are kept busy with the construction and maintenance of buildings. A father puts up a building; his son inherits it and, because he mismanages his money, he allows it little by little to fall into ruin; the cost of keeping it in good order would have been small, but in the end his grandson, when he inherits in his turn, is forced to rebuild from scratch, at great expense. Then it's common enough for someone to build a new house at vast expense; someone else acquires it, but its new owner thinks it's in poor taste. He spends nothing on it, so that it soon tumbles down, and then he builds another one, somewhere else, costing just as much money as the first. But among the Utopians, where everything is well managed and the government properly ordered, it's very rare indeed for them to choose to build on a previously empty site; and not only do they take prompt action to repair deterioration, but they have a regular program of maintenance to prevent it. The consequence is that their buildings last indefinitely, with very little work being expended on them; and builders have scarcely enough work to keep them busy. They have to be told to occupy themselves sawing planks and squaring and trimming stones, so that if any work does come along they will be able to complete it more quickly. *Keeping building costs down*

Then consider how little work is involved in making their clothes. When they are working they don't worry about their appearance but cover themselves in leather or fur overalls, which last for years on end. When they go out in public they put a woolen cloak on top of their shabby work clothes. Wherever you go on the island the cloaks are of the same color: the color of undyed wool. The result is that they use much less woolen cloth than other peoples do, and what they do use requires much less labor to produce. *And clothing costs*

---

59. "Son of Zeus."
60. "The Ruler without a People."

But, since linen cloth requires even less labor to produce, they usually use it. They like their linen to be as white as possible, and their wool to be as clean as possible; but they don't care whether it is woven out of fine or coarse thread. In other countries people may feel that they can barely get by with only four or five cloaks of different colors and the same number of silk shirts, and those who are only a little bit fussy feel that ten of each isn't enough. But there nobody feels they need more than one cloak or shirt, and they usually make it last for two years. After all, there is no reason why anyone should want more, for they would be no better protected against the cold, and they wouldn't look the slightest bit more elegant.

Since there's bound to be an abundant supply of everything, because on the one hand everyone works at a useful trade, and on the other they need less labor to produce the goods they use, they are on occasion able to commit enormous numbers of people to work on the roads (if they have fallen into disrepair). And when they have no need for any more work of this sort to be done, then they decree that the working day be shortened, for the magistrates never force the citizens to carry out more work than is necessary unless they wish to. For their political system is designed to pursue one objective before all others. As far as society's needs permit, all citizens should have as much of their time as possible released from productive labor so that they can devote themselves to the free development of their minds. For true happiness, they believe, is to be found in spiritual development.

Their Social Relations

At this point I should explain the terms on which citizens relate to each other, the interactions that take place between them, and the way in which goods are distributed among them.

Each city is made up of households, and the members of each household are usually related by birth or marriage.[61] When girl children grow up they are given away in marriage and go to live in the households of their husbands. But sons, and their sons in turn, remain in the household, and obey the eldest male inhabitant, unless his faculties have been diminished by old age, in which case the

---

61. This was not true in the England of More's day. Adolescent children left the home to work in other people's households and were replaced by other people's children.

next eldest takes over from him. There are six thousand house- *The number*
holds in each city, not counting the surrounding countryside. In or- *of citizens*
der to ensure that their cities have neither too many inhabitants nor
too few, care is taken to ensure that no household has more than
sixteen or fewer than ten adult members. Obviously they cannot pre-
determine the number of children, but it is easy for them to transfer children when they reach adulthood from larger households to
smaller ones. But if a city simply has too many inhabitants, the excess number is used to make good shortages in other cities on the
island. Whenever the population of the island as a whole becomes
excessive, they select inhabitants from every city to emigrate to the
nearby mainland and establish a colony governed according to their
own laws. They select a location where the indigenous peoples have
land to spare, land that lies uncultivated. They welcome into their
number those inhabitants who are willing to live according to their
principles and adopt their way of life. The two groups easily blend
together, to their mutual benefit. The Utopians' procedures ensure
that the land, which its original inhabitants had found infertile and
barren, produces plenty to support its increased population. But
those who refuse to live under their laws they drive out of the territory that they have claimed for themselves, and they go to war
against any who resist them. For they believe it is entirely legitimate to wage war against any society that does not use the land it
owns but leaves it waste and uncultivated, while at the same time
preventing others from using and owning it, though they are entitled by the law of nature to use it to feed themselves.[62]

If some crisis should cause any city to lose so many inhabitants
that they cannot restore the population without reducing other
cities on the island below their quota, then they bring back people
from the colonies to make up the numbers. Only twice in their
whole history has this been necessary, on both occasions because of
a dreadful outbreak of plague. They would rather see their colonies
wiped out than allow any of the cities on the island to go into decline.

But let me get back to the way of life that citizens share. I have
already told you that the oldest male member of each household is *How to*
in charge. Wives take orders from their husbands, children from *avoid*
their parents, and in general the younger from the older. The whole *having large*
numbers of
idle servants

---

62. Here, as in the discussion of slavery, More's argument prefigures that
of Locke's Second Treatise.

city is divided into four equal districts, and in the middle of each district there is a market where all sorts of goods are to be found. The products of each household are brought here and left in a store-room belonging to that household. They are then redistributed into warehouses, each of which contains goods of a particular sort. To these warehouses the head of each household comes to look for those goods which he and his family need. When he finds what he is looking for he takes it away without handing over any money or making any sort of payment. Why should anything be denied him? There is more than enough of everything, and no one worries that someone will want to claim more than his household needs. Why suspect someone of taking away too much, when you know he is

The cause confident that there will always be enough to go around? Fear of
of greed hunger makes every species of animal acquisitive and grasping. Human beings are unique in that they amass possessions out of sheer pride, for they glory in outdoing each other in the conspicuous display of wealth. But given the way Utopian society is organized, there's not the slightest opportunity for greed to gain a foothold.

Next to the markets for dry goods, which I have just described, are the food markets. To them are brought vegetables, fruits, and
Putrefying loaves of bread, and the edible parts of fish, beasts, and fowl. There
refuse causes are places set aside outside the town where fish and meat can be
epidemics in prepared for market. They have plenty of running water to wash
cities. away the blood and guts. The Utopians carry the carcasses to market after they have been slaughtered and cleaned by slaves. They do
By not want their citizens to become hardened to the butchering of an-
slaughtering imals. For engaging in such activities, they believe, slowly destroys
beasts we our capacity for compassion, which more than any other sentiment
learn to is the one that distinguishes human beings from other animals.
butcher They are also concerned with ensuring that nothing dirty or filthy
men. is brought into the city for fear that the stench of putrefaction will corrupt the air people breathe and spread diseases.

Every street has a number of large assembly rooms. They are set at equal distances apart, and each has a name by which it is known. There is a syphogrant in charge of each of these halls, and each has thirty households assigned to it—in other words, the fifteen houses to left and right of it—which eat there together. The catering managers of all the halls meet in the food markets at a fixed time and lay claim to a supply of food appropriate for the number they have to feed.

Looking But the first priority is the care of the sick, who are looked after
after the in public hospitals. Every city has four of these within its jurisdic-
sick

tion, though they stand a little outside the walls. They are so large that they might be compared to four little towns. Their size is intended to ensure that no matter how many sick people they may have to care for, the patients will not be squeezed in together and so made uncomfortable, and to make it possible to isolate effectively those who are infected with contagious diseases, which would otherwise be transmitted to other patients. These hospitals are so admirably designed, they are so well supplied with the resources needed for treating the sick, the care received there is so considerate and attentive, highly skilled doctors do the rounds so frequently, that, though it is a rule that no sick person is to be sent there against their will, nevertheless there is scarcely a single person in the whole city who, if they were ill, would not rather be in a hospital bed than their own.

When the catering manager of the hospitals has taken delivery of the food prescribed for the patients by their doctors, then the best of what remains is divided fairly between the various assembly rooms in proportion to the number each has to feed. The only exceptions are that special consideration is given to the governor, the high priest, and the tranibors. Moreover, foreign ambassadors and other visitors from abroad (when there are any in town—which isn't very often) also receive special treatment. There are never many of them, but those that do come are given special furnished houses to live in. At set hours a bronze trumpet sounds to warn all *Meals are* the inhabitants of the syphogranty that it is time to go to lunch or *taken* dinner in the assembly room. Only those who are sick in bed at *together by* home, or are away in the hospital, are excused. After the assembly *all and* rooms have received the supplies to which they are entitled, there is *sundry.* nothing to prevent a private individual from collecting food from *The* the market and taking it home. But they know no one would do this *principle* except in abnormal circumstances. For though there is no law *of liberty* against eating at home, people avoid doing it if they can. They re- *is always* gard it as impolite behavior, and in any case it would be foolish to *respected* go to the effort of preparing a second-rate meal at home when there *to ensure* is a fine and fancy one already prepared almost next door in the as- *there is no* sembly room. *coercion.*

In the assembly rooms all the especially dirty or heavy tasks are done by male slaves. But female citizens are the only people em- *Women cook* ployed in preparing and cooking the food, laying the tables, and *and serve* serving. Each household is assigned this task in turn. The assem- *the meals.* bled households sit at three or more tables, depending on how many are dining. The men sit with their backs to the wall and the women opposite them, so that if a woman has an attack of cramps, which happens frequently to women of childbearing age, they can get up without disturbing the others and go off to join the nursing mothers.

The nursing mothers and their babies eat separately in a dining room of their own. They always have a fire going and have clean water and cots at hand, so they can put the babies down to sleep, or if they prefer pick them up, take off their diapers, and cheer them up by playing with them in front of the fire. Each mother breast-feeds her own child, unless death or illness prevents her. When that happens the syphogrant's wife is responsible for quickly finding someone who can be a wet nurse. It's usually straightforward, for those who can give suck volunteer more enthusiastically than they would for any other task, since society as a whole applauds such tender-heartedness, and the child grows up to regard his wet nurse as his true mother.

Praise and kindness are the best way of persuading people to act well.

All the children that are under the age of five also sit with the nursing mothers. The rest of the young people—and they regard as children all those, whether boys or girls, who are too young to marry—either wait on table, or, if they are not yet old and strong enough, stand to one side without making the slightest sound. Both groups eat whatever is passed to them by those sitting at table—and this is the only meal time they have.

Bringing up children

The syphogrant and his wife sit halfway along the first table, both because this is the place of honor, and because from it (since this table is elevated and placed crossways to the room) the syphogrant can see the whole assembly. Two of the eldest sit next to them, for the places are laid at each table in groups of four. But if there is a temple within that neighborhood of thirty houses, the priest and his wife sit beside the syphogrant as being of equal status with them. On both sides of them sit a group of younger people, and then beyond them sit a group of older people, and so young and old alternate through the hall. By this arrangement they allow those of the same age to sit together, and at the same time they make young and old sit next to each other. The intention, they say, is that the authority and dignity of the old will inhibit the young from using improper language or engaging in immodest behavior, for nothing can be said or done during the meal without the old be-ing aware of it, since every young person has an older person sitting next to them.

Rulers defer to priests. But now even bishops are treated like slaves by the secular authorities.

Young and old mixed together

The food is not served from one end of the table to the other, but first all the older people (whose places are distinctive so that they

Respect shown to the elderly

can easily be identified) are served with the most desirable portions, and then equal portions are given to the rest. But the old people, if they choose, share with their neighbors the delicacies that were in too short supply for them to be distributed to everyone. Thus the elderly are treated with proper respect, and at the same time everyone eats well.

At the beginning of every lunch and dinner someone reads aloud a passage that concerns good behavior and morality; but they keep it short, so that no one is bored. The elders follow on by raising appropriate subjects of conversation, but they avoid being dull or gloomy. But they do not talk right through the meal, for they are also keen to listen to the younger people. In fact, they take pains to draw them out, so that they can assess each individual's natural abilities and character, which are revealed during the relaxed give-and-take of mealtime conversation.

Nowadays even monks scarcely bother to do this.

Table talk

Their lunches are no more than snacks; but they eat heartily at dinner. After lunch they must go back to work; dinner is followed by a quiet night of rest, which they think is much better for the digestion. At dinner the main course is always followed by dessert, and there is always a musical interlude. They burn incense and sprinkle perfume about, and do everything possible to ensure that the diners enjoy themselves. They are more inclined than we are to the view that no kind of pleasure should be forbidden, providing no harm comes of it.

Contemporary medical opinion would disapprove.

Music at mealtimes

Innocent pleasures are not to be despised.

This is the way they live together in the city; but in the countryside, where each household is at a much greater distance from its neighbors, they eat in their own homes. Even in the country no household is short of food, since they are the source of all the food that is consumed in the cities.

ON THE TRAVELS OF THE UTOPIANS

If anyone wishes to go and stay with friends who live in another city, or if they simply want to see the city itself, then they can easily get permission from their syphogrants and tranibors, unless there is some reason that they cannot be spared. A group of travelers is assembled, and they carry a letter from the governor, which specifies the day on which they have permission to set out, and the day on which they are expected to start back. They are given the use of a wagon and of a public slave, who drives the oxen and takes care of their needs. But if there are no women in the group they usually leave the wagon behind, as it would be a nuisance and would slow them down. They take no provisions with them, yet everywhere they go they are well supplied, for the whole of Utopia is their home. If they remain for more than a day in one place, then each of them practices his craft wherever he happens to be and is given a friendly welcome by his fellow craftsmen.

Anyone who leaves their own territory for reasons of their own, and is caught traveling without the governor's passport, is regarded as having disgraced themselves, is brought back as if they were a fugitive from justice, and is severely punished. If they dare do it again, they are condemned to slavery. Anyone who is taken with the urge to stroll through the fields surrounding their town is free to do so, providing they have the consent of their father and the permission of their spouse. But no matter where they go in the countryside, they will be given no lunch until they have completed a morning's stint of work, and no dinner until they have completed what they regard as a normal afternoon's. Subject to these conditions, they may go anywhere they please within the territory of their city, for wherever they go they will be as useful to their fellow citizens as they would have been had they stayed in town.

A holy community! Christians ought to imitate it.

Now you can see that no one ever has permission to loaf, nor any excuse for idleness. There are no wine bars, no pubs, no whorehouses. There are no opportunities for wickedness, no hiding places; there is no scope for conspiring in secret. They are always under the observation of their fellow citizens and have no choice but either to work as hard as the next person, or else engage in respectable pastimes. Such discipline inevitably produces an abundant supply of goods. And since they all receive their fair share of

Equal treatment means there's enough to go around.

society's wealth, it's a necessary consequence that nobody is ever reduced to poverty, and nobody ever has to beg.

In the senate at Amaurot[63] (to which, as I have explained, three representatives come from every city each year), the first order of business is to establish what goods are oversupplied in a particular area, and where there are shortages; they then straightforwardly agree to transfer surpluses to where there are shortages. These transfers are gifts, not loans, for those who receive are not required to make any repayment to those who give. But though a city that gives to its neighbor gets nothing in return, it has the right to get

---

63. *Mentirano* in the first edition; evidently a survival from an earlier version, in which Utopia was called Nusquama and all the other names had Latin roots.

what it needs from another city to whom it has given nothing. *A political*
Thus, the whole island is like a single household. *community*

Once the Utopians have stored up enough to satisfy their own *is really a*
needs (and they only consider they have done this when they have *family writ*
two years' supply in store, for then they need not worry if next *large.*
year's harvest fails), they export large quantities to neighboring
countries: grain, honey, wool, flax, timber, scarlet and purple dyes,
fleeces, wax, tallow, hides, and also livestock. One seventh of all *Utopian*
that they export they give to the poor of the importing country. *commercial*
The rest they sell at a reasonable price. In exchange they import *activities*
into Utopia not only those goods that they are short of at home
(they have virtually everything they need, except iron), but also
vast quantities of silver and gold. Since they have been carrying on
trade for many years on these terms they have by now accumulated
a stockpile of precious metals, which is larger than anyone would
believe possible. As a result, it is now a matter of virtual indifference to them whether they are paid in cash or extend credit to their
purchasers. Most of their sales are in exchange for promissory
notes, but in these cases they always insist that the purchaser must *Thus they*
never be a private individual but that payment must be guaranteed *never forget*
by an enforceable contract with the foreign city itself. When the *the interests*
due date comes the city collects the money owing from the private *of their*
individuals who have taken delivery of the goods and puts it in the *community.*
government treasury. It then enjoys the use of the money until the
Utopians request payment. And usually they never ask to be paid. *How there*
For they have no use for money, and they think it scarcely fair to *can be an*
deprive those who do have need of it of the chance to use it. But if *oversupply*
circumstances require them to lend some of the money to another *of money*
nation, then they request payment. They also call in their loans
when they find themselves at war. Indeed, war is the only purpose
for which they keep all that treasure which they have accumulated
at home, so that they may use it to protect themselves in moments
of extreme or unforeseen danger. Primarily they use it to hire foreign mercenaries, to whom they pay enormous salaries, for they
would rather endanger the lives of strangers than those of their
own citizens. They also realize that if you're prepared to spend *Better to*
enough, many of the enemy soldiers themselves can be induced to *avoid war*
turn against their own side and will either secretly betray their own *by bribery*
forces or even embark upon a civil war. *or cunning*
than to
This is why they have filled their treasury with gold and silver; *engage in*
except they don't keep them in a treasury, or even regard them as *large-scale*
precious. I'm rather ashamed to report exactly what they do with *bloodshed.*

them, for I fear you won't believe what I say. It's not surprising that I expect you to be incredulous, for I am fully aware that it would have been almost impossible to persuade me to believe such a thing on the strength of someone else's report. I believe it only because I saw it with my own eyes. In general the more the practices of another society are at odds with our own, the harder it is to persuade us that they really behave that way. However, if you think it through you may realize that it isn't particularly astonishing that in a society that is completely different from ours in so many respects, the way in which gold and silver are used will correspond to their way of thinking, not to ours. For they have no use for money in their daily lives but merely keep it in case they need it in circumstances that may arise, but on the other hand may never occur. Meanwhile they put gold and silver (which is what money is made of) to a use that ensures that no one will put a higher value on them than that to which their physical attributes entitle them. For anyone can see that iron is much more useful than the so-called precious metals. Iron is as essential to human existence as fire and water, while the natural attributes of gold and silver are such that we could easily make do without them. It is we who in our stupidity have chosen to value them merely because they are in short supply. Nature, by contrast, like a loving parent, has placed everything we need out in the open, where we can get at it. Air, water, and the earth itself are all around us, while we have to search high and low for those materials that are of no practical use to us.

Since the common people are often too clever for their own good, there was an obvious danger that if the Utopians locked these metals away in some fortress, the populace would begin to suspect that the governor and the senate were planning to work some scam and make a profit at the nation's expense. Alternatively, if they were to have craftsmen turn them into plate and other finely wrought objects, then if a time came when they had to be melted down and used to pay an army's wages, they realized, people would be loath to part with objects in which they had begun to take pleasure. In order to eliminate these risks they thought of a strategy that fits in perfectly with the rest of their social institutions, just as it is completely at odds with ours (for we take it for granted that gold should be highly valued and carefully locked away). But that strategy will seem incredible to you, for you have not seen it in practice. For while they eat and drink from dishes and cups made of earthenware and glass—beautifully made, it is true, but very cheap to make— they make their chamber pots and all the other vessels that they use for shameful purposes out of gold and silver; not just the ones they use in their assembly rooms, but all the ones they use in their private homes. In addition, the chains and heavy shackles they put on their slaves are also made from the same materials. Finally, people who have been convicted of some disgraceful act are required to wear gold rings in their ears, gold rings on their fingers, gold chains around their necks, and even gold headbands. Thus they employ every possible measure to ensure that in Utopia gold and silver are associated with shame and disgrace, and this strategy guarantees that if they had to part with their whole stock of these metals all at once, whereas other nations would suffer almost as much at the prospect as if they were being disemboweled, the Utopians would feel the loss was too insignificant to mention. *What magnificent contempt for gold!*

Golden ornaments as symbols of disgrace

Similarly, they pick up pearls when they find them by the seashore, and diamonds and garnets that are sticking out of fallen rocks. They never go looking for them, though, but only collect them when they come across them by chance. They polish them up and give them to their children to wear. Little children take immense pleasure and pride in such baubles, but then when they grow a little older they realize that only kids care about such trifles. Their parents don't have to say a thing. They become ashamed to wear jewelry of their own accord, just as our own children give up jacks, marbles, and dolls when they grow up. *Jewels delight children.*

These customs, which are so different from those of all other nations, result in a people with quite different values and dispositions. The most striking example of this for me was their attitude to the Anemolian[64] ambassadors. They came to Amaurot while I was there. Since the matters they had come to discuss were of the first importance, the three citizens representing each city had assembled before their arrival. The ambassadors from neighboring countries, who had sent missions to Utopia before and were familiar with the customs of the Utopians, knew perfectly well that they put no store by fancy clothing, that they despised silk and held gold in contempt. So they knew to come dressed in their plainest clothes. But the Anemolians, since they lived far away and had had few previous dealings with the Utopians, had merely heard that they all dressed alike and wore simple clothes. They assumed that if the Utopians dressed cheaply, it was because they were impoverished. Since they had more pride than wisdom, they decided to *A first-rate story!*

---

64. From the Greek for "windy."

dress in such gorgeous outfits that they would look more like gods than men, believing they would dazzle the poor Utopians with their sparkling attire.

And so the three ambassadors made their entry with a hundred retainers, all dressed in shimmering colors, and most of them in silk. The ambassadors themselves, who were after all noblemen in Anemolia, wore cloth of gold, with gigantic necklaces and earrings of gold. They had gold rings on their fingers, and sparkling strings of gems and pearls hung from their caps. In short, they were dressed in exactly the way the Utopians dress slaves to punish them, wrongdoers to disgrace them, and children to amuse them. I wouldn't have missed for anything the sight of them strutting and preening themselves as they compared their own fine outfits with those of the Utopians, who had rushed out of their houses to line the streets. And there was just as much pleasure in knowing how completely mistaken their hopes and expectations were, and how far they were from being greeted with the admiration to which they thought they were entitled. To all the Utopians who were staring at them—with the exception of a very few, whose business had taken them to foreign countries—their fancy outfits looked contemptible. So they bowed low to the lowliest servants as they went by, as if they were great lords, while they mistook the ambassadors themselves, since they were wearing gold chains, for slaves, and showed them no respect at all. There were children there who had recently given up their pearls and gems and were astonished to see such toys dangling from the ambassadors' caps. They nudged their

What skill! mothers and said, "Hey, Mother, look at that big idiot wearing pearls and gems as if he were a little kid." And the mother would reply straight-faced, "Hush child, I think he must be one of the ambassadors' jesters." Others found fault with the gold chains, arguing that they were so flimsy as to be useless, since any slave could easily snap them, and so loosely fastened that he could wriggle out of them and run off wherever he wanted to, as free as a bird.

When the ambassadors had spent a day or two there, had seen such quantities of gold put to shameful uses, and had realized that gold was as closely associated with disgrace in Utopia as it was with honor in their own country; when they had realized that the gold and silver that had been used to make the chains and shackles of a single runaway slave would easily pay for the fancy clothes and precious ornaments of all three of them, they didn't feel so cocky, and, shamefaced, changed out of the fancy clothes that they had been so proud to wear—and they felt even more foolish once there had

been an opportunity for them to talk informally with the Utopians
and to learn about their customs and values.

The Utopians can scarcely believe that any human being can be
delighted by the uncertain sparkle of a little jewel or gem when
they can admire any of the stars in the sky, or even the sun itself.
Equally, they can't understand why anyone would think themselves
a finer character because their clothes are made of exceptionally
fine wool. No matter how finely spun it may be, the wool was once
worn by a sheep, and the sheep wasn't so fine that she stopped being a sheep.[65] They are astonished that gold, which has so few practical uses, is now everywhere valued so highly by human beings
that people themselves are thought to be worth much less than
gold, though the value of gold derives entirely from the uses to
which people put it. So much so that a complete idiot, someone
with the intelligence of a fencepost, and someone who is as wicked
as he is stupid, can have many good and wise men at his beck and
call merely because he happens to have a purse full of gold coins. If
some stroke of fortune or some trick of the law (for the law goes
about raising the low and plucking down the high as arbitrarily as
fortune herself) should transfer his gold from him to the lowliest
serving boy in his household, before you know it he would become
the servant of his serving boy, as if he was a mere adjunct to his
coins, and whoever owned them owned him. But even greater than
their astonishment at this is their dismay and horror to see people
so confused that they treat the rich with almost as much respect as
they would show to the gods themselves: rich men to whom they
don't owe money, and whom they have no particular reason to fear,
but over whom they fawn simply because they are rich. And they
carry on like this even with people who they know are so penny-
pinching, so mean, that they can be confident that, no matter how
long they live, not a single penny out of their great heap of wealth
will ever come their way.

The Utopians come to have these views, and other views like
them, in part because of their upbringing, for they have been raised
in a society where people are taught to behave in a way that is directly opposite to idiocies of this sort. But their upbringing is reinforced by their education and the books they read. Although only a
very small number of individuals in each city are permitted to give
up manual work and are assigned full-time to a life of study (these

He calls it uncertain, as jewels are often fake, and certainly one can say their sparkle is feeble and pathetic.

How true, and how well put!

How much wiser the Utopians are than the vast majority of Christians.

---

65 See Lucian, *Demonax*, sect. 41.

being people who from early childhood have demonstrated exceptional abilities, extraordinary intelligence, and a natural inclination
for scholarship), every child receives a sound education, and
throughout their lives a substantial proportion of the population,
both male and female, gives over that part of each day which, as I
have explained, they have free from physical labor to study.

The
education
of the
Utopians
and the
subjects they
study

They conduct their studies in their own native language.[66] It has
an extensive vocabulary and is easy on the ear, and one can express
oneself as well in it as in any other. This same language, or versions
of it (for everywhere outside Utopia it is to some degree corrupted), is diffused throughout that region of the world. As for all
those philosophers and scientists whose names are so well known in
our part of the world, the Utopians had never even heard of any of

Music, logic,
arithmetic

them before our arrival. Yet in music, logic, arithmetic, and geome-
try they have discovered more or less the same body of knowledge
as was taught by the great men of our past. But while their knowl-

This passage
seems
sarcastic.

edge is equal in most respects to that of classical Greece and Rome,
our new logicians have far outstripped them.[67] For the Utopians
have not devised a single one of those extremely subtle rules regarding restrictions, amplifications, and suppositions that have
been introduced into textbooks of elementary logic and are taught
to all our children. Furthermore, they are so far from being able to
conceptualize abstractions that not a single one of them was able to
see what we meant by humanity's species-being, as the philosophers call it, though (as you well know) Man is enormous, bigger
than any giant, and we had no difficulty in pointing him out to
them. On the other hand, though, they have a wonderful knowl-

Astronomy

edge of the courses of the stars and the movements of the planets.
They have invented a number of different ingenious instruments,
which they use to portray with great exactness the movements and

Yet
nowadays
no one
questions the
truth of
astrology.

position of the sun, the moon, and the various stars that are visible
in their hemisphere. As for the conjunctions and oppositions of the
planets, and all the rest of that pretended science which people
claim enables them to foretell the future by the stars, it's never even
crossed their minds. As a result of long and careful observation,

---

66. In contrast to the Europeans of More's own day, who conducted their
studies in Latin.
67. Around the same time that he mocked the new logicians in Book Two
of *Utopia*, More wrote an extended attack on contemporary philosophy in
his open letter to Maarten van Dorp.

they have identified certain indicators that enable them to predict rain, storms, and other changes in the weather. But as to the underlying causes at work, as to explaining the ebb and flow of the tides, or the saltiness of the sea, not to mention the origin and the nature of the heavens and the earth, on these questions they tend to agree with our ancient philosophers. That is to say, much of the time they agree to disagree. They do, however, sometimes invent new explanations, at odds with any known to us; but on these questions they disagree among themselves as to whether to agree.

Physics the least established of all the sciences

In that part of philosophy concerned with human behavior, they carry on the same disputes as we do. They analyze those qualities that justify one in talking about a good mind, a good body, and good circumstances. They argue about whether the word "good" can properly be applied to all of these, or whether it should be reserved for good qualities of the mind. They discuss virtue and pleasure, but their main topic of debate, their primary concern, is the understanding of human happiness, for they disagree about whether there is one thing that makes for happiness, or many different things. On this question they seem rather too inclined to side with those who defend the claims of pleasure, for they hold that if happiness cannot be identified with pleasure, then at least pleasure is the main factor that makes for happiness.[68] You'll be even more surprised to learn that they turn to their religion for arguments in support of this self-indulgent view, though their religion is serious and strict, one might even say gloomy and inflexible. For they never discuss happiness without joining to the rational arguments of philosophy certain principles founded in religious conviction. They believe reason alone, without the support of such principles, is weak and ineffectual when it comes to investigating the nature of true happiness.

Ethics

Ranking differing goods

The ultimate good

The Utopians hold honest pleasure to be the measure of happiness.

Philosophical argument to be grounded in religious premises

These are the principles on which they rely. The human soul is immortal and intended by a loving God to be happy; our virtues and good deeds will be rewarded in a life after death, while our evil deeds will be punished. Although these are religious principles, they believe that reason leads us to believe and adopt them. They are absolutely confident that, without these principles to rely on,

Utopian theology

The immortality of the soul, about which nowadays even quite a few Christians have doubts

---

68. The Utopians therefore agree with Epicurus, and with some humanists, such as Lorenzo Valla (*De voluptate*, 1431). They differ from Epicurus, however, when they insist on belief in the immortality of the soul. Their views are also, as the marginal annotator rightly remarks, close to those of the Stoics.

anybody who could add two and two to make four would recognize
that he or she should seek pleasure without worrying about a di-
vinely ordained moral law. His or her only concern would be to ensure that the pursuit of a lesser pleasure did not prove to be an
obstacle to attaining a greater one, and to take care to avoid pursu-

Just as not
every
pleasure is to
be pursued,
so pain is to
be avoided,
except when
inseparable
from virtue.

ing pleasures that are outweighed by the pains to which they give
rise. They think you would have to be completely mad to live a life
of strict and demanding virtue if it involved not only giving up
life's pleasures but willingly enduring pain with no prospect of personal benefit. And what benefit can you obtain by being virtuous if
there is no reward for virtue in the next life, and it involves contin-
uously giving up pleasure—and consequently living miserably—in
this life?

But if their principles are granted, then happiness is not to be
found in any and every pleasure, but only in those that are good and
honest. One school of thought holds that virtue itself leads us to
pursue honest pleasure as the supreme good for creatures like ourselves; another maintains that virtue is itself true happiness.

This sounds
like the
Stoics.

Either way, they define virtue as living according to nature and
maintain that God himself has designed us so that nature's purposes are his. When people listen to reason before deciding what
objectives they will pursue and what dangers they will try to guard
themselves against, then they are realizing their true nature. And
reason, above all else, fans in us the flames of love and devotion towards God himself, for it teaches us that we owe our existence to
him, and that it is he who has made us capable of achieving happiness. Next, reason advises and urges us to lead a life that is as free
of worries and as full of delights as possible. And it obliges us to
come to the assistance of all our fellow human beings in their quest
for happiness, for we are all engaged in a common enterprise. After
all, there has never been anyone (even among those who believe
that to love virtue you must hate pleasure) so miserable and inflexible that, at the same time as he urged you to adopt a life of toil,
sleepless nights, and deprivation, he would not also order you to do
everything you could to relieve the poverty and distress of those
around you. Even such a devotee of pain would agree that we
should praise people who ensure the comfort and welfare of their
fellows, and that we should praise them for their humanity. Nothing is more humane than to relieve the sufferings of others and, by
eliminating the causes of misery, enable them to live a life of happiness, that is of pleasure, and humanity is the virtue above all others
that human beings should strive to exemplify. Surely, then, nature

must require us to treat ourselves with the same kindness we are supposed to show to others. For either a life of happiness (or, for it amounts to the same thing, of pleasure) is evil, or it isn't. If it is evil, then not only is it wrong to bring a little happiness into someone's life, but you should positively seek to destroy happiness wherever you find it on the grounds that it is not merely harmful, but deadly. But if you are not only allowed but are actually obliged to help others attain happiness, on the grounds that happiness is good, then why shouldn't your first concern be to make yourself happy? For you ought to treat yourself at least as well as you treat other people. Or do you imagine that when nature tells you to be kind to others, she intends you to understand the opposite when it comes to yourself; that you should be cruel and merciless? Therefore, they say, we can see that nature herself orders us to make a life of happiness (that is to say, a life of pleasure) the goal of all our actions; and we have already seen that they define virtue as behavior in accord with nature's commands. Nature is certainly right to urge human beings to cooperate in making each other's lives happier, for no one has been created to be so superior to their fellow human beings as to be able to claim that their own welfare is nature's sole concern; indeed, nature cherishes equally all those creatures that share the same biological identity, and it follows that she warns you over and over again to take care that in seeking your own advantage you do not cause harm to others.

But nowadays some people embrace pain as if it were inseparable from true religion, rather than being something to bear if it happens to be a consequence of acting morally, or if it is imposed upon us by natural necessity.

   They believe it follows that not only must one fulfill a private contract once one has entered into it, but one must also obey valid government decrees. Laws about the distribution of resources— and resources are the raw material of pleasure—are to be obeyed if they have been decreed by a good king or approved by the representatives of the people, provided they are not oppressed by tyranny or deliberately misinformed. To pursue your own interests within the framework set by the law is prudence; to go beyond that and pursue the public welfare is patriotism. But to deprive someone else of pleasure in order to obtain it for yourself is unjust. On the other hand, to deprive yourself of something so that others may benefit is to act in a fashion that is humane and benevolent, although what you give up will always prove to have been wisely invested. For good deeds bring reciprocal favors; and in any case the knowledge that you have acted properly, and the memory of the affection and goodwill of those you have benefited, will give you more spiritual pleasure than the goods you have given up would have given you physical pleasure. Lastly, religion will easily convince

Contracts and laws

Helping each other

anyone who is willing to have faith that God will repay the loss of a brief and slight pleasure with an eternal and exquisite delight. And so this is how they conclude, having given the matter careful thought and due consideration, that all our actions (even our virtuous deeds) are directed towards pleasure as their goal and fulfillment.

Pleasure defined

They define pleasure as any movement or state of body or mind in which we naturally take delight. They are right to specify that the pleasure must be natural, for both our senses themselves and right reason pursue pleasures only if they are natural, that is, if they do not involve harm to others, do not involve the loss of a greater pleasure, and do not give rise to pain. Some sensations that

False pleasures

are not naturally delightful human beings pretend to themselves are pleasurable and conspire together to call pleasures (as if one could change the real nature of things as easily as one can change the name for something), but the Utopians believe that all such pleasures do not make for true happiness and are often an obstacle to it. This is because once one has become preoccupied with these so-called pleasures they displace the genuine delights one would otherwise have pursued, and the mind becomes entirely preoccupied with a false idea of pleasure. For there are very many things that of their own nature contain no pleasantness; indeed for the most part they involve a good deal of suffering, yet through the perverse attractions of distorted desires they are not only taken to be the most exquisite pleasures but are even thought to be among the few things that make life worth living.

The mistake of those who take pride in appearance

Among the counterfeit pleasures they include one I mentioned earlier: the conviction many people have that the better the clothes they wear the better people they are. Such thinking involves not one mistake but two, for they are just as mistaken when they think their clothes are better than other people's as when they think they themselves are better. If you judge a garment by its usefulness, why should you assume that a finer thread is superior to a thicker one? But they, as if they were genuinely superior and did not merely take themselves to be, puff themselves up and think their fancy clothes increase their own value. They are convinced they are entitled to be treated with respect because of the way they are dressed, while if they were more plainly attired they wouldn't dare assume they should be singled out. And if someone passes them on the street without a mark of respect they become indignant.

Honors for fools

Isn't the same kind of error involved in taking meaningless and purely honorific titles seriously? For what natural and authentic pleasure is to be derived from the fact that someone bares his head or bends his knee to you? Will this cure you if your own knees are stiff and sore? Will this help you think straight if your brains are scrambled? It's astonishing how much deranged pleasure people take in imaginary, counterfeit delights. They relish the thought of their own nobility and congratulate themselves on the ancestors they chance to have, generation after generation of whom have been taken for rich (for wealth is the only nobility these days), and rich not just in money but in landed estates. They don't even think themselves the slightest bit less distinguished if none of their ancestors' wealth has come down to them, or if they themselves have squandered their own inheritance.

Empty nobility

As I have explained, the Utopians include in the same category people who are preoccupied with jewels and precious stones and who think they're in heaven if they acquire a first-rate specimen, particularly if it is of whatever particular type of rock is especially fashionable at that moment in their social circle—for at different times, in different places, different rocks are prized. And no one will buy a stone until they've had it out of its gold setting and inspected it all over; and even then they will insist that the vendor swear it is genuine and give a written guarantee. They're terrified that they'll mistake a counterfeit for the real thing. But why should you get any less pleasure out of looking at a fake if your eyes can't see the difference between it and the genuine article? Both should be worth the same to you, just as they would be equally valuable, goodness knows, to a blind person.[69]

The ridiculous pleasure afforded by jewelery

Fashion increases or decreases the value of jewels.

And what's one to make of people who stockpile money? They have no use for such quantities but simply take pleasure in the sight of them. Are they experiencing a genuine pleasure, or are they being taken in by an imaginary one? Or what about those whose covetousness takes a different form: they bury gold coins they are

---

69. The following passage from *Praise of Folly* would appear to be a story about More: "I know someone of my name who made his new bride a present of some jewels which were copies, and as he had a ready tongue for a joke, persuaded her that they were not only real and genuine but also of a unique and incalculable value. Now, if the young woman was just as happy feasting her eyes and thoughts on coloured glass, what did it matter to her that she was keeping such trinkets hidden carefully away in her room as if they were some rare treasure? Meanwhile her husband saved expense, enjoyed his wife's illusion, and kept her as closely bound in gratitude to him as if he'd given her something which had cost him a fortune." (trans. B. Radice, ed. A. H. T. Levi, Penguin, 1971, rev. ed. 1993, p. 72)

A
remarkable
hypothesis,
and very
telling

never going to use and perhaps may never see again. They're afraid of losing their wealth, and so they ensure that it's as good as lost. For what difference does it make that it's still yours when you can make no use of it, and perhaps nobody will ever be able to use it again, now that it's back in the earth? And yet once you've hidden your gold, you feel like dancing with delight, as if you no longer had a care in the world. What if someone comes along and steals it, and you die ten years later without ever learning of the theft? Throughout those ten years that you remained alive after the money was gone, what difference did it make to you whether it was there or was gone? For it was just as useful to you one way as the other.

Dice

In their list of absurd pleasures they include gambling (for they've heard how crazy gamblers can be, though none of them gamble themselves), along with hunting and hawking. Where is the pleasure in throwing dice on a table over and over again? Even if it was fun the first time, wouldn't doing it again and again lead one to grow bored with it? Is it possible to experience a pleasant sensation when listening to the yapping and howling of dogs? Doesn't it

Hunting

rather hurt the ears? Why should the sight of a dog chasing a hare cause more pleasure than the sight of a dog chasing a dog? For what's going on is identical in both cases, and if you enjoy watching dogs run you should enjoy the second case as much as the first. But if you really go to see blood, if the hope of seeing a living creature torn apart in front of your eyes is what draws you, then what you ought to feel is pity, not pleasure, at the sight of the little hare being savaged by the hound, the weak falling prey to the strong, a de-

Yet today
this is the
favorite
recreation of
our masters
at court.

fenseless and timorous creature falling victim to an aggressor, an innocent life being taken by a ruthless murderer. And so the Utopians, who regard every aspect of hunting as demeaning, insist that it be conducted only by butchers, who, as I have already explained, are all slaves. They regard hunting as the vilest form of butchery. Other methods of killing animals they believe to be more useful and more respectable. The slaughterman feeds more people and kills only so that others may eat, while the hunter is only after pleasure when he kills some poor little creature and butchers it. If one takes pleasure at the sight of killing, even if it is only animals that are being killed, then, they believe, this means one either has a cruel disposition to begin with, or else will end up brutalized by the continuous pursuit of such cruel pleasures.

The average person regards these activities and others like them (there are too many even to be counted) as pleasures; but the

Utopians firmly believe that they bear no resemblance to genuine pleasures, since there's nothing naturally pleasurable about them. They concede that they are often associated with pleasant sensations, which seems to imply that they are indeed pleasures, but they hold to their view despite this. In such cases the pleasure derives not from the nature of the activity itself, but from the deformed habits of ordinary people. Their corruption causes them to take pleasure in bitter things, mistaking them for sweet, just as *The peculiar* pregnant women have distorted sensations and think tar and candle *tastes of* wax are sweeter than honey. A person's sensory responses may be *pregnant* rendered unreliable either by disease or by acquired habits, but this *women* does not mean that whether something is naturally pleasurable or not is subject to change, any more than it means that other natural characteristics are mutable.

They classify what they take to be genuine pleasures into several *Categories* different categories. Some they term pleasures of the mind, others *of true* of the body. Among the pleasures of the mind they include under- *pleasure* standing and the satisfaction one feels on reflecting on true knowledge. To these they add the way one can savor the memory of a life well spent and the confident expectation of happiness in the life to come.

The pleasures of the body they divide into two types. In the first *Pleasures of* the senses are pervaded by a distinct feeling of pleasantness. This *the body* happens, for example, with the restoration to vigor of organs that have been worn out by our bodily functions: food and drink, we know, renew and refresh us. Or it happens with the elimination of some excess from the body. We experience this pleasure when we evacuate our bowels, or engage in sexual congress, or relieve the itching of any part of our body by rubbing or scratching it. Sometimes pleasure arises not from making good some deficiency that we sense in our body, nor by eliminating some discomfort, but through some mysterious but unmistakable force that tickles and excites our senses and makes them alert to its influence. Music affects us in this way.

They say that the second type of bodily pleasure consists in the peaceful and harmonious condition of the body, that's to say, the health of the individual when undisturbed by any discomfort. This state, when the body is free of pain, is pleasurable in itself, even if the body is receiving no pleasurable stimulation from outside. Although this form of pleasure excites the senses and captures the attention much less than the desire to eat or to drink, nevertheless many hold this to be the most exquisite pleasure of all. Virtually all

To be happy the Utopians agree that this is not only a significant pleasure in it-
you must be self but also the foundation and basis of all the other pleasures. On
healthy. its own it makes life peaceful and satisfactory, and without it there
is no scope for any other pleasure. But to be simply free of pain,
without the sensation of well-being, is, they say, to be numb, not to
experience pleasure.

They long ago rejected the arguments of those who maintained
that a steady and peaceful condition of good health is not to be considered a true pleasure, although at the time this view provoked
considerable debate among them. Its proponents maintained that
one can experience a sensation only through the stimulus of something external to the body, but now almost everyone holds the alternative view, that health is one of the greatest pleasures. For they
argue that pain is an attribute of disease, and that pain is the implacable enemy of pleasure in the same way that disease is the enemy of health. Why then should not pleasure be an attribute of
peaceful good health? They think it makes no difference to the argument whether you think pain and disease are one and the same
thing, or whether you think pain is an attribute of disease, since it
amounts to the same thing in the end. Health may be a pleasure in
itself, or it may inevitably engender pleasure, as fire engenders
heat; either way, the result is that those who have uninterrupted
good health cannot but experience pleasure.

They maintain that what is going on when we are eating is that
health, which was beginning to be weakened, takes food as its ally
in the struggle against hunger. As our health slowly regains the up-
per hand in this conflict, the process of recovering our accustomed
strength gives us pleasure, which in turn reinvigorates us. If our
health takes pleasure in its struggle with hunger, will it not also rejoice when it has conquered it? Throughout the conflict its goal
was to recover its original strength; when it achieves its objective
will it immediately become insensible and fail to recognize and embrace its own good? The claim that there can be no sensory experience of good health is, they believe, far from the truth. Surely any
human being, providing he is awake, can feel that he is healthy; unless of course he is ill. Is there anyone so overwhelmed by numb-
ness or by lethargy that he will not admit that being in good health
gives him satisfaction, even delight? And what is delight but pleasure under another name?

They are primarily interested in the pleasures of the mind, for
they consider them to be the most important and the most satisfying. And the most important of the intellectual pleasures, they be-

lieve, is achieved through the practice of the virtues and the sense of a life well lived. Of those pleasures that derive from physical sensation, they think good health is the most important. For the delights of eating and drinking, and of other similar pleasures, are, they argue, worth pursuing, but only because they lead to good health. Such experiences are not really pleasurable for themselves, but because they are associated with resistance to the scouting parties of ill heath. Just as the wise want to avoid falling ill and regard being successfully treated for illness as a second best; just as they think that never experiencing pain is preferable to being relieved of it; so, equally, it would be preferable not to have a need for pleasures of this sort, and wallowing in them is far from ideal.

If anyone thinks that true happiness lies in this kind of pleasure, then they are obliged to admit that the pinnacle of pleasure for them would be to lead a life in which they were constantly assailed by hunger, thirst, and itching, constantly eating, drinking, scratching, and rubbing. Surely anyone can see that such a life would not only be disgusting, but wretched! These pleasures are unquestionably the lowest of all, for they are the most imperfect. You can never experience them except in conjunction with the pains that are their opposites. The pleasure of eating, for example, is inseparable from the pain of hunger, but unfortunately the two are not equally matched, for the pain is sharper and lasts longer than the pleasure. Indeed, the pain not only precedes the pleasure, but it disappears only as the pleasure itself fades away. Thus they think it is wrong to set much store by pleasures of this sort, though no one can do without them. Of course, they too enjoy eating and drinking, and they are thankful that Mother Nature is an indulgent parent who entices her children with delicious pleasures to do what otherwise they would have to be constantly forced to do by pressure of necessity. How miserable life would be if the daily diseases of hunger and thirst had to be treated with bitter potions and sour medicines, as we have to treat the other diseases that infect us less frequently!

Yet fitness, strength, agility—of these, as special and pleasant gifts of nature, they make much. They also seek to enjoy the pleasures of sound, sight, and smell, as they think they add savor and spice to life. They maintain that nature intended them to be a particular and unique characteristic of humankind, for no other species of animal takes pleasure in the construction and beauty of the natural world, or enjoys scents (except when distinguishing the edible from the inedible), or distinguishes between harmonious

and dissonant musical intervals. But in all their activities they respect this principle: that the lesser pleasure should be sacrificed to
the greater, and that no pleasure should be pursued if it will lead to
pain. For they believe that pleasures that cause pain are by defini-
tion dishonorable.

They think it is completely mad for someone to despise fitness,
to allow their strength to atrophy, to transform agility into slug-
gishness, to run down their body with fasts, to injure their health,
and to turn their back on nature's other pleasures, unless they are
sacrificing their own welfare so that they can more effectively secure the welfare of others or the public good. In such a circum-
stance they can expect that God will repay them for their efforts
with a pleasure greater than any they have gone without. Otherwise
it is crazy to give up one's own pleasure for the pointless appearance of virtue if no one actually benefits thereby, nor should one do
without pleasure in order to prepare oneself to withstand suffering
with greater equanimity, for the evil day may never come. In their
view this is evidence of people who are cruel to themselves and
completely lacking in gratitude for nature's kindness. It is as if they
were too proud to be in her debt and so refused to accept her gifts.

*Take very
careful note
of this!*

These are the views they hold on the question of pleasure and
pain. They believe that human reason can make no further
progress towards truth, unless a religion sent down from heaven
should inspire human beings with more sacred convictions. We do
not have the time to determine whether the conclusions they have
reached are right or wrong, nor is it important for us to do so, since
my purpose here is to describe their principles, not to defend them.

*The
happiness
of the
Utopians,
and their
appearance*

But I certainly do believe that, whatever one makes of their principles, one cannot find anywhere else a more excellent people or a
happier society.

They are physically agile and energetic, and stronger than you
would think judging by their size, which is not to say they are
small. Their soil is not particularly fertile, but they work hard to
improve it. Their climate is not especially healthy, but they avoid
its ill effects by temperate living. You won't find anywhere else
grain and cattle in more ample supply, or people's bodies more vigorous or less prone to illness. There not only might you watch farmers doing to the best of their ability all those things that farmers do
elsewhere in order to improve poor soil by the application of sweat
and skill, but you could see a whole forest dug up by the roots and
replanted elsewhere, a task in which all the inhabitants worked together. They undertook this not in order to increase the yield of

timber but in order to make it easier to transport, by producing it closer to the sea, to navigable rivers, and to the cities themselves. For it is relatively easier to transport grain any significant distance over land than timber.

The people are gentle, cheerful, and clever. They enjoy their free time but are able to put up with hard work when needs be (though they certainly don't take pleasure in it for its own sake). It is when they turn to intellectual activities that they are tireless. When we told them about the literature and learning of the Greeks (for we thought that there was nothing in Latin that they would appreciate, with the exception of the historians and the poets), it was remarkable to see how eagerly they begged that they should be given the opportunity to learn that language through our instruction. We began therefore to give them lessons. At first we were mainly concerned with showing that we were prepared to go to some trouble; we scarcely expected them to learn anything. But we hadn't been at it for long before we realized that they were diligent students, and that consequently our own efforts would not be wasted. We were astonished to see how easily they learned to copy the Greek alphabet, how quickly they learned to pronounce the words, and how speedily they memorized them, so that they could soon recite whole passages accurately. It is true that most of our students were scholars of exceptional ability and mature years, and that they were not simply eager to learn but were also instructed by the senate to do so. As a result, in less than three years they had learned the language perfectly and could read the best authors fluently, provided they had a reliable copy of the text. I suspect that they learned the language all the more easily because it is somewhat related to their own. I believe the Utopians are descended from the Greeks because their language, though it resembles Persian in other respects, retains some traces of Greek in the words used for the names of cities and for the titles of public officials.[70]

The usefulness of learning Greek

The Utopians' remarkable aptitude for learning

But now dolts and dunderheads take up the vocation of scholarship, while the finest minds are destroyed by a life of self-indulgence.

Before I set out on my fourth voyage I loaded on board a decent-sized bale of books, instead of trade goods, for I had made up my mind that I would certainly be away for a long time and knew that I might never return. So I was able to give them my copies of most of Plato's works, and even more of Aristotle's, along with Theophrastus on plants, although I am sorry to say that book was somewhat

---

70. This is of course a clue to readers to help them decipher the names of Utopia.

damaged. For while we were at sea a monkey came across the book—I had carelessly left it lying about—and picked it up to play with. He thought it great fun to tear pages out at random and rip them up. They have only one grammar book, that of Lascaris, for I had not taken a copy of Theodorus with me. And the only dictionary they have is the one by Hesychius, plus Dioscorides. They love the works of Plutarch, and they also greatly enjoy the witticisms and jokes of Lucian. Of the poets they have Aristophanes, Homer, and Euripides, and a copy of Sophocles in Aldus's pocketbook format.[71] Of the historians they have Thucydides and Herodotus, and also Herodian.

As far as medical books are concerned, my companion Tricius Apinatus[72] brought with him some of the shorter works of Hippocrates and Galen's *Microtechne.* They valued these books very

Nothing more useful than the study of medicine highly, for although there is scarcely any country in the world that is in less need of medical expertise, medical science is nowhere regarded with more respect, for they believe that medicine is one of the most beautiful as well as one of the most useful branches of knowledge. They are convinced that when, with the help of this

Contemplation of nature particular type of natural philosophy, they search out the hidden secrets of nature, they are not only giving themselves an exquisite pleasure but are also winning the warmest affection of nature's author and fabricator. For they think that he, as craftsmen do, constructed the amazing structure of this world and put it on show so that it could be admired by humankind, human beings being the only creatures he had created capable of understanding his achievement. Consequently, he is bound to have more affection for the inquisitive and astonished observer and admirer of his workmanship than for someone who behaves like an animal lacking the capacity for understanding and pays no attention to so grand and marvelous a spectacle, remaining blind and unmoved in its presence.

The intellects of the Utopians, well trained through their studies, are remarkably successful at inventing techniques that pay off in making life more comfortable. But there are two techniques that they owe to us—or at least partly to us, and partly to their own skills. These are the casting of metal type and the manufacture of

---

71. Aldus, who was based in Venice, was one of the greatest publishers of the day, comparable in importance to Froben. Erasmus worked in collaboration with both of them.
72. The Roman poet Martial had said of his poems, *sunt apinae tricaeque:* 'they're trifles and toys."

paper. For when we showed them books made of paper and printed with type made by Aldus, we chatted about the material out of which paper is made and the technique of printing letters—I say we chatted, for we were hardly in a position to provide a proper explanation, since none of us had any practical experience of the procedures involved. At once they brilliantly worked out what was involved. And whereas before they had written only on vellum, bark, and papyrus, they now set about making paper and printing letters. At first they weren't particularly successful, but after making numerous attempts they soon produced satisfactory results in both paper manufacture and printing. They are so successful that if they had copies of the works of Greek authors they would have no trouble reproducing them. At the moment all they have are the works I have mentioned, but these they have replicated by printing thousands of copies.

Any traveler who comes to see their country and who has some exceptional intellectual capacity, or who as a result of his journeying has acquired a knowledge of the methods employed in many different countries, is warmly received, which is why our own landfall was welcome. They love to hear news of what is going on anywhere in the world. But their opportunities are limited, as few merchants come to them. What cargo could they bring, except iron, or else gold and silver, which merchants prefer to carry home with them? And then when it comes to exporting goods, the Utopians think it wiser to transport them themselves, rather than have others come to fetch them. That way they learn more about a wide range of foreign countries, and their own technical skills when it comes to deepwater sailing are kept up to scratch.

On Slaves

Slaves in Utopia are not people who have been captured in battle, except by the Utopians themselves. The children of slaves are not born into slavery. They do not purchase from other countries people who have been enslaved there. Slaves are either people who have been condemned to slavery because of some dreadful crime they have committed in Utopia, or else people who have committed crimes in foreign cities and been condemned to death. By far the majority are of the second sort, for the Utopians import them in large numbers. Sometimes they buy them cheap. Usually they are given them for nothing. Slaves of both kinds work without respite and are always chained. But the Utopians subject their own citizens

The remarkable fairness of this nation

to the harshest regime, as they believe they are more at fault, and deserving of greater punishment, for despite having received an absolutely first-rate moral education, it has still proved impossible to prevent them from turning to crime. A third type of unfree laborer consists of hard-working, poverty-stricken servants who have chosen of their own free will to indenture themselves to the Utopians. They are decently treated, living lives almost as good as the citizens themselves, except that they are expected to do a little bit of extra work, since they're accustomed to it. They are free to leave if they choose, which they rarely do, despite the fact that they receive a payment on their departure.

The sick   As I explained earlier, the sick receive extremely sympathetic care, and nothing that might help their recovery, whether it involve medicine or diet, is neglected. Those who are suffering from incurable diseases receive the best possible palliative care, and people come and sit with them and talk to them. But if their disease not only is incurable, but also causes them unremitting, excruciating pain, then the priests and public officials urge the patients to recog-
Choosing to nize that they are no longer capable of fulfilling any of life's duties,
die   that they are now a nuisance to others and a burden to themselves, and that they are alive although it is past time for them to die. They tell them that they should not allow this dreadful disease to feed on them any longer, and, now that it is torture to be alive, they should not hesitate to die. They should put their hope in the life to come, and they should either break out of this present life, as they would escape from a prison or a torture chamber, or else agree to let others rescue them. In so doing they would be acting wisely, for their death would put an end not to pleasure, but to terrible suffering. Moreover, they would be following the advice of the priests, who interpret to us the will of God, and so their action would be pious and godly.

Those who are persuaded by these arguments either choose to starve themselves to death or are released from their sufferings in their sleep and are never conscious of dying. But they never dispatch anyone against their will, and those who choose to live on they continue to tend as gently as before. Those who are urged to end their lives and do so die an honorable death, but those who kill themselves for reasons that have not been approved by the priests and the senate they regard as disgraced and unworthy of either burial or cremation, so they unceremoniously throw their bodies into a bog.

Marriage   Women do not marry until they are eighteen, while men are required to be four years older. If a man or a woman is convicted of secretly engaging in premarital intercourse he or she is severely punished, and both parties are permanently forbidden to marry, unless the governor's pardon releases them from their sentence. Both the father and mother in charge of the household where the offense was committed suffer disgrace for having been negligent in fulfilling their responsibilities. They punish this crime so severely because they reason that otherwise few people would join together in married love, realizing that they will be obliged to spend the rest of their life with the same person and that they will also have to put up with all the vexations that implies, unless they were strictly prevented from engaging in promiscuity.

There is a custom that they solemnly and strictly observe when it comes to choosing a marriage partner, which seemed to us absolutely silly and completely ridiculous. The woman, whether she be a virgin or a widow, is shown naked to her suitor by a responsible and respectable married woman; similarly, a man of good reputation shows the naked suitor to the young woman. We mocked this custom and thought it ridiculous, but they for their part were just as astonished by the complete stupidity of every other nation. When people go to buy a colt, although very little money is at stake, they are so cautious that, although the greater part of the animal is exposed to view, they refuse to buy unless the saddle and the harness are taken off, in case there is some sore lurking beneath these coverings. Yet in the choice of a spouse, which will result in either pleasure or disgust for the whole of the rest of one's life, people are so careless that a man will judge a woman on the basis of the mere handsbreadth of her body which is visible—that's to say her face, which is all he can usually see, for the rest of her is shrouded in clothes. And thus they are joined together, though there's an obvious danger of their being ill suited, should some aspect of one partner's body prove later to be repulsive to the other. For most people aren't wise enough to judge others by their character alone; and even the truly wise regard attractive physical characteristics in their marital partners as a significant supplement to moral qualities. There's no question but some disgusting deformity may lie hidden under a woman's clothing, one bad enough to alienate a man's affections from his wife, and yet one that he discovers only when he has lost the right to separate his body from hers. Of course, accident or disease may bring about some dreadful deformity after the marriage has been contracted, and then there's nothing that can be done about it, but there ought to be a law to

Prudence will approve, though modesty protests.

protect people before they enter into marriage from being deliberately deceived.

The Utopians have all the more reason to take precautions because they are the only nation in that part of the world of people who are faithful to their partners. Marriages there are rarely dissolved except by death, although they allow divorce for adultery or for intolerable behavior.[73] The innocent party in such a divorce is given permission by the senate to remarry; the guilty party not only suffers disgrace but also is condemned to a lifetime of celibacy. But they never permit a spouse to put away a partner against his or her will if he or she has done nothing wrong but has simply suffered some physical calamity. They think it cruel to abandon someone at the time when they are most in need of support, and maintain that old age, which is itself an infirmity and leads to other infirmities as well, deserves more than an uncertain and unreliable fidelity.

Occasionally a husband and wife turn out to have incompatible characters, and both of them find other people with whom they believe they could live more harmoniously. Provided they first obtain permission from the senate they may separate by mutual consent and enter into new marriages. The senate will not approve such a divorce until the senators and their wives have carefully inquired into the circumstances. Even then they will be reluctant to consent, since they know that the affection that partners should express towards each other will be undermined, not reinforced, if each nurtures the hope of entering into a new marriage without much difficulty.

Those who fail to remain faithful to their spouses are punished with the strictest form of slavery. If both the offenders are married, then those they have wronged may, if they choose, divorce them and marry each other, or anyone else they choose. But if either of the injured parties is determined to go on loving a spouse who is so undeserving, then the law does not prohibit the continuation of the marriage, provided the innocent partner shares in the labors of the guilty one. Sometimes it happens that the penitence of the guilty partner, and the earnest diligence of the innocent one, move the governor to take pity on them, and he restores them to their freedom. But if the guilty partner offends again, he or she suffers the death penalty.

Divorce

---

73. More would have been aware that Erasmus was exceptional in advocating divorce and remarriage for the injured party in cases of adultery. Church law was opposed to divorce for any reason.

There is no fixed punishment for other crimes; the senate decrees an appropriate punishment for each infraction, taking into account the extent to which it seems outrageous, or the nature of any mitigating circumstances. Husbands discipline their wives and parents their children, unless the offense committed is so dreadful that it needs to be punished in public as an example to others. Generally serious offenses are punished with slavery, for they think this deters potential offenders as effectively as would the death penalty, and society benefits more than it would if they were in a hurry to do away with the guilty. For if they live, the community benefits from their labor, and at the same time they are a continuing reminder to others who might be tempted to follow in their footsteps. But if those who are condemned to slavery rebel and prove disobedient, then they are put to death as though they were wild beasts who could not be tamed by cages and chains. Yet if they submit patiently, then their situation is not completely hopeless. For if their behavior suggests that they regret their evil deeds even more than they dislike their punishment, their servitude will be lightened or brought to an end, either because the governor chooses to exercise his prerogative or because the people as a whole vote to show clemency. *The judges determine the penalty.*

Anyone who tries to seduce another person will be punished as severely as if they had succeeded, for they take the view that a deliberate and indubitable attempt to commit a crime is morally indistinguishable from the criminal act itself. The fact that they failed should not count in favor of someone who made every effort to succeed. *Punishment for attempted seduction*

They take great delight in simpletons.[74] Anyone who mocks them is held in contempt, but there is no objection to people being amused by their antics. Indeed they believe that idiots are much the happier for giving pleasure to others. If anyone is so severe and so solemn that nothing that a fool can do or say makes them laugh, then they do not allow them to be responsible for looking after such a person, for they would be concerned that they would not treat them as gently as they should. After all, fools are of no practical use to anyone; the one good thing they can do is give amusement. *Fools delight.*

---

74. The Latin word, translated here as "simpleton" and "fool," is *morio*, which would have reminded readers of More's own name and of Erasmus's *Praise of Folly* (*Encomium moriae*). More himself kept a fool, Henry Patenson.

To laugh at someone because they are deformed or crippled is regarded as an indication that there is some moral deformity in the mocker, not the victim, for otherwise they would not be so stupid as to blame someone for something outside their own control.

Counterfeit beauty

In their view anyone who fails to make the most of the physical endowments nature has given them is lazy and slothful, but on the other hand to use cosmetics to improve on them they regard as disreputable and vain. Experience has convinced them that no physical attractions are as effective in making husbands think well of their wives as a good character and a respectful demeanor. Beauty alone may be enough to make some men fall in love; but for love to endure, virtue and obedience are essential.

Rewards provide incentives for good behavior.

They do not only deter people from committing crimes by punishing defaulters; they also incite them to good behavior with the prospect of honor and status. They set up statues in public places of distinguished human beings and of people who have placed the nation in their debt, both to preserve the memory of noble deeds, and so that the glory of their ancestors may spur their descendants on to comparable behavior.

Canvassing forbidden

Anyone who campaigns to be elected to a public office is regarded as having permanently disqualified himself from any office at all. They live on good terms with each other partly because none

Respect for public officials

of their public officials is overbearing or awe-inspiring. They call them 'fathers,' and that's how they behave. The people treat their officials with respect (as they should) because they want to, not because they are forced to. The governor himself does not dress dif-

The governor's badge of office

ferently or wear a crown; what marks him out is a handful of grain that is borne before him, just as the high priest is identified by a candle that precedes him wherever he goes.

Few laws

They have very few laws, for they are so well trained that they hardly need any. One of their main criticisms of other nations is that they have innumerable volumes of laws and of commentaries on the law, but even these are not enough. They think it is completely wrong to oblige people to obey laws that are too numerous to be read from beginning to end, or too obscure to be understood by the person in the street. They will have nothing to do with

The useless swarm of lawyers

lawyers, for they only quibble about the meaning of the laws and try to get around them. They think it best if each person pleads his own case and tells the judge exactly what he would have told his own lawyer. As a result there is less confusion, and it is easier to get at the truth. The defendant speaks frankly, without having been trained in deception by some lawyer, and the judge carefully weighs up everything he says and comes to the assistance of naïve witnesses who otherwise might fall victim to the false accusations of the cunning and deceitful. This sort of fair treatment is hard to find in other countries, where they have vast numbers of virtually incomprehensible laws. In Utopia, by contrast, everyone has an expert knowledge of the law. For, as I have said, there are very few laws, and they believe that it is always fairest to interpret the law in its simplest and most obvious sense. They argue that the only reason for having laws is to inform every citizen of their duty, and subtle interpretations are scarcely helpful in telling people what to do, for very few can follow them. The obvious and straightforward meaning of the law, by contrast, is one that everyone can make out. The majority of the population consists of ordinary people without much education, and they are precisely the people who are most in need of being told what they may and may not do. As far as they are concerned you might as well have no laws at all as have laws that you interpret as meaning things which no one could find in them unless they brought to them not only exceptional intelligence but also a profound knowledge of the arguments of previous interpreters. The simple minds of ordinary people aren't sharp enough to follow such reasoning, and even if they were they don't have a lifetime to devote to the task, since they have a living to earn.

Many of the countries neighboring Utopia are free and autonomous—often because the Utopians themselves earlier freed them from subjection to tyranny—and these states are so impressed by the admirable features of the Utopian legal system that they acquire their legal officers and civil servants from Utopia, sometimes offering them one-year contracts, and sometimes five-year ones. At the end of their term of office they bring them back to Utopia, praising and honoring them for the service they have done, and return to their own countries accompanied by their successors. These peoples have certainly come up with an excellent and foolproof way of running their countries. For whether a political system fares well or badly depends on the moral caliber of those in charge. And where could they find wiser governors than these? For they are quite uninterested in taking bribes, since money will be useless to them when they return home, as they soon will. Moreover, since they are outsiders, they have no factional commitments or hidden allegiances. Wherever the legal system is tainted by the two evils of partisanship and bribery justice itself ceases to exist, and justice is the cement that holds society together. The Utopians call these peoples who come to them to find their judges and civil

servants their allies; other nations to whom they have provided
other forms of assistance they call their friends.

On treaties   Other nations are constantly making, breaking, and renewing
treaties with each other. The Utopians never sign anything. "
"What's the point of treaties?" they ask. They believe nature herself ensures that the interests of different peoples coincide. "Why
would a government that has no respect for the natural order of
things take mere words to heart?" They are strongly reinforced
in this view by the fact that in their part of the world treaties and
alliances between princes are not usually respected as they ought
to be.

Here in Europe, of course, the authority of treaties is everywhere recognized as sacred and inviolable, and this is especially
true in those countries that are properly called Christian. This is
partly because our rulers are all just and honest; but it is also because they all respect and fear the authority of the pope. The popes
not only set an example by never promising to do something and
then failing to perform; they also order all other rulers to fulfill
their promises, no matter what. Those who try to refuse are forced
to obey by pastoral censures and public condemnation. The popes
take the view (as indeed they should) that it would be shocking if
you couldn't put your faith in treaties entered into by people who
call themselves "the faithful."[75]

But in this newly discovered part of the world, whose manners
and morals are miles apart from ours—after all, it's far off in the
other hemisphere—nobody expects anyone to respect their treaty
obligations. The more elaborate and solemn the ceremonies that
accompany the signing of a treaty, the sooner it is broken. It doesn't
take long to find some defect in the wording, for they have the fore-
sight to insert defects when the treaties are drawn up. Nobody can
negotiate terms that don't leave some loophole or other through
which a government can slip, in the process making a mockery both
of the treaty and of their claim to have negotiated it in good faith. If
it was discovered that such sharp practice (not to say fraud and deception) was being exploited by the parties to private contracts,
there would be an immediate outcry, and people would protest that
such behavior was unconscionable, and sacrilegious, and ought to
be harshly punished. Leading the protest, you can be sure, would
be the very people who take pride in having advised rulers on how

---

75. This passage is sarcastic.

to avoid fulfilling their promises. The result is that people think of justice as a humble and inferior virtue, one that it would be far below the dignity of a king to cultivate. Or else they conclude that there are two distinct kinds of justice. One is suitable for ordinary people. It is humble and lowly, tied down with chains and fetters, quite incapable of breaking free. The other is a virtue peculiar to princes. Naturally, it's much more distinguished than its popular cousin, and a great deal freer to do as it pleases. Indeed, the only rule it has to obey is that it must never do anything it doesn't want to do.

I take it that this habit, peculiar to rulers in that part of the world, of not respecting the terms of treaties is the explanation for the Utopians' refusal to enter into any. Probably they would change their minds if they had Europeans to deal with, although they take the view that, even if treaties were faithfully adhered to, it would still have been infinitely preferable for them never to have been invented. For a treaty implies that neighboring peoples are naturally each other's enemies and competitors, as if two peoples who are separated only by a few yards of space, by a hillside or a river, were not linked together by a natural community of interests. It implies they are right to try to slaughter each other whenever no treaty stands in the way. Moreover, they argue that signing a treaty does nothing to promote true friendship. Indeed, it leaves both parties free to prey on each other, for you can be sure that the final wording of the treaty won't be tight enough to exclude such an interpretation completely. The Utopians take the opposite view. They maintain that nobody is to be regarded as an enemy until he has done you an injury, that the natural fellowship between peoples makes any treaty unnecessary, and that people are more united by mutual goodwill than by paper contracts, more by their hearts than by their tongues.

OF WARFARE

They utterly detest war as a truly beastly activity, though admittedly none of the beasts is as bellicose as a human being.[76] They are unlike almost every other nation, for there is nothing in their view that is less deserving of admiration than the glory won in battle. Yet

---

76. Compare Erasmus's 1515 commentary on the adage, "Sweet is war to those who have not tried it" (*Dulce bellum inexpertis*, IV.i.1).

they drill and practice for war with real dedication. There are fixed days set aside for military training, and not just the men but the women train too, in order to ensure that there is nobody who would not be able to play their part in the event of war. Still, they don't enter upon a war without strong reasons, such as the need to defend their own frontiers; or to drive enemies off the lands of their friends; or to use their forces to liberate an oppressed people, bowed down under tyranny and reduced to servitude. In such cases they act out of compassion and fellow-feeling. They are prepared to come to the assistance of their friends, not only when they are engaged in self-defense, but also when they are seeking compensation and taking their revenge for injuries they have received in the past. But they will act in such cases only if they have been consulted in advance, if they believe the cause to be just, and if compensation has been requested and denied. And then they insist on overall military command. They are prepared to go on the offensive, not only when there is an enemy incursion onto friendly territory and plunder is seized, but also, and even more implacably, when their or their friends' merchants are unfairly treated but have no recourse in law, either because the local laws are themselves unfair or because they have been unfairly applied.

This, as it happens, was the cause of the war that the Utopians waged on behalf of the Nephelogetes and against the Alaopolitans[77] shortly before our own arrival. What they took to be a wrong, although it was not condemned by the local courts, had been done to some Nephelogete businessmen who lived in Alaopolis. There may be some doubt as to which side was in the right; but there's no question that the war fought over this supposed injustice was ferocious. Neighboring countries added their expertise and resources to support the troops and inflame the animosities of the warring parties. Some wealthy societies paid dearly, while others were nearly destroyed. Things went from bad to worse, until the Alaopolitans were forced to surrender and accept servitude. The Utopians, since they hadn't been fighting to protect their own interests, handed them over to the Nephelogetes, although in the days of Alaopolitan glory the Nephelogetes had been no match for them.

So you can see that the Utopians harshly punish injuries done to

---

77. "The People Born from the Clouds," and"The Citizens of a Country without People."

their friends, even when only money is in question. But they are
not so implacable when it comes to their own interests. If property
is seized from them anywhere abroad, providing nobody has been
wounded, their angry response is limited to cutting off trade with
that nation until they receive compensation. This is not because
they care less about the welfare of their own citizens than their allies. Rather, the loss of money is more serious for the latter, because
the merchants of these friendly societies lose their private property
and so are gravely affected by its loss. But the citizens of Utopia
only lose public property; moreover, there's plenty more of anything they lose in the stores at home, more than they can use, in
fact, since otherwise the goods would not have been exported in the
first place. The result is that nobody feels the poorer. They think it
would be excessively cruel to avenge an injury that does not endanger the life or diminish the standard of living of a single one of their
citizens by the deaths of many people. But if a citizen of Utopia is
crippled or killed abroad, whether by agents of a foreign government or by private individuals, their ambassadors establish the true
circumstances; after that the only thing that will satisfy them is
that the culprits should be handed over. Otherwise they declare
war. If the culprits are handed over, they are punished with either
death or slavery.

The Utopians are not merely dismayed when they win a victory *Costly*
at the price of leaving many dead on the battlefield, but ashamed. *victories*
For they think it incompetence to pay too much, even for goods of
the finest quality. But if they are victorious as a result of skill and
cunning, then they wholeheartedly celebrate the enemy's defeat.
They march in triumph through the streets and erect a monument
as if they were commemorating a hard-fought battle. They boast
that their actions have been truly manly and praiseworthy whenever they win a battle by methods no animal other than a human
being could have used, in other words by force of reasoning. Bears,
lions, boars, wolves, dogs, and other wild beasts fight with their
bodies, and some of them are stronger and more vicious than we
are. But all of them fall victim to mental agility and intellectual
acuity.

Their only objective when they go to war is to obtain the conces-
sions which, had they been made earlier, would have made war unnecessary. If circumstances make this impossible, then they seek so
harshly to punish those they hold responsible that in the future
they won't even dare think of repeating the offense. Having decided on their objectives, they try to achieve them as quickly as

possible, while always bearing in mind that the first priority must be to avoid unnecessary risks, not to win fame or glory.

Thus, the moment war is declared they arrange for numerous posters to appear, as if from nowhere, in the most conspicuous places throughout the enemy's territory. They bear the official seal and promise huge rewards to anyone who eliminates the enemy's ruler. They also offer smaller, but still substantial, rewards for the assassination of any one of a number of individuals whom the same posters declare to be condemned as outlaws. These are the people who they believe are, after the head of state, primarily responsible for the policies that have damaged their interests. The reward for a successful assassin is doubled for anyone who abducts one of the proscribed men and hands him over still alive. Moreover, they offer the same rewards, plus their protection, to any of those they have condemned who betray their associates. It doesn't take long for those they have singled out to begin to fear that the whole world is out to get them; they stop being able to trust each other, for each knows he has become untrustworthy. They fear the worst and are right to do so. For over and over again the outcome is that a significant proportion of those on the wanted list, and the head of state in particular, are betrayed by those in whom they placed most trust. This just goes to show that people will do anything for money, especially the vast sums that the Utopians put up. They are well aware of the risks they are asking people to take on their behalf, so they make sure that the rewards on offer represent more than adequate compensation for the dangers involved. They offer not only enormous quantities of gold, but also outright ownership of valuable estates in the safest of locations on the territory of their closest allies; and what they promise they deliver.

This custom of putting a price on your enemy's head, this black market in human beings, is condemned by other nations, who regard it as a bloodstained crime engaged in by a degenerate people. But the Utopians insist that their actions are admirable. They claim their policy is one that any wise person would approve, for it enables them to bring great wars to a successful conclusion without a single battle being fought. Moreover it is humane and merciful, since the death of a few guilty men enables them to save numerous innocent lives that would otherwise be lost on the battlefield. The lives of their own citizens are saved; but so are those of the enemy, and they empathize with the common soldiers on the other side almost as much as with their own men, for they realize that they do not choose to go to war but are forced into it by the madness of their rulers.

If bribery does not work, then they sow seeds of dissension among the enemy and nurture them. For example, they win the ruler's brother, or some other leading nobleman, over to their side by encouraging him to aspire to the throne. If these internal divisions come to nothing, then they stir up neighboring peoples and seek to involve them in the fighting by reminding them of some long-forgotten claim they have to their neighbors' territory, for it is never hard to turn up such claims if one goes back through the history of any monarchy.

When they promise material support to an ally who is going to war they give money without counting the cost, but they endanger the lives of as few of their own citizens as possible. For they place such a high value on their own citizens—or rather, they reciprocally value each other so highly—that there is not a single Utopian whom they would willingly agree to barter for an enemy ruler. But gold and silver, which they use for this one purpose, they spend without reluctance, for they know their standard of living will not be affected even if they spend all they have. Moreover, they can supplement the wealth they have at home, for they have limitless reserves abroad, since, as I explained, many different countries have borrowed from them. So they hire mercenaries wherever they are available and send them to the front; many of these mercenaries are Zapoletes.[78]

The Zapoletes live five hundred miles in an easterly direction from Utopia; they are barbaric, brutish, and ferocious.[79] They are happiest when in the midst of dark forests and surrounded by high mountains, for this is the landscape of their homeland. They are tough and withstand heat, cold, and hard work. They live without even the most elementary luxuries and have no interest in plowing, sowing, and reaping. They don't care what they wear or what sort of buildings they live in. They are a pastoral people, but many of them depend on hunting and banditry. First and foremost they are trained to fight; they are always on the lookout for opportunities to go to war and eagerly seize on those that come their way. Many of

---

78. "The Busy Traders."

79. The 1518 editions omit the marginal annotation that appeared in the first two editions: "A people not unlike the Swiss." It may be that Froben, who was Swiss, took exception to this comparison.

them go abroad and offer to fight on behalf of anyone who is in need of soldiers, even if the wages are dreadful. The only way of life they know depends on others dying so that they can live.

For those who pay their wages they fight bravely, and they never betray them once battle is joined. But they never oblige themselves to serve for any particular period of time. The contract by which they commit their support to one side leaves them free so that if on the next day they are offered more money by someone else, even the enemy, they can switch their allegiance; and if a day later they are offered a little bit more by their original employer, then back they go. It's unusual for there to be a war in which significant numbers of their troops are not to be found fighting on both sides. This means that it's commonplace for men who are not only related to each other by blood but have campaigned together and have become close comrades, to find themselves a few days later serving in opposing armies and trying to kill each other. The ties of kinship and of friendship are forgotten, and, with murder in their hearts, they try to run each other through, though they have no reason at all for wishing each other harm, except for the fact that they have accepted a pitiful wage to serve under rulers at odds with each other. They take money so seriously that they believe they have no option but to change sides if they are offered an extra cent a day. They've quickly become infected with avarice, although in their case it serves no purpose, for every cent they earn as hired killers they immediately spend on bad wine and ugly women.

The Zapoletes will fight on behalf of the Utopians against anybody and everybody, for the simple reason that the Utopians pay them higher wages than anyone else. And the Utopians, who are proud of making good use of good men, also make a point of using up these evil men. For when there's a need for it, they promise them vast sums so that they can put them in the front line. Usually only a minority of them return to collect their wages. The Utopians pay the survivors exactly what they've promised in order to incite them to take similar risks again. They simply don't care how many Zapoletes get killed, for they take the view that the whole of humanity would be eternally in their debt if they could exterminate every last surviving Zapolete, so disgusting and evil do they consider them to be.

Their second preference is to make use of troops belonging to the nation they are trying to defend; and after them, they enlist as auxiliaries squadrons drawn from their other allies. Lastly they enroll their own citizens. But they always appoint one of their own men who has demonstrated his military capacity to be commander in chief of the whole army. They also nominate two alternate commanders. As long as the original commander is fit and free the alternates have no authority; but if he is killed or captured one of the two inherits his position; and if something then happens to him, then the third takes over, so that, despite the inevitable risks of battle, the whole army will not be thrown into confusion if the commander happens to be killed.

In the cities of Utopia men are invited to volunteer for military service, and it is from among the volunteers that a selection is made. No one is forced to serve in the armed forces that are sent abroad, for they hold the view that if someone is cowardly by nature then one can be sure that he will prove feeble on the field of battle; worse, his fear may prove infectious and spread to his comrades. But if their own island is invaded, then they call to the colors even timid soldiers of this sort, provided they are physically fit. They place them on board ship, mixed in among reliable troops; or post them here and there among the troops on guard in castles and along city walls. Either way, they have no choice but to stand their ground. In these circumstances they hope that the desire to earn the respect of their comrades, the immediate danger from the enemy, and the impossibility of escape will overcome their fear, and indeed often mortal danger makes brave soldiers of them.

Not only do they insist that no Utopian should be forced to serve in the army abroad against his will, but they also permit the wives of soldiers to accompany their husbands abroad if they wish. Indeed, they go so far as to encourage them to go and they praise those who do so. They march alongside their husbands and stand shoulder-to-shoulder on the battlefield. Around each soldier they place any of his children and relatives by blood or marriage who are serving in the army, so that those are nearest at hand to help each other who are naturally keenest to look after each other. There is nothing more shameful than for one member of a married couple to return from battle without the other, or for a son to survive when his father dies. Thus when they join battle, if the enemy stand their ground, the outcome is decided by a long and deadly struggle, which continues until there is no one left alive.

They go to great lengths to avoid having to put themselves in the line of battle, trying instead to make use of mercenaries to serve in their place. But when they have no option but to commit themselves to the fight, they prove themselves to be as brave when needs must as they were cautious in trying to avoid unnecessary danger.

In the first clash of arms they are not especially terrifying, but as time and the battle go by they grow steadily more powerful. They are so resolute that it is easier to kill them than to make them retreat. For they know that if they are defeated those they have left behind will be looked after, and they have no need to worry about providing for their heirs (an anxiety that often makes cowards of the bravest men). Therefore, they are noble of spirit and scornful of defeat. In addition, their confidence is reinforced by their sense of their own military expertise. Finally, their values make them all the more trustworthy: values that they are explicitly taught in childhood and that they pick up unconsciously as a result of living in a well-ordered society. They neither set so little store by their lives that they are willing to throw them away through foolhardy actions, nor are they so enamored of them that they shamefully cling to life when duty obliges them to embrace death.

The attack concentrated on the enemy general so as to cut short the war   When the battle is at its height, a select group of young men, bound together by ties of loyalty and affection, set themselves the task of hunting down the enemy general. They charge straight at him, or they try to creep up on him. They shoot at him from a distance, or grapple with him hand-to-hand. He is attacked by a phalanx of troops who are never injured and never die, for reinforcements rush to take the place of those who are exhausted. They nearly always succeed in killing him or taking him alive, unless he takes refuge in flight.

When they win, their victory never degenerates into a massacre. They take more pleasure in capturing those who are running away than in killing them. Moreover, they always ensure that when they are pursuing a routed enemy they retain at least one line of troops in battle array. If their other troops have been driven back, and they have only achieved a victory by committing these final reserves, then they would normally allow the enemy forces to escape intact rather than pursue the fleeing troops with their own ranks in disorder. They are well aware that on more than one occasion the bulk of their own army has been beaten and smashed, and the enemy, rejoicing in their victory, have scattered in every direction to pursue individuals as they ran away. Then a small force of Utopians held in reserve, waiting for the right moment, have suddenly thrown themselves on the dispersed and disorganized enemy, who, feeling safe from attack, have been caught completely unprepared. Thus the outcome of the battle has been transformed, and a victory that had already been achieved and celebrated has been snatched from the enemy's hands. The Utopians, though conquered, have conquered their conquerors.

It is not easy to decide whether the Utopians are more notable for the cunning with which they lay ambushes or the slipperiness with which they avoid falling into them. You would think that they were on the point of running away when that is the last thing on their minds; on the other hand, when they really have decided to retreat there is nothing to betray their intention. If they believe that they are badly outnumbered, or if the enemy occupies a superior position, then they strike camp in the dark and slip silently away, or employ some other stratagem to escape unnoticed. If they have to retreat in plain view, then they keep their troops in such good order that it is as dangerous to attack them while they fall back as when they are advancing. They go to great lengths to fortify their camps, digging a deep and wide ditch, and throwing the earth inward [to form a rampart]. They don't make use of laborers to do such work. The soldiers do it with their own hands. The whole army is put to work, except only for an armed guard, which stands ready outside the fortifications in case of a surprise attack. With so many people hard at work they construct high ramparts surrounding large areas of ground faster than one would have thought possible.

Their armor is solid enough to withstand an enemy's blows, but flexible enough to allow the arms and legs freedom of movement. They can even swim in it without difficulty, and learning to swim in armor is a normal part of basic training for recruits. The projectile weapon they rely on is the arrow, which they shoot accurately at long range. Not only their infantry but even their cavalry achieve this. When fighting hand-to-hand they use not swords but battle-axes. These are both heavy and sharp, a lethal combination, and can be used for both cutting and stabbing. They are extremely ingenious at inventing engines of war. Once they have constructed them they go to great lengths to conceal their existence, since if the enemy knew of them before they were employed in battle they might provoke laughter rather than fear. When they are constructing them, their first concern is to ensure that they will be easy to transport when disassembled and to deploy when assembled. *The design of their armor*

When ceasefires are negotiated with the enemy they observe them so faithfully that they do not break them even if provoked. They do not lay waste to the enemy's territory or set fire to his crops. They try their best to prevent both men and horses from trampling the growing crops, recognizing that they may have need *On ceasefires* of them themselves. They do no injury to unarmed men, unless they are spies. They do no harm to cities that surrender to them, and even those that they have to storm they do not sack, though they execute those who spoke out against surrender and condemn the rest of the defenders to slavery. All the unarmed civilians they leave untouched. If they identify any inhabitants who recommended that the city surrender itself, they reward them with a share of the property of those they have condemned. The remainder they hand over to their auxiliary forces, for no Utopian citizen ever takes any plunder.

But nowadays the victors pay the bulk of the costs. Once a war is finished they make good the expenses they have incurred, not by charging their allies, but by confiscating some of the wealth of the conquered. They make up a proportion of the required sum by taking cash, which they put aside to be used in future wars, but the balance consists of landed estates, which they retain within their former enemy's territory indefinitely, and which bring in a substantial annual revenue. They now have income of this sort in many different countries, from estates acquired gradually and under many different circumstances. The revenue amounts to more than seven hundred thousand ducats a year. They send some of their citizens abroad to live on these estates and collect the rents. They live in luxury and conduct themselves like great noblemen. But most of the income remains after their expenses have been covered and is sent to the Utopian treasury, unless they prefer to bank it with the local people. They often do this until they have need of it, and even then they rarely have to reclaim the whole amount. As I have already mentioned, they assign a portion of these estates to those individuals who have taken risks in response to their urgings.

If any ruler takes up arms against them and prepares to invade their territory, then they send a large force to meet him before he reaches their borders. For they do their best to avoid fighting a war on their own soil, and no matter how bad the situation is they never bring foreign troops to help them defend their own island.

On the Religions of Utopia

There are a number of different religions in Utopia. Indeed, each city contains adherents of different faiths. Some worship the sun as their god, others the moon, and others one of the planets. Some Utopians believe that a certain human being, who was remarkable, long ago, either for his virtue or for his vanity, was not only a god, but the supreme god. But a substantial majority of Utopians, including nearly all the wiser citizens, believe in none of these religions. They believe there is one divinity, which is unknown, eternal, unmeasurable, inexplicable, beyond the capacity of man's understanding, and present throughout the universe, though not as a physical body, but rather through its influence. They call it the parent of all that exists. The origins, progress, multiplication, vicissitudes, and ends of all things they attribute to him alone, and they do not worship any other being as divine.

Though all the other religions hold beliefs that differ from those of the religion of the majority, they all agree that there is one supreme power responsible for the construction of the universe and its fate. In the local language he is known by all as Mithra.[80] But they disagree among themselves in that they describe this spirit in different ways. Each takes the characteristic that it believes to be most important and claims this is the fundamental attribute of that supreme being whose absolute authority over all creation is recognized by the common consent of every nation. But slowly over time they are abandoning the present variety of superstitions, and uniting in one religion, which seems more rational than all the others. Indeed, there can be no doubt that the others would all have disappeared long ago, if people thinking of changing their religion did not, out of fear, interpret any unlucky event that occurred to them as the result not of chance but of divine intervention, as if the god whose worship they were thinking of abandoning was punishing the impiety they were planning to commit.

But after they heard us speak of Christ and describe his teaching, his way of life, and the miracles he performed, and recount the equally extraordinary constancy of so many martyrs, whose blood, willingly shed, has brought so many nations, scattered far and wide, to adopt their religion, you would not believe how enthusiastically they too were converted. Perhaps God was invisibly at work, or perhaps Christianity seemed to them very similar to the religion that is most popular among them. One might think it was of considerable significance that they were told that Christ approved of the communal way of life practiced by his first followers, and that among the most authentic Christians common ownership *Monasteries* is still practiced. In any case, whatever their motivation, a large

---

80. The supreme deity for the ancient Persians (whose language is close to that of the Utopians).

number of them agreed to join our faith and were washed in holy water.[81]

Since among the four of us (there were only four of us left, for two had died) there was, to my continuing regret, not a single priest; although we could instruct them in the principles of our religion, we could not confer on them those sacraments which we believe can be administered only by a priest. But they understand what they are missing and desire it more than anything else. Indeed, they even argue vigorously among themselves as to whether, if no Christian bishop is sent to them, one chosen from among themselves could be appointed to exercise the powers of a priest. They seemed to be on the point of making an appointment, but when I left they had not yet done so.

Those who have not adopted the Christian religion make no attempt to deter others from doing so. They do not turn against the converts, although while I was there one of our new Christians was punished. As soon as he had been baptized, he began to preach the Christian religion in public with more enthusiasm than good sense. We advised him to be more prudent, but he grew more and more hot-headed. He not only maintained that our religion was better than any of theirs, but insisted that theirs were worthless. He ranted away, saying that their religions were wicked, and that those who believed in them were godless and sacrilegious, and would be condemned to eternal damnation. After he had held forth in this

Men should be drawn to the true religion by praise of what is good.

manner on numerous occasions they arrested him. They tried him, not for insulting their religions, but for behavior likely to provoke a riot, found him guilty, and sentenced him to exile. For they believe that one of the oldest principles, respected by their legal system, is that no one should be punished for his religious beliefs.[82]

They attribute this principle to Utopus himself and to the founding of Utopia. For Utopus had heard that the natives, before his arrival, were in bitter conflict over religious differences. And he recognized that where a community is divided into conflicting sects, these sects are unable to cooperate to defend their country against an outside attack, for it was this that had given him the opportunity to defeat them one by one. Once he had conquered them, one of his first decrees was that every individual should be free to

---

81. That is, baptized.
82. By contrast, when More became Lord Chancellor in 1529 he played a leading role in intensifying the persecution of Protestants.

follow the religion of his or her choice, and even to make every effort to convert others to it, as long as he makes the case for his own beliefs calmly and moderately and relies on rational arguments. If urging the merits of his own religion proves ineffectual, he may not bitterly attack the beliefs of others. He must abstain from abuse and must never threaten violence. Anyone who blatantly enters into conflicts over religion is to be punished with exile or slavery.

Utopus introduced this law, not only in order to ensure peace, which he saw being utterly extinguished by constant conflicts and irreconcilable enmities, but also because he believed such a law would serve the interest of religion itself. In matters of faith he thought it would be foolhardy to dogmatize, for he considered it possible that God wants to be worshipped in varied and diverse ways, and so inspires different peoples with different faiths. In any event, he was certain that to try to compel everyone else by means of threats and violence to believe what you yourself happen to believe is both arrogant and ineffectual. Should it be the case that there is only one true religion, and all the rest are false, he was quite confident that, as long as people confined themselves to moderate and reasonable discussion, the truth would have the advantage and would eventually prevail. But if riots and wars are allowed to decide the outcome, then, since the worst men are also often the most determined, the best and most sacred religion would die out, smothered under foolish superstitions, just as wheat is overgrown by thorns and weeds. Therefore, he left the question of which is the true religion open, so that each person is free to believe what he thinks right. The only exception was that he solemnly and severely forbade anyone to deny the fundamental dignity of his own nature to the point of believing that the soul perishes with the body, or that the world is governed by mere chance and providence has no part to play.

Thus they all believe that after we die our vices will be severely punished and our virtues will be generously rewarded. Anyone who denies this they do not think worthy to be called a human being, since in such a person's own opinion their soul, which is truly sublime, is fundamentally no better than the foul body of a mere beast. Even less are they willing to consider them as a fellow citizen, for they know that, but for the fear of punishment, they would have nothing but contempt for the laws and customs of society. For who can doubt that someone who has nothing to fear but the authorities, and who has no hope of surviving after death, will not hesitate to break the communal laws of their own country for the sake of some private advantage, as long as they think they can avoid detection or can resist arrest. Consequently, anyone who holds such views is barred from receiving any honors, is condemned never to be promoted to any position of authority, and is excluded from all positions where others would depend on them. Everyone treats them as if they were congenitally worthless and good for nothing. But they impose no punishment, for they are convinced that no one has the capacity to freely choose what they believe. Nor do they bring pressure to bear on such people to ensure that they conceal their convictions; on the contrary, they do not tolerate any form of deceit or misrepresentation, and they loathe dissimulation, in the belief that it is a short step from deception to crime. They merely forbid them to muster arguments in support of their beliefs when they are in the presence of the uneducated. But when they are alone with the priests and people of standing, they not only permit them but positively encourage them to enter into debate, for they sincerely believe that in the end even the mad will acknowledge the force of superior arguments.

A remarkable opinion regarding the souls of animals

There are others who make the opposite mistake and believe that animals have immortal souls, though not souls that are anything like as admirable as our own, nor intended to attain the same degree of happiness. Indeed, this is a widespread view, and one that is perfectly respectable, as there are arguments in its favor and it is not synonymous with immorality.

Nearly all the Utopians are completely convinced that for human beings the delights of the next world will be utterly exquisite. So, while they grieve over each person who falls sick, they mourn no one's death, the only exception being those whom they see torn from life against their will and fearful of what is to come. They regard this as a very bad omen, for it is as if the soul, conscious of its burden of guilt and abandoning all hope, was terrified of dying because it had some secret premonition of the punishment that awaits it. Moreover, they think that God is scarcely likely to take pleasure in the arrival of someone who does not come willingly when called, but is dragged off against their will, resisting all the while. Those who are present at such a death are horrified by it and bear the body away in melancholy silence. They pray that God in his mercy will pardon the failings of this soul, and they bury the body in the ground. By contrast, whenever someone dies cheerfully and full of optimism, they do not grieve over them, but follow their bier singing and commend their soul to God with expressions of genuine affection. They cremate the body as a gesture of respect rather than to signify their loss, and they mark the place by erecting a column on which the deceased's titles are recorded. When they have returned home they remind each other of the ways they behaved and the things they did, and no episode in their life is discussed more frequently and more eagerly than their joy in dying.

They think that remembering the admirable qualities of the dead in this way is a very effective way of encouraging the living to live virtuously. They also think that this form of commemoration gives pleasure to the dead themselves, who, they believe, are present, listening to what is said of them, though to the dull eyesight of the living they are invisible. Given that the virtuous dead have every desire satisfied, they must be able to go wherever they please, and they would be hard-hearted if they were to have completely lost the desire to see their friends, to whom in life they were bound by mutual ties of love and esteem. They conjecture that affection, like other good qualities, is increased rather than diminished in the virtuous after death, and conclude that the dead come and go among the living, hearing what they say and seeing what they do. This gives them greater confidence in all their undertakings, for they believe themselves to be under the protection of these invisible spirits, and their conviction that they are overseen by their ancestors serves to deter them from any evil deed that they might hope to conceal from the living.

They never engage in fortune-telling or other misleading and superstitious methods for predicting the future. They realize other societies set great store by divination, but they mock them for it. But when miracles occur without any assistance from nature they revere them, considering them to be the works of God and as testifying to his presence. Indeed, they say that miracles can often be seen to happen in Utopia, and sometimes, when important and difficult decisions have to be made, they hold public prayers asking for a miracle, and their conviction that they will be heard is always rewarded.

They think the contemplation of nature and the sense of awe that it fosters represent a form of worship acceptable to God. But there are some—indeed a significant number—who believe it is a religious duty to turn away from a life of scholarship and who refuse to engage in the study of nature. This does not mean they have time for leisure, for they are convinced that the only way to earn happiness after death is to give oneself over to hard work and to doing good to others. So some take care of the sick; others mend roads, clear drains, repair bridges; or dig peat, sand, or gravel; or

The active life

fell trees and chop them up; or cart lumber, grain, or other bulky commodities into the cities. Not only when they are working on public projects but also in their private lives they serve others, even more than the slaves do. Find a job that is backbreaking, dirty, and difficult, so that the effort, frustration, and disgust would put most people off, and these people will be delighted, positively thrilled, if they can have it all to themselves. By dedicating themselves to unremitting labor they make it possible for others to have leisure. They ask for no reward, and neither criticize others nor sing their own praises. The more they put themselves at the service of others, the more everyone admires and respects them.

These laborers belong to two different sects. The members of one sect never marry, and abstain not only from sexual intercourse but also from eating meat, and some of them from fish and fowl as well. They reject all the pleasures of this life as being wicked, but long for the pleasures of the next, which they hope to attain through dedication and hard work. Trusting that death will soon take them away, they live meanwhile vigorous and happy lives. The other sect are just as keen on hard work but prefer to marry. For they see no reason to despise the companionship of marriage and believe that just as they are under a natural obligation to labor, so they are under a civil obligation to produce children. They welcome pleasures of all sorts, providing they do not interfere with their labors. They prefer to eat meat, as they think it makes them stronger and helps them in their work. The Utopians think the second sect have better judgment, but they think the first sect are more pious. They would laugh at them if they claimed their preference for celibacy over marriage, for a hard life over an easy one, was rational; but as they claim their motives are religious, they admire and respect them. There is no principle they observe more carefully than the principle that it is not easy to sit in judgment on someone else's religion. For these people they have a special word in their own language, Buthrescas. Perhaps we can translate this as "god-fearing."

Their priests are men of extraordinary sanctity, and consequently there are very few of them. There are no more than thirteen of them in each city, corresponding to the number of temples, except during time of war. Then seven of them are assigned to serve with the army, and seven more are appointed to fill their places in the meantime. When the army returns, they take up their old posts; the supernumerary priests step into the places of the others when they die. Meanwhile they serve as attendants to the high priest, for one of the thirteen has authority over the others. Priests are elected by the people, in the same way as all the other magistrates, and the ballot is secret in order to avoid factional conflict. Once they have been selected they are ordained by their fellow priests. They look after the holy places and take charge of public worship, and they censure the moral failings of the people. It is a terrible disgrace to be identified or criticized by them for leading an immoral life. But as it is their job to praise good behavior and criticize bad, so it is the job of the prince and the other magistrates to condemn and to punish the guilty, though the priests do exclude *Excommu-* from religious ceremonies those who are notorious for their evil *nication* lives. There is scarcely any punishment that is more feared than this, for those excluded have their public reputations destroyed, while in private the fear of supernatural sanctions gnaws at them. Even their bodies are not safe for long, for unless they rapidly demonstrate their penitence to the priests, they will be seized by the civil authorities and punished for impiety.

Children and adolescents are educated by the priests. Reading and writing are not given priority over good behavior and morality. They go to great lengths to inculcate the young, while they are still unformed and malleable, with good opinions and with attitudes that help ensure the stability of their society. For once such opinions have lodged in the minds of the young, they accompany the adult throughout his life and are of tremendous value, in that they place the social order on a sound footing. For societies are corrupted only by the vices of individuals, and vices always originate in false values.

The priests choose as their wives the very best women in the whole country—I'm assuming the priests are men, though strictly *Women* speaking women are not excluded from the priesthood. However, *priests* they are rarely chosen and only elderly widows are eligible.

There is no official in Utopia whose standing is higher than that of the priest. It is even the case that if a priest commits a crime, no court will condemn him; he is left to the mercy of God and his conscience. They do not think it right to lay mortal hands on someone who, no matter how wicked he may be, has been dedicated as a gift to God in so singular a fashion. It is all the easier for them to respect this principle because they have so few priests and they choose them so carefully. For it scarcely ever happens that someone chosen for his outstanding moral qualities and elevated to such a high position solely on account of his virtue slips into a life of degeneracy and vice. Were it to happen, even in an extreme case (which is not inconceivable, for human nature is subject to change), given the fact that there are so few priests, and that they are entrusted with no authority beyond that which derives from the respect in which they are held, there is no reason to fear that they could bring about any great harm to society at large. Indeed, they *And think* have so few priests in order to ensure that the office, which is now *what* held in such respect, should not be devalued by being made widely *swarms of* available. Moreover, they think it would be difficult to find many *them we* men good enough to be worthy of such a position, for it requires *have!* virtues above and beyond the ordinary.

They may have a high opinion of their priests, but other peoples think equally well of them. I think it is easy to show why this is so, and how it came to be. For when Utopia's armies join battle with the enemy, their priests are never far away, kneeling on the ground *O, how* and dressed in their sacred robes. They raise their hands to the *much holier* heavens and pray, first of all for peace, then for the victory of their *these priests* countrymen, and, above all, that there should be no massacre. If *are than our* their own side are victorious they run onto the battlefield and re- *own!* strain their own men from murdering their defeated enemies. If the enemy soldiers merely see them and call out to them, it is enough to save their lives; if they reach out and touch their flowing robes, their property is guaranteed against plunder and confiscation. It is this which has won them such a remarkable reputation among each and every nation, and ensured that they exercise such extraordinary authority that they have often been able to save as many of their own citizens from the enemy as the enemy from their own citizens. It is well known that there have been occasions when their own forces have first given ground before the enemy's assault and then turned in flight. The enemy have rushed forward to slaughter and plunder, but the Utopian priests have intervened to halt the massacre and separate the armies; with the result that a peace has been negotiated and concluded upon terms that are fair to both sides. One cannot find a people so savage, cruel, and barbarous that it does not respect their persons as sacrosanct and inviolable.

Public The Utopians celebrate the first and the last day of each month *holidays* as a public holiday, and they also celebrate the first and last day of *observed by* the year. They divide the year into months by the waxing and wan-*the* ing of the moon, and the course of the sun marks out the year. In *Utopians* their language they call the first days Cynemerns, and the last days Trapemerns, for which the equivalent in our language would be Firstholiday and Lastholiday. Their temples are remarkable, not only for the labor that has gone into their construction, but also for their vast size, since, as they have so few temples, each one must be capable of holding an enormous congregation. They are all rather dark inside, not because they do not know how to build light buildings, but because, they say, the priests were of the view that bright light scatters the thoughts, while in semidarkness it is easier to concentrate and pay attention to one's religion. *Their temples described*

In Utopia they do not all share the same religion, yet for all their differences (of which there are many) they all agree in worshipping a divinity of the same nature, like travelers heading for the same destination by different routes. So nothing is seen or heard in their temples that does not conform to the beliefs they have in common. If one of the sects has a rite of its own that it believes essential, then someone performs it in a house rather than a temple; the public ceremonies are performed according to a ritual that in no way denies the legitimacy of any private ceremonies. No image of any religion's god is displayed in the temples, so each individual is free to conceive of God as their own religion teaches. In public they do not invoke God by any name that belongs to the god of a particular religion, but use the common name of Mithra. By that name they all agree to refer to the universally accepted nature of the divine majesty, even while they disagree about many of God's characteristics. No prayers are authorized except ones that anyone could say without offending against the principles of their own sect.

They gather in the temple on the evening of Lastholiday, after a day of fasting, in order to thank God for what has gone well during the month or year that ends that night. Next day, which is Firstholiday, they assemble at the temple in the morning to pray for good fortune and success during the coming month or year whose beginning this holiday marks. On Lastholidays, before families go to the temple, while they are still in their homes, wives prostrate themselves at the feet of their husbands, and children at the feet of their parents, and confess their wrongdoings, whether they be things they have done which they ought not to have done, or things which they have not done as they ought to have, and beg for forgiveness. Thus, if any black cloud of domestic conflict has cast its shadow over them, this apology disperses it, so they can attend the ceremonies with a clear conscience—for it is forbidden to participate in them if one is troubled in mind. If they are conscious of feeling anger or hatred towards anyone, then they do not attend the ceremonies until they have been reconciled and no longer feel hostile towards them, for they fear that if they were to conceal their true feelings and attend, they would meet with a swift and terrible punishment. *Confession in Utopia*

While among us the wicked jostle each other to get close to the altar

When they enter the temple they separate, the men going to the
right-hand side and the women to the left. They organize themselves so that all the men of the household file in and sit down before the male head of that household, while the female head of the
household sits between the womenfolk and the exit. The intention
is that whatever anyone does in public is overseen by those who are
responsible for their management and discipline at home. They
also take great care to ensure that young people sit alternately with
their elders, for if children were supervised by other children they
might be horsing around during the very time when they ought to
be developing a devout fear of the gods, which is the greatest and
very nearly the only inducement to a life of virtue.

They slaughter no animals during their ceremonies, for they do
not believe that a merciful God, who bestowed life on living creatures so that they might live, can take pleasure in bloodshed and
slaughter. They burn frankincense and other sweet-smelling substances and light great numbers of beeswax candles; of course, they
know that God has no need of such gifts. Indeed, he has no need
even of the prayers we offer him. But they take pleasure in what
they regard as a harmless form of worship and are convinced that
sweet odors, flickering lights, and ritualized activities work on us
imperceptibly to elevate our thoughts and serve to involve us more
wholeheartedly in worship of the divine.

The congregation are all dressed in white while the priests wear
multicolored robes, exquisitely tailored, although the material of
which they are made is not particularly expensive. They are not
embroidered with gold or encrusted with precious jewels; but extraordinary skill and delicacy goes into embellishing them with the
feathers of many different sorts of birds, such that one forgets that
the material of which they are made is inexpensive in one's admiration for the handiwork that has gone into making them. Moreover,
in the selection of the feathers on the priests' robes and in the pat-
terns made with them they say that certain esoteric mysteries are
concealed. The interpretation of these symbols is carefully passed
on from one generation of priests to the next, and they serve as a
constant reminder of God's goodness toward them, of the love and
honor they owe in their turn to God, and of their obligations towards each other.

As soon as the priest in all his finery enters from the sanctuary,
the congregation immediately prostrate themselves as a mark of respect. The complete silence of so vast a gathering is in itself

enough to strike terror into each heart, as if they were indeed in the presence of a divinity. When they have been lying on the ground for a short period, the priest gives a sign and they rise. Then they sing praises to God to the accompaniment of musical instruments, most of which are quite different in design from those that are familiar in our part of the world. Some of our instruments far surpass theirs in the sweetness of their tone; but some of theirs are infinitely superior to ours. But there is one respect in which their music is unquestionably preferable to ours. All their music, whether they produce it by playing on instruments or by singing, expresses and conveys natural emotions, and the sound always fits the subject. The words of the song may be supplicatory, happy, peaceful, troubled, or angry; the melody is designed to represent the sense to be conveyed, and it is astonishing how effective it is in moving, stirring, and inflaming the hearts of the audience. Finally, the priest and the people together recite a fixed form of prayer, the words of which are such that all can say them together while each individual applies them to their own particular circumstances.

Music in Utopia

In these prayers everyone acknowledges God to be their maker and ruler, and the author of all the good things that befall them. They thank God for all the benefits they have received and especially for his kindness in making them a member of the happiest of all earthly societies, and for the good luck they had in being born into what they trust is the truest of all religions. If they are mistaken in this respect, if there is any religion or society that is better and preferable in God's eyes, they pray that God in his goodness will ensure that they acquire knowledge of it, and they declare themselves prepared to follow God's guidance wherever it may lead. But if the principles of their society are the best, and the beliefs of their religion are the truest, then they pray that God will keep them faithful and will bring all other human beings to adopt the same way of life and the same religious doctrines—unless there is something about the sheer variety of religious beliefs that gives delight to God, whose will is unfathomable.

Then they pray that they will die without pain and that God will gather up their soul; but they insist that they would not be so bold as to express a wish to die young or live long. Nevertheless, if they might express an opinion without seeming disrespectful, then they would much prefer to come to God by an early death, no matter how painful, than to be kept away from him for longer, even if all their earthly aspirations are fulfilled in the meantime. Having reached the end of this prayer, they briefly prostrate themselves once more and then rise and go off to lunch. The remainder of the day they spend in recreation and in military training.

I have described for you as accurately as I can the structure of the commonwealth of Utopia, which I believe to be not only the best social order in the world, but the only one that can properly claim to be literally a commonwealth. Everywhere else people talk about the public good but pay attention only to their own private interests. In Utopia, where there is no private property, everyone is seriously concerned with pursuing the public welfare. Both here and there people act with good reason, for outside Utopia there can't be anyone who doesn't realize that unless they take care of their own welfare they may die of hunger, no matter how much the commonwealth prospers. Sheer necessity obliges them to choose to look after their own interests, rather than those of the public, that is to say of other people. By contrast, in Utopia, where everything belongs to everybody, there is no need to fear, so long as the public warehouses are kept full, that any individual will ever be short of what they need. There are no shortages; no one is poverty-stricken or reduced to begging. No one owns anything, but everyone is rich.

For who is wealthier than those who live happily and peaceably, free of all cares? No one has to worry about where their next meal is coming from. No man is subjected to constant nagging by his wife. No one has to fear that his son will be impoverished, or worry that his daughter will have no dowry. They are all confident that there will be food and happiness enough for themselves and their nearest and dearest—their wives, their sons, their grandsons, great-grandsons, and great-great-grandsons, all that long succession of descendants that in our society only the nobility feel entitled to foresee. Indeed, there even those who used to work but are now no longer able-bodied are as well looked after as those who have taken their places.

Is there anyone who would dare compare the fair dealing that characterizes Utopia with what passes for justice in other countries? For my part, I can't for the life of me find the slightest trace of justice or fairness among them. For what sort of justice is it when a nobleman, or a goldsmith, or a moneylender, or anyone else who either does no sort of work at all, or who works at some occupation that is not of the slightest use to the commonwealth, has a way of life that is splendid and luxurious on the basis of doing nothing or else nothing useful? Meanwhile a laborer, a carter, a carpenter, or a plowman works so hard and unremittingly that a beast of burden could hardly support it. Their work is so necessary that without it no society could survive for as much as a year, but they earn such a miserable income and live such a pathetic life that draft animals would seem to find themselves in much better circumstances. For beasts are allowed to rest from their labors, and the food they are given is not much worse—indeed to their taste it's rather better—while they have no fear for the future. But manual workers not only must suffer the harsh discomforts of unrewarding and underpaid work here and now; they are also tortured by the prospect of a destitute old age, for what they earn each day is not enough to meet their daily expenses. There's no hope of their being able to put something aside each day for use in their old age.

Isn't this an unjust and ungrateful social order, which squanders largesse on gentlemen, as they are called, jewelers, and others who are no better, who are either men of leisure, or fawning flatterers and manufacturers of worthless pleasures. But plowmen, colliers, laborers, carters, and carpenters, without whom society could not survive for a single day, are not generously looked after. Their best years are spent in backbreaking labor, and then, when they are broken down by old age and ill-health, when they are completely penniless, this hard-hearted society, forgetting their unremitting efforts, unmindful of all that they have done for others, repays them by leaving them to die a miserable death. Moreover, every day the rich steal part of the daily wages of the poor, not only by the cheating and swindling of individuals, but also by the government's laws. Previously anyone could see that it was unjust that those who deserved to receive the most from society should be given the least; but now they have passed a law requiring everyone to accept that this evil practice is just and right. And so, when I consider all the different societies around the world that thrive at the moment and assess their qualities, I am forced to conclude that they are nothing but a conspiracy of the rich, whose objective is to increase their own wealth while the government they control claims to be a commonwealth concerned with the common welfare. There's no end to the ways and means they invent to ensure that, first of all, they can hang on to the wealth they have accumulated by deception and deceit, and then that they can extract from the poor workers the maximum effort for the minimum reward. These tricks the rich then turn into laws, passed in the name of society as a whole—that is to say, in the name of the poor themselves—requiring that everyone practice them.

These contemptible men! Their insatiable greed compels them

Make a note of this, reader!

to divide up among themselves all the wealth that would have been sufficient to provide for everyone, and yet in the end they have nothing like the happiness experienced by ordinary citizens in Utopia. There, by abolishing money they have abolished greed itself. Conflict and crime are eliminated from society, just as a cancer is cut out of a body, or a crop of weeds is dug up by the roots. Is there anyone who does not realize that fraud, theft, mugging, brawling, rioting, looting, sedition, assassination, treason, poisoning—all the crimes for which the hangman each day exacts retribution, though the gallows each day proves useless as a deterrent—would cease the moment money stopped changing hands? Moreover, fear, anxiety, stress, long days, and sleepless nights would all disappear the moment money lost its power. Even poverty, which exists only when people are in need of money, begins to disappear the moment no one has any.

Let me convince you by taking the example of a year in which the crops have failed and many thousands of people have died of hunger. I am convinced that if, when the famine was at its worst, the granaries of the rich had been searched, then sufficient grain would have been found stored in them to ensure that, if it had been distributed among those dying of emaciation and infection, no one would have felt the slightest adverse effect from nature's parsimony. That's how easy it would be to provide everyone with the means of subsistence, if only sacred money, which appears to be a brilliant invention to enable people to obtain the means of subsistence, were not in fact the only barrier keeping the hungry from the food they need. I am sure that even the rich understand this. They know perfectly well that it is far better to have a state of affairs where no one lacks the bare necessities than one where a few have vast wealth for which they have no practical use, that it would be much better to be rid of all our present problems than to continue to be obstructed wherever we turn by wealth itself. Indeed, I have absolutely no doubt that either the logic of each individual's personal interest, or the authority of Christ our savior (for Christ in his great wisdom could not but know what was for the best, while his goodness was such that he had to recommend what he knew to be best) would long ago have been easily sufficient to induce the whole world to adopt the laws of this commonwealth, were it not for the resistance of one monster, and one only, the princess and mother of all mischief: pride.

A remarkable sentiment

Pride causes us to measure our welfare not by our own well-being, but by whether we have things that others lack. Pride would not be willing to become a goddess except on condition that there be others left in misery over whom she could domineer and triumph. Her good fortune shines brightly when compared with the miseries of others. She flaunts her riches in order to vex and inflame their sense of their own poverty. This serpent from hell infests the hearts of men and prevents them from choosing a better way of life, as the remora slows down ships and brings them to a halt.[83]

Pride has too firm a grip on the human heart to be easily torn out. So, though I might wholeheartedly wish that the whole world would imitate the structure of the Utopian society, I am delighted that there is one place at least where it has been realized in practice. The way of life they have adopted has served as the foundation for a community that is not only the happiest, but which, insofar as one can make judgments about the likely course of future events, seems certain to last forever. They have eradicated at home the causes of ambition and faction, along with many other vices, and so there is no danger of their being troubled by internal conflict; this alone has been enough to destroy the wealth of many cities that seemed to have taken every precaution against attack. And while they preserve harmony at home and ensure that their institutions are flourishing, the envy of the rulers of all the neighboring countries will not be capable of shaking or alarming their government, since in the past they have often attacked them, but have always been beaten back.

When Raphael had finished his report I was left with the impression that many of the customs and laws established in that country were simply absurd: not merely in their approach to warfare and in their views on religion and spiritual matters, along with other practices of theirs, but especially as regards that principle that is the keystone of their whole system, their communal way of life and common ownership without any exchange of money. All nobility, magnificence, splendor, and majesty is utterly destroyed by this one principle, yet these are generally held to be the true ornaments and splendors of any commonwealth. But I knew that Raphael had tired himself out with so much talking, and I was not sure whether he would be able to tolerate the expression of views at odds with his

---

83. The ancients believed the remora or suckfish was able to bring a ship to a halt by attaching itself to it.

own, especially as I remembered that he had been critical of people who seem afraid that they will not be thought sufficiently knowledgeable unless they can find something to find fault with in the ideas of others. So, praising both their system and his account of it, I took him by the hand and led him in to dinner. But first I said that on another occasion we would be able to think more deeply about these matters and discuss them more thoroughly. And I still hope that some day we will have an opportunity to continue our discussion.

Meanwhile, though I cannot agree with everything he said, yet he is unquestionably someone who is both immensely learned and extraordinarily widely experienced in the affairs of humankind, and so I am happy to admit that there are many aspects of Utopian society that I would like to see established in our own political communities, even though I don't expect to see my wishes realized.

END OF BOOK TWO

THUS THE AFTERNOON DISCOURSE

OF RAPHAEL HYTHLODAY ON

THE LAWS AND INSTITUTIONS OF THE ISLAND OF UTOPIA,

UNTIL NOW KNOWN BY ONLY A FEW,

AS REPORTED BY A MOST DISTINGUISHED

AND LEARNED MAN,

MASTER THOMAS MORE, CITIZEN AND UNDERSHERIFF

OF LONDON,

ENDS.

BUSLEYDEN TO MORE

Jerome Busleyden to Thomas More

It was not enough for you, oh most distinguished More, to have already dedicated all your care, efforts, and energy to fostering the interests and welfare of individuals; you wanted also to put them at the service of the public at large, for such is your generosity and concern for others. Whatever the merits of your service to the public, you realized that you would deserve more applause, would win more gratitude, and would seize more glory the more widely it was distributed, the more people had access to it, the more numerous those who were helped by it. You've always striven to excel, and now you've achieved it to an astonishing extent—by writing down that afternoon's discussion about a just and well-ordered commonwealth (something we all long to see) found in Utopia.

In your fine description of a wonderful way of life there is nothing lacking that either profound learning or an extraordinary practical understanding of human behavior could contribute. Both qualities compete with each other in your work on terms of such perfect equality that neither gives ground to the other, and both lay equal claim to a glorious victory. The range of your learning is so impressive, and then again your practical experience is so extensive and so reliable, that anything you write you write as an expert, and anything you decide to say is truly learned. Your success in this respect is remarkable and exceptional; and all the more exceptional in that such success is not available to the many, but is only possible for a few: those few who have what it takes to give advice on public affairs, that is, whose desires are upright, whose learning is profound, whose confidence is well grounded, whose authority is extensive, and who are consequently able to act as honorably, rightly, and prudently as you do now. You do not think of yourself as born for yourself alone but for the whole world. Your extraordinary ability will have enabled you to recognize that your labors will be rewarded and that the whole world is in your debt.

There was no more appropriate and effective means of achieving your end than to set before men of exceptional intellectual capacity

the idea of such a commonwealth, the principal and perfect image
of a good way of life. No one has ever seen a society more soundly
constructed, more self-sufficient, more desirable. It is much superior to, it easily outstrips those most celebrated republics that have
been so much praised: Sparta, Athens, and Rome. If they had been
founded under the same auspices as your community and had been
governed by the same institutions, laws, decrees, and customs, then
certainly they would not yet have fallen into ruin and been leveled
to the ground, so that now, alas, they are destroyed beyond any
hope of reconstruction. The opposite would be true. They would
still be undamaged, happy and successful, blessed with good fortune, in control of events, and dividing among themselves an empire extending far and wide over land and sea.

Taking pity on the pitiable fate of these republics, you were
afraid that other states, which now seem to be securely in control of
their own destinies, would meet the same end. The result is this,
your perfect commonwealth, whose efforts are directed not so
much to formulating the best laws as to educating the best men to
rule. Nor was this a mistake, for without good rulers, all laws, even
the best—we are assured by Plato—are ineffectual. The whole organization and the characteristic activities of any ideal commonwealth should be constructed in order to present the image of such
rulers, models of probity, perfect examples of good conduct, the
living embodiments of justice. And priority should be given to prudence in the rulers, bravery in the soldiers, moderation among ordinary citizens, and justice in all.

Since your republic, which you praise so much, is so marvelously
constructed, as anyone can see, it will not be surprising if it should
not only provoke fear in many other states, but also be admired by
all nations and indeed if it should be commended to future generations. It is admirable because in it there is no scope for conflict over
property, for no one has any property of his own, but everything is
held in common by everyone, in order to foster the common good.
Every object and every action (even the most insignificant) is entirely directed to maintaining one principle of justice, equality, and
cooperation. Where that principle is fully recognized, anything
that might be a spark or tinder for ambition, luxury, envy, and injustice must be eliminated. Private property, or the burning desire
to acquire it, or ambition, the most wretched characteristic of human beings, drive human beings forward, even against their own
better natures and to their own immense, indeed immeasurable,
detriment. They frequently result in clashes between individuals,

armed conflicts, and, worst of all, civil wars. These do not merely utterly destroy societies that are flourishing and wealthy, but entirely obliterate the glories they had previously achieved, their triumphs, their illustrious trophies of battle and captured standards taken from defeated enemies.

If what I have said is less convincing than I would wish, then there are plenty of entirely trustworthy witnesses to whom I can entrust you. I can call on the many cities destroyed in the course of history, the political communities shattered, the republics crushed, the villages set alight and burned up. Scarcely any traces or vestiges of all these calamities are visible today; and not even their names are reliably recorded by the histories, even the oldest ones that have been added to by generation after generation.

Such dreadful disasters, devastations, destructions, and other calamities of war our commonwealths (if that is what they are) could easily escape if they would only strictly regulate themselves according to the fundamental principle of the Utopian republic, deviating from it, as the saying goes, by not so much as a hair's breadth. If they finally succeed in doing this they will be able to clearly recognize from the outcome how much they have benefited from the good deed you have done to them, particularly as by adopting your recommendation they will have learned how to ensure that their commonwealth remains healthy, secure, and victorious. To you, their most efficacious deliverer, they will owe just as much as is owed to someone who has not rescued a single citizen, one of many, but rather the whole society.

But for now, farewell. Carry on successfully thinking out, discussing, and developing ideas that if put into practice in the state will ensure that it survives for ever and will acquire for you an immortal reputation. Farewell, most learned and well-educated More, you who are the glory of your Britain and of this world of ours.

From my home at Mechlin, 1516

Gerald Geldenhouwer of Nijmegen on *Utopia*:[84]

Reader, do you enjoy the delightful?
Here is all that is most delightful.
If you seek the useful, you can read nothing more useful.
If you desire both, this island abounds in both,
So that you can both enhance your speech and inform your mind.
Here the wellsprings of right and wrong are revealed
By the accomplished More, his London's foremost glory.

[1516]

---

84. Geldenhouwer was a humanist who worked closely with the printer of the first edition of *Utopia*.

De Schrijver on *Utopia*

Cornelis de Schrijver to the reader:

Do you wish for new marvels, now there's a new-discovered world?
Do you want new ways of life, different in kind?
Do you seek the fount of all virtue? Seek the origin of all
Evils? And that great void lying at the heart of everything?
Read here, what More has depicted in diverse colors,
More, the flower of London's celebrated men.

[1516]

MORE TO GILES

Thomas More to his friend Peter Giles, warmest greetings.[85]

Dearest Peter, I was tremendously pleased by the criticism of that very intelligent person whom you know, who posed this dilemma regarding our *Utopia*:[86] if the account we are given is supposed to be truthful, then there are a number of things in it that border on the absurd; but if it is made up, then it has some features that seem at odds with More's characteristically penetrating good judgment. Peter, I'm extremely grateful to this chap, whoever he is: I suspect he is learned, and I can tell he is a friend. This frank assessment of his pleased me more, I think, than any other of which I've heard since the book was published. In the first place, he must have been led on by a liking either for me or for the book, for he does not seem to have been so wearied by reading it as to have given up, but to have read right to the end. And he did not read carelessly and hastily, as priests usually read the divine office (those who read it at all), but slowly and laboriously in order to give careful consideration to every detail. Then, having marked certain issues, and only a few of them, he announced that he approved of everything else, and that he did so not carelessly, but after serious thought. Finally, his criticisms may seem severe, yet they imply a higher opinion of the book than those who set out on purpose to praise it. For he shows very clearly what a high opinion he has of me when he complains that he feels let down when he reads a passage that is not sufficiently well formulated, while I think myself lucky if there are any passages in the whole book that are not completely absurd.

But, if I may in my turn be as frank with him as he has been with

---

85. This letter appeared only in the second edition.
86. Just as the French *vous* can mean either "you" singular or "you" plural, so the Latin *noster* can mean either "mine" or "our." It is thus unclear whether *Utopiam nostram* should be translated as "my *Utopia*" or "our *Utopia*": I have opted for the latter, as it seems an appropriate recognition of Giles's role in the publication of *Utopia*.

me, I can't see why he should think himself so sharp-sighted or, as the Greeks say, so beady-eyed because he detects some near-absurdities in the institutions of the Utopians, or because he catches me making some suggestions as to how a society should be constructed that aren't entirely helpful. As if there were no absurdities to be found outside Utopia! As if not a single philosopher among the many who have produced an outline for an ideal society, ruler, or private household had made the least proposal that needed to be changed! Now that I mention it, but for the respect I have for the long-established reputation of certain famous men, I could easily produce from the works of each one of them examples of views that I am sure everyone would agree should be rejected outright.

But when he expresses uncertainty as to whether my account is factual or imaginary, then I begin to have doubts about his good judgment. Now, I don't deny that if I had decided to write about the state, and I had had the idea of writing a story of this sort, then I might not have been unwilling to employ such a fiction by which the truth might slip into people's minds a little more agreeably, as if smeared with honey. But I would certainly have managed my narrative in such a way that, while I might actually have intended the unsophisticated to be misled by their own ignorance, I would have left for the more educated some clues that would have made it easy for them to make sense of our undertaking. Thus I would have needed only to give such names to the ruler, the river, the city, and the island as would alert the more expert reader to the fact that the island was nowhere, the city a chimera, the river without water, and the ruler without subjects. This wouldn't have been hard to do and would have been much wittier than what I actually did. You can be sure that if the obligation to produce an accurate account had not been overriding, I am not so stupid as to have actually wanted to use such barbarous and meaningless names as Utopia, Anyder, Amaurot, and Ademus.

But, my dear Giles, I now see that some men are so cautious that, whereas you and I, being simpleminded and credulous chaps, wrote down without question what Hythloday told us, they, being wise and wary, can scarcely be persuaded to believe a word of it. Lest both my own credibility in particular and the reliability of nonfictional reports in general should come into question among such people, I am glad I can say about my own offspring what Mysis says in Terence's play about Glycerium's boy, in order to ensure that no one thinks he's trying to pass someone else's child off as his own: "Thank God," he says, "that there were some reputable women present at his birth." Similarly, it's extremely lucky for me that Raphael told his story not just to you and me, but to many other people, people who are highly respectable and completely reliable. I don't know whether he told them more, and more remarkable, things than he told us; but he certainly told them as much as he told us, and what he told them was as significant as what he told us.

But if the skeptics are unwilling to believe even their accounts, then they should speak with Hythloday himself, for he is still alive. Only recently I heard from some travelers arriving from Portugal that on the first day of last March he was as healthy and fit as he has ever been. Let them extract the truth from him, or chisel it out of him with their questions, as long as they understand that I guarantee only the accuracy of my own work, and that I do not vouch for anyone else's honesty. Farewell to you, my dearest Peter, and to your delightful wife and beautiful little daughter. My wife sends them both her warmest best wishes.

[1517]

Erasmus's "The Sileni of Alcibiades"

"The Sileni of Alcibiades" seems to have turned into a proverb among the learned; certainly it appears as a proverb in the Greek collections.[1] It can be used about something which on the surface and at first sight (as the saying goes) seems worthless and ridiculous, but which on closer and inward consideration proves admirable, or about someone whose clothes and physical appearance are much less promising than what they hide in their heart. It seems the Sileni were statuettes divided in half and put together so that they could be opened up and the interior displayed. When closed they portrayed some ridiculous and monstrous flute player, but when opened all of a sudden they displayed a god. The amusing deception was designed to show off the skill of the carver. The exterior subject of these figures was taken from that ridiculous character Silenus, the schoolteacher of Bacchus, and the jester of the gods as portrayed in poetry, for they have their buffoons like the princes of our own day. Thus, in Plato's *Symposium*, Alcibiades begins his speech in praise of Socrates by comparing him with these Sileni, on the grounds that like them he was quite different when you got to know him properly from what one would imagine from his outward appearance and manner.[2]

Anyone who took him at face value, as they say, would not have paid a nickel for him. He had the face of a country bumpkin, a bit like that of an ox, and a snub nose always running with snot. You would have thought he was dull and stupid, good only at pulling faces. His appearance was scruffy, and his speech was plain, elementary, and working-class, for he was always talking about carters and cobblers, clothmakers and blacksmiths. It was from them that he drew his examples. He had hardly any money, and his wife was someone that a charcoal burner—and you can't sink lower than that—would have turned away from. He seemed to admire the bodies of young men, and to be susceptible to love and jealousy, though

---

1. In fact this is untrue; Erasmus obviously thought it *ought to be* a proverb.
2. Plato, *Symposium*, 215a.

even Alcibiades eventually realized that he was a long way from having such emotions. He was always cracking jokes, which meant that he seemed to be something of a clown. In those days it was the height of fashion among the stupid to appear to be an intellectual, and Gorgias was not unique in claiming that there was nothing he did not know. Pompous asses of this sort were to be found at every turn. Socrates alone said that there was only one thing he knew, and that was that he knew nothing. He seemed unsuited to any position of responsibility, so much so that once when he stood up to make a speech in public there was too much laughter for him to be heard.

But if you open up this Silenus, who is outwardly so ridiculous, you find within someone who is closer to being a god than a man, a great and lofty spirit, the epitome of a true philosopher. He despised all those things for which other mortals strive and sail the seas, sweat and go to court, even go to war. He was untouched by insults, and neither good fortune nor bad had any impact on him. He feared nothing, not even death, which scares everybody. He had the same look on his face when he drank the hemlock as when sipping a glass of wine at dinner, and as he lay dying he was telling a joke to his friend Phaedo, telling him to sacrifice a cock to Aesculapius, as he owed him one as a result of a vow he had taken, "for now I have taken my medicine I begin at last to feel truly healthy."[3] For he was leaving the body, in which all the diseases of the soul pullulate like maggots. So it was perfectly fair that, at a time when people who called themselves philosophers were thick on the ground, this buffoon was the only person whom the oracle declared wise. He who said he knew nothing was judged to know more than those who proudly claimed to know everything. Indeed, that was the very reason why he was judged to know more than they did—because he alone admitted he knew nothing.

Another Silenus of this sort was Antisthenes.[4] He may only have had a staff, a pack, and a cloak, but he was richer than an emperor. Another Silenus was Diogenes, who was thought by most people to have the manners of a dog.[5] Yet Alexander the Great, whom one would think the first and foremost of all princes, seems to have recognized something divine in this dog, since he so admired his

---

3. Plato, *Phaedo*, 118a.
4. A pupil of Socrates and one of the founders of the Cynic school.
5. Most famous of the Cynics (fourth century B.C.E.).

nobility of mind that he said that if he couldn't be Alexander he would want to be Diogenes—though the fact that he was indeed Alexander should have made him all the keener to have the spirit of Diogenes. Epictetus was yet another Silenus.[6] He was a slave, poverty-stricken and crippled, as we learn from his epitaph. He was also—and one can't have better luck than this—loved by the gods. But then he had earned his good fortune in the only way one can, by integrity of life, and by wisdom as well.

This is the nature of things truly worth having: what is most valuable about them is hidden away and concealed, while what is visible on the surface appears beneath contempt. They hide their treasure beneath a coarse and worthless shell, and do not let the uninitiated catch even a glimpse of it. Vulgar and trivial things have a quite different character. They please at first sight, and their best qualities are immediately visible to any passerby. But if you look more closely, you will find that they are the opposite of what you would think from their appearance and reputation.

And was not Christ, too, a marvelous Silenus—if I may be permitted to speak of him in such terms? I cannot see why all those who take pride in calling themselves Christians do not feel an obligation to make their best efforts to copy this aspect of his nature. If you look at the outside of this Silenus, what, judging by normal standards, could be more contemptible or despicable? His parents were insignificant and penniless. His home was a shack. He was poor himself, and his disciples were few in number and equally insignificant, drawn from the tax collector's office and the fisherman's nets. Then think of his life—a life without pleasure, during which he endured hunger and exhaustion, insults and mockery, that finally ended on the cross. The mystical prophet was looking at him from this perspective when he gave us this description of him: "He hath no form nor comeliness; and when we shall see him, there is no beauty that we should desire him. He is despised and rejected of men"—and much more to the same effect, which follows this passage.[7]

But if you have the opportunity to look at the inside of this Silenus, if Christ deigns to show himself, our immortal God, to the purified eyes of your soul, what an indescribable treasure you will find; in this muck, what a pearl; in this humility, what grandeur; in

---

6. A Stoic philosopher of the first century A.D.
7. Isaiah 53:2–3.

this poverty, what wealth; in this weakness, what immeasurable strength; in this disgrace, what glory; in these labors, what perfect peace; and finally in that bitter death, the never-failing source of everlasting life! Why are the very people who take such pride in bearing his name so revolted by this way of seeing him? Nothing would have been easier for Christ than to make himself the ruler of the whole world. He could have achieved what the rulers of ancient Rome tried and failed to do. He could have had more soldiers than Xerxes, more gold than Croesus. He could have silenced all the prattling philosophers and exposed the stupidity of the sophists. But instead he chose to be a Silenus, and it is this example that he wanted his disciples and friends, that is, all Christians, to imitate. He chose a philosophy which was worlds away from the teaching of the philosophers and from the judgments of the world, but which is the only philosophy to offer the one thing that all the others, each in its different way, is after—happiness.

Once upon a time the prophets were Sileni of this sort: exiles, wanderers, living in the wilderness in the company of wild beasts. They ate grasses and wore the skins of sheep and goats. But he who said "the world was not worthy of them" had looked right inside these Silenus images.[8] John the Baptist was a Silenus of this sort. He was clothed in camel hair, with a leather belt knotted around his waist; yet he outshone the purple gowns and bejeweled girdles of kings. He dined on locusts; yet his meals were more delicious than those of princes. The treasure that lay hidden beneath that peasant's cloak was recognized by one person, who summarized all the praise he was due in this marvelous phrase, "Among them that are born of women there hath not arisen a greater than John the Baptist."[9] Such Sileni were the apostles: poor, unsophisticated, uneducated, base-born, powerless, rejected, spared no insult, ridiculed, hated, cursed, the public laughingstock, and the abomination of the world. But open the Silenus, and what tyrant has had powers to equal theirs? Devils obeyed their slightest word; they raised a hand, and the raging seas quieted; they spoke, and the dead returned to life. Even Croesus would seem poor compared to them, for by the touch of a shadow they make healthy the sick, and by the touch of a hand they impart the Holy Spirit. Even Aristotle would seem stupid, ignorant, irrelevant compared with them, who draw heavenly

8. Hebrews 11:38.
9. Matthew 11:11.

wisdom from its very source, wisdom compared with which all human wisdom is pure stupidity. In those days the kingdom of heaven really was symbolized by a grain of mustard seed, minuscule and insignificant in appearance, but immensely powerful.[10] And, as I have said, in this it differs utterly, diametrically, as the saying is, from the mindset of this world.

A Silenus of this sort was Martin, who was mocked and treated with contempt.[11] Such were the early bishops, exalted in their humility, rich in their poverty, and famous because they thought nothing of fame. Even today you can find Sileni if you look for them, but unfortunately they are very rare. The majority of men are Sileni turned inside out. Anyone who looked carefully at the underlying motives and true nature of men would find that none are further from true wisdom than those whose grand titles, professorial robes, richly worked belts, and bejeweled rings advertise their claim to perfect wisdom. Indeed, you will often find more true and authentic wisdom in one insignificant individual, who most people think is simpleminded and half-mad, who has been taught what they know not by the subtle (as he is commonly called) Scotus,[12] but by the heavenly spirit of Christ, than in many people who play the part of theologians and claim to be able to teach us. They are windbags blown up with Aristotle, sausages stuffed with a mass of theoretical definitions, conclusions, and propositions. Similarly, there is nowhere you will find less true nobility than in those Thrasos[13] who, with their ancient pedigrees, golden chains, and splendid titles, boast that they are the acme of nobility. You won't find anyone who is further from having true courage than those who are thought to be supremely strong and totally unconquerable because they are foolhardy and brutal. No one is more abject and servile than someone who thinks themself (as the saying is) a companion of the gods, and lord of all they survey. No one is in as much trouble as someone who seems most completely successful. Those who are truly impoverished are the very people whom public opinion worships for their wealth. Those who are the least bishops hold the best dioceses. If only this were not the truth; very often the people who are furthest from true religion are those who are sticklers

---

10. Matthew 13:31.
11. St. Martin, bishop of Tours.
12. The medieval theologian Duns Scotus.
13. A reference to Terence's *Eunuchus*.

that the correct forms of address be used, the right vestments be worn, the ceremonies be exactly performed, and who believe that this proves that it is they who are truly religious.

Wherever you look you will find it is always true that the most significant part of something is the least conspicuous. Take trees: the flowers and leaves charm the eye, and their spreading branches can't be missed. But their seed, which contains the whole life force, how tiny it is, how hidden away! There is nothing about it that entices the eye, nothing that draws attention to itself. Similarly, nature hides gold and jewels in the deepest recesses of the earth. Among the elements, as they are called, the more important they are, the more they escape our senses, like air and fire. In living creatures, the organs that are crucial and that do the most work are hidden away on the inside. In human beings, the part that is most divine and is immortal is the only one that is invisible. In every kind of thing, the material of which it is made is the baser part and at the same time the most accessible to the senses. The principle that underlies its construction and its function can be discovered from the role it plays, but this is not something that is immediately apparent from sense perception. Thus in the makeup of our bodies, we often encounter blood and phlegm because they are palpable; but the most important thing in keeping the body alive is least apparent—I mean the breath. In the cosmos, the most important entities escape our vision, such as what are termed the separate substances.[14] And the most important of all of these is the furthest removed from our senses. God, the unique source of all things, can be neither imagined nor understood.

One can even see some similarity to the Sileni in the sacraments of the Church. You see the water, you see the salt and the oil, you hear the words of consecration; these are like the outward image of the Silenus. The heavenly power you neither hear nor see, yet in its absence everything else would be completely ridiculous. The Holy Scriptures also have their Sileni. If you stay on the surface, much of it seems absurd. If you penetrate to the spiritual meaning, you will be full of admiration for God's wisdom. Let us take the Old Testament as an example. If you pay attention to nothing but the literal meaning, and you hear that Adam was made out of clay, and his little wife was taken secretly out of his side while he was sleeping; that the serpent tempted the woman using an apple as his bait; that

---

14. That is, noncorporeal beings or angels.

God went for a walk in the cool of the day; that a great sword guarded the gates of Paradise lest the exiles should return—would you not think that this was an imaginary tale, produced by some apprentice Homer? If you read about the incest of Lot; the adultery of David, and the girl who slept in his arms when he was old and cold; about Hosea's marriage to a prostitute—would not anyone who was reasonably easy to shock turn away, thinking this was an obscene story? And yet under these veils, goodness me, what splendid wisdom lies hidden! The parables of the Gospel, if you judge them by their outward shell, surely anyone would agree, must have been written by someone hopelessly unsophisticated. But if you crack open the shell, you will find within hidden wisdom, a wisdom truly divine and very like Christ himself. I don't want to become boring by giving you too many examples. It is the same in both the natural and the supernatural realms: the more significant something is, the deeper it is hidden, the more effectively it is concealed from prying eyes.

It is the same with questions of knowledge. The real truth always lies deeply hidden, so that it cannot be easily attained, nor by most people. Most people are stupid and have a distorted vision of the world. They judge everything according to the first impression made on their senses. Over and over again they make mistakes, they go astray, they are misled by false images of the good and the bad. It is the inside-out Sileni that they admire and respect. I am speaking here of the bad; I mean no harm to the good, nor for that matter to the bad. I am engaged in a general discussion of moral failings, not in the criticism of any individual. But it's a shame there aren't fewer people who match my description. When you see the scepter, the badges of office, the bodyguards, when you hear the titles, do you not revere your ruler like a god on earth, do you not think that you have the privilege of seeing someone more than human? But open up this inside-out Silenus and you find a tyrant, even an enemy of his people, a thief, someone who commits sacrilege and incest, a gambler, or, in summary, what the Greek proverb calls "an Iliad of evils." There are those who are officially magistrates and guardians of the public good, and who if you take them at face value appear to correspond to their titles; but really they are wolves and pirates who prey upon the community. There are some who, having caught sight of their shaven heads, you would respect as priests; but if you look inside the Silenus they are worse than laymen. You may even find some bishops—if you saw their solemn consecrations, if you caught sight of their new vestments, the miter shining with gold and jewels, the crozier encrusted with jewels, the whole mystic panoply that covers them from their head to their feet, you would think they were heavenly beings and certainly not mere mortals. But turn the Silenus inside out and you will find you have in front of you nothing but a man of war, a man of business, even a tyrant. You will realize that all those splendid symbols of holiness were props for a theatrical effect. There are some men—I only wish one didn't run into them everywhere one goes—who, judging by their unkempt beards, their pallor, the fact that they go about hooded and belted, with supercilious and cantankerous expressions on their faces, you would think to be new Serapios or Pauls.[15] But if you look inside you will find they are mere buffoons, and the treasure, as the proverb has it, turns out to be a lump of coal. Again, I must stress that no one need be offended by what I have to say, since I don't identify anyone by name. If you don't fit the description, then you are free to think it has nothing to do with you. But if you recognize your own faults, then consider yourself to have a lesson to learn. If you're of the first sort, then congratulate yourself; if of the second, then you owe me your thanks.

Finally, everywhere, among all kinds of human beings, there are those of whom you would think, judging by their physical appearance, that they are not only people, but fine examples of humankind. But if you open the Sileni you will find that on the inside they are perhaps a pig, or a lion, or a bear, or a donkey. In their case the opposite has happened to that which happened, according to the poets' stories, with Circe's spells. Her victims had the bodies of beasts and the minds of men, but these have the appearance of being human while concealing their true natures, which are worse than those of the beasts. Their opposites are those I have already discussed, who from their appearance you would think were scarcely human, while deep inside they are inhabited by the spirits of angels.

This then is the difference between a worldly person and a Christian. The first bases their responses and opinions on what is most obvious to the eye, on what is most coarsely material. The other aspects of reality they either completely ignore or else attribute the least importance to them. The second, contrariwise, is only drawn to those things hardest to perceive, which are at the greatest distance from material reality. The rest they either pay no attention to or else regard with contempt, basing their judgment of

---

15. Egyptian hermits famed for their sanctity.

all things on their hidden characteristics. Among the good things, as they are termed by Aristotle, which are not intrinsically part of a person's own nature, wealth is the least worth having.[16] But among the common people—indeed, among almost everybody—those who have wealth are the most highly thought of, no matter how they obtained it. Everybody is after wealth and will walk on coals to get it. Next after wealth comes noble birth, though birth on its own amounts to nothing, a ridiculous and empty name. Someone who can trace their descent from Codrus, King of Athens, or from Brutus the Trojan (personally I'm not sure he ever really existed), or from the mythical Hercules is regarded as semidivine; while someone who has become famous for their learning and their virtue is dismissed as being of humble birth. One person is called illustrious because their distant ancestor proved himself a particularly bloody murderer on the field of battle, and another is a plebeian because they have no famous ancestors to point to, though their intellectual gifts have benefited the whole world. In the third place is physical well-being. Anyone who happens to be tall, strong, handsome, and robust is held to be one of the lucky ones, though of course not nearly as lucky as someone who is rich, nor as lucky as someone who is of noble birth. The well-being of the spirit is their last concern.

But if, following St. Paul, you divide human beings into three parts, the body, the soul, and the spirit (for I am using his terminology),[17] the lowest part, condemned by the apostle but most accessible to the senses, is the part the common people value most. The middle part, which he approves of only it if is linked to the spirit, is considered valuable by many. But the spirit, the best part of us, from which, as from a fountain, all our happiness flows, the part by which we are joined to God, they are so far from considering precious that they do not even ask whether it exists or what it is, although Paul emphasizes its importance so often. And so ordinary people end up with a scale of values that is upside down. What we should particularly honor is regarded as being of no account, an also-ran, and what we should strive after with might and main is regarded as being absolutely worthless. Gold is valued more than learning, blue blood more than integrity, physical strength more than intellectual ability, religious ceremonies more than true piety, man-made law more than God's decrees. The mask is preferred to

---

16. Aristotle, *Politics*, VII.1323a; *Rhetoric*, I.1360b.
17. I Thessalonians 5:23.

the face, the shadow to the reality, the artificial to the natural, the fleeting to the substantial, the momentary to the eternal.

Upside-down values mean that the meanings of words have to be displaced. The lofty they now call lowly; the bitter is sweet; the precious is worthless; life is called death. Let me give you one or two examples in passing. Someone is said to love someone else if they seek to corrupt them by indulging them, or if they set out to destroy their reputation and their sense of shame. If this is love, what would hostility be like? They call it justice when evil is deterred by evil, a crime is repaid with a crime, and any injury you have received is paid back at an exorbitant rate of interest. People are said to be hostile to marriage if they attack adultery and maintain that married life should have more in common with celibacy than with the goings-on in a brothel. They call a man a traitor and an enemy of his ruler if he thinks the ruler should be prevented from acting outside the law and contrary to justice—that is, if he wants him to act like a true ruler and in no way to resemble a tyrant, the foulest of all wild beasts. They call someone a counselor, a friend, a supporter of government if he corrupts the ruler with an inappropriate education, inculcates him with idiotic ideas, deludes him with flattery, gives him bad advice so that he ends up being hated by his subjects, and involves him in wars and violent upheavals. They say the majesty of the ruler is enhanced if he shows himself to be a bit of a tyrant—that is to say, if he to a significant degree becomes the worst species of human being. They accuse anyone who wishes to reduce the taxes extorted from the public of robbing the public purse.

Goodness, wisdom, and power are the three most important qualities a ruler should have, and through them he represents God, the only true king. Can someone properly be called the ruler's friend if he robs him of two of these qualities, goodness and wisdom, leaving him only with power—or rather with the appearance of power, power that in any case isn't truly his own? For power, if it is not combined with goodness and wisdom, is not power, but tyranny. And just as the ruler's power comes from the consent of the people, so the people can take it away. But if he should be deprived of his throne, he will retain goodness and wisdom as his personal attributes. Death is the punishment for attacking the symbols of the king's authority; and are men to be rewarded for corrupting his character and turning him from a good ruler into a cruel one, from a wise man into a cunning one, from a legitimate prince into a tyrant? One death is not punishment enough for someone who tries to poison the prince's drink; and is there to be a reward for those who corrupt and poison his mind with false opinions? Their actions are comparable to poisoning the public water supply, thereby inflicting the greatest harm on the whole community. They talk about a ruler's position as if it were his personal property, when in fact the sum total of being a ruler consists in administering what belongs to the community. Dynastic marriages and the constantly changing alliances between rulers, they say, serve to cement peace between Christians, when in fact we see that these are the source of nearly all wars and most of the great upheavals in our lives. By their way of calculating, a ruler's dominions are enlarged when he acquires the title to one or two little towns, no matter how high the price that has been paid, no matter how many citizens have been pillaged, how much blood has been shed, how many wives have been made into widows and children into orphans.

In just the same way they call the priests, bishops, and popes "the Church," when in principle they are only the servants of the Church. The Christian people are the Church. Christ himself said the Church is superior to its servants,[18] so the bishops should wait on the people while they sit at the table, treating them with deference, even though from another point of view they could establish their superiority if they were to take on in their turn the office he fulfilled, and reform their morals and way of life in imitation of him. Although he was in every possible respect the lord and master of all things, yet he took on the role of a servant, not a master. The full force of a thunderbolt is hurled at those who steal small change from the priests' collection; they are called enemies of the Church and are nearly branded as heretics. Now, I am no supporter of those who cheat and steal, don't misunderstand me. But I ask this: If we should hate the Church's enemies, could the Church have an enemy more destructive and more deadly than a godless pope? If there has been some slight reduction in the assets or income of the priesthood, the cry goes up on all sides that the Church of Christ is being oppressed. But now, when the world is on the brink of war, when the unconcealed immorality of the clergy threatens to bring about the destruction of so many thousands of souls, no one bewails the fate of the Church, though it is now that the Church is really suffering. They talk about the Church being honored and adorned, not when piety is increasing among the people, when vice

---

18. Luke 22:24.

is less prevalent and good behavior is on the increase, when Christian learning is flourishing, but when the altars glisten with gold and
jewels; worse, when the altars are neglected, and landed wealth,
servants, luxury, mules, horses, the construction of costly buildings
(palaces would be a better word), and the rest of the bustle of life
have made the priests indistinguishable from satraps.[19] I don't want
even to mention those who spend the Church's wealth on immoral
activities, to the outrage of ordinary people. If they become wealthier, we congratulate them and say the Church of Christ is better
off, when the only respect in which the Church can be better off is
if more people are living a Christian life.

They call it blasphemy if someone speaks of Christopher or
George with insufficient reverence, and fails to treat all the stories
about all the saints as if they were equal in authority to the Gospel.
But Paul uses the term "blasphemy" for occasions when the un-
godly behavior of Christians causes the name of Christ to be dis-
credited among the Gentiles.[20] What can one expect the enemies of
the Christian religion to say when they have seen Christ in the
Gospels urging us to have contempt for riches, to turn away from
the pursuit of pleasure, and to stop being concerned about reputation, and then they see the leaders and representatives of the
Christian faith live according to principles that appear to be diametrically opposed to those of Christ, so that they outdo the Gentiles
in their efforts to accumulate wealth, in their love of pleasures, in
their splendor of life, in the ferocity of their wars, and in almost
every other vice. The perceptive reader will understand how much
I am passing over in silence out of respect for the honor of the
name of Christian, and how deeply I sigh within myself.

They call it heresy if anyone says or writes something that dis-
agrees in any way—even over a question of grammar—with the
pettifogging propositions of those who instruct us in theology. But
is it not heresy for someone to claim that a principal part of human
happiness lies in pleasures which Christ himself repeatedly says
are worthless? Or to promote a way of life that is clearly at odds
with the teaching of the Gospels and the practice of the apostles?
Or, directly contrary to the intention of Christ, who sent the apostles out to preach the Gospel armed only with the sword of the
spirit (which alone, by cutting out all earthly attachments, can

---

19. The governors of provinces in the Persian empire.
20. Romans 2:24

make it possible to do without the sword), arms their successors with steel, so that they can defend themselves against persecution?[21] (There's no doubt that the word "sword" was intended to include crossbows and cannon, siege engines, and the rest of the apparatus of war.) And then weighs them down with a wallet in which they can carry money, presumably so that they will never have to go without? (And the word "wallet" was intended to refer to anything that is used to ensure a supply of material goods.) Yet this is how the words of Luke are distorted by the great Lyranus, whom many respect more than Jerome![22]

It is regarded as an unforgivable sacrilege if someone steals something from a church; but it seems to be a minor offense to plunder, cheat, and oppress the poverty-stricken and the widowed, although they are the living temple of God. It is profanity to pollute the sacred building by fighting or by an emission of semen; but we do not curse the man who uses endearments, gifts, promises, and flattery to violate, corrupt, and profane that temple of the Holy Spirit, a pure and chaste virgin. As I've already said, I'm not coming to the defense of wrongdoing. My point is that ordinary people pay much more attention to what they see with their eyes than to those things which are all the more real for being less exposed to view. You can see the consecration of a physical building; because you cannot see the dedication of a soul, you pay no attention to it. You will fight to the death to protect its ornaments, but no one will pick up the sword of the spirit to protect the integrity of morals, though Christ ordered each one of us to sell the shirt on his back in order to buy such a sword. It is called the height of piety to take up arms to defend or increase the dominion and wealth of the priesthood and to throw things sacred and profane together into the maelstrom of war. But while the priest's money—something of no spiritual significance at all—is being defended, war, like a vast flood, sweeps away all religious feeling. For what sort of evil is there that war does not bring in its wake?

But perhaps at this point my reader's unspoken thoughts will break in. "What's the purpose of all this foul-smelling stuff?" you ask. "Do you want every ruler to have the exceptional qualities that Plato attributed in his *Republic* to the guardians? Do you want to equip priests with only the wallet and staff of the apostles, wresting

---

21. Luke 22:35ff.
22. The medieval theologian Nicholas of Lyra (c. 1265-1349).

from them their power, dignity, status, and riches?" Good questions. I am not wresting their possessions from them, but enriching them with more valuable ones; I am not depriving them of their status, but challenging them to set their sights higher. I ask you, which of us has a more exalted view of kingship? You, who want your king to be free to do whatever he likes, to choose to be a tyrant, not a legitimate ruler; who stuff him with pleasures, abandon him to luxury, make him the captive and slave of his appetites; who weigh him down with the things that even the Gentiles always thought it was noble to despise? Or I, who want him to be as similar as possible to God, whose representative in some measure he is? I want him to be wiser than everyone else, for wisdom is the true glory of a king. I want him to be far removed from all base passions and diseases of the soul, which corrupt the stupid and vulgar masses. I want him to set his sights above the commonplace, to rise above the pursuit of wealth, to be, in short, to the state what the soul is to the body and God to the universe.

Which of us has a more accurate assessment of the dignity of a bishop? You, who weigh him down with worldly wealth, entangle him in base and sordid cares, embroil him in the violence of war? Or I, who want him, as the vicar of Christ and the guardian of his heavenly spouse, to be completely uncontaminated by earthly contagion, and to resemble, as closely as possible, him whose place he occupies and whose job he does? The Stoics say that one cannot be a good person unless one is free of all diseases of the spirit. By diseases of the spirit they mean desires or emotions. Christians have a much greater obligation to free themselves of them, and the ruler a greater obligation than anyone else. And the ruler and father of the Church, of a heavenly community, has an even greater obligation. I want the priest to rule, but in my view mere earthly power is too sordid for someone who exercises a heavenly authority to be burdened with it. I want to see the pope triumphant, but not riding in those bloody triumphs that were held by evil Marius and godless Julius, which were so ostentatious that the satirists mocked them. If Democritus had been present I do believe he would have died laughing![23] Rather in truly magnificent and apostolic triumphs, of the sort that Paul (a warrior and general far more glorious than Alexander the Great) describes and even boasts about:

---

23. Erasmus had watched Pope Julius II enter Rome in triumph in 1507. Democritus was known as the "laughing philosopher."

In labors more abundant, in stripes above measure, in prisons more frequent, in deaths often. Of the Jews five times received I forty stripes save one. Thrice was I beaten with rods, once was I stoned, thrice I suffered shipwreck, a night and a day have I been in the deep; in journeyings often, in perils of waters, in perils of robbers, in perils by mine own countrymen, in perils by the Gentiles, in perils in the city, in perils in the wilderness, in perils in the sea, in perils among false brethren; in weariness and painfulness, in watchings often, in hunger and thirst, in fastings often, in cold and nakedness. Besides those things that are without, that which cometh upon me daily, the care of all the churches. Who is weak, and I am not weak? Who is offended, and I burn not?[24]

Again, a little earlier, there is this:

In all things proving ourselves the ministers of God, in much patience, in afflictions, in necessities, in distresses, in stripes, in imprisonments, in tumults, in labors, in watchings, in fastings; by pureness, by knowledge, by longsuffering, by kindness, by the Holy Ghost, by love unfeigned, by the word of truth, by the power of God, by the armor of righteousness on the right hand and on the left, by honor and dishonor, by evil report and good report; as deceivers, and yet true; as unknown, and yet well known; as dying, and behold, we live; as chastened, and not killed, as sorrowful, yet always rejoicing; as poor, yet making many rich; as having nothing, and yet possessing all things.[25]

Here you can see his battle honors, his victory, his apostolic triumph. This is the glory by which Paul sometimes swears, as if it were sacred. These are the heroic deeds for which he believed a crown of immortality had already been set aside as his reward.[26] Surely those who lay claim to the status and authority of the apostles will find it no hardship to follow in their footsteps. I want the popes to be as rich as possible, but rich with the pearl of the Gospel, rich with heavenly treasure. Then they will find that the

---

24 II Corinthians 11:23–9.
25. II Corinthians 6:4–10.
26. II Timothy 4:8.

more of their wealth they give away, the richer they will be. Then there will be no danger that generosity now will be at the expense of their capacity to be generous in future. I would wish them to be defended against all attacks, but with the armor of the apostles, with the shield of faith, the breastplate of righteousness, and the sword of salvation (which is the word of God).[27] I want them keen to fight, but against the true enemies of the Church: simony, pride, lust, ambition, anger, godlessness. These are the undying enemy, the Turks, against whom Christians must always stand on guard, against whom they must always be planning their next attack. This is the battlefield on which a bishop should prove himself a resourceful general and an inspiring leader. I would like priests to be the people to whom everyone else defers, but not on account of their noisy bullying; rather on account of their excellent knowledge of the doctrines of Christianity and their outstanding virtues. I would like them to be revered, but on account of their integrity and their ascetic lives, rather than on account of their titles or their fancy outfits. I would like them to be feared, but as fathers, not tyrants. Finally, I would like them to luxuriate in delights, but rare delights, delights much sweeter than most people will ever experience.

Would you like to know what the true riches of the papacy are? Then listen now to the prince of popes: "Gold and silver have I none, but such as I have I give thee: In the name of Jesus arise and walk."[28] Do you want to hear the splendor of the name "apostle," which is worth more than any title, any monument or statue? Listen to Paul, the truly illustrious: "For we are to God a sweet savor of Christ in every place."[29] Do you want to hear of a power that is greater than any king's? "I can do all things," he says, "through Christ who strengtheneth me."[30] Do you want to hear of true glory? "You are my joy and crown in the Lord."[31] Do you want to hear the titles that are worthy of a bishop, the terms in which one should honor a true pope? Paul describes such a person for you: "sober, blameless, prudent, modest, given to hospitality, apt to teach; not given to wine, no striker, but patient, not a brawler, not

---

27. Ephesians 6:14–17.
28. Acts 3:6.
29. II Corinthians 2:15.
30. Philippians 4:13.
31. Philippians 4:1.

greedy of filthy lucre, not a novice; moreover he must have a good report of them that are without, lest he fall into reproach and the snare of the devil."[32] Look at the ways in which Moses does honor to Aaron, the high priest: the wealth with which he presents him, the many-colored embroideries in which he envelopes him, the jewels shining like stars with which he adorns him, the gleam of gold with which he embellishes him. If you know the interpretation of Origen and of Jerome, then you will know the meaning of all this, and you will know how a bishop should be fitted out.

Who should the popes imitate in their lives, if not those whom they portray on their seals, whom they recall in their titles, whose places they occupy? Can it be more appropriate for the vicar of Christ to model himself on Julius or Alexander, Croesus or Xerxes, who were nothing but very successful bandits, than on Christ himself? Who could the successors of the apostles imitate better than the prince of the apostles? Christ directly denied that his kingdom was of this world, and do you think it right that Christ's successor should not only agree to be an earthly ruler, but should use political skills to acquire power and should, as the saying goes, leave no stone unturned in his quest for it?

In this world there are really two worlds, in conflict with each other in every possible way. One is gross and physical, the other heavenly and already straining every nerve to practice being what it one day will become. In the first world the most successful person is held to be someone who has least to do with all that is truly good and is most heavily burdened with fictitious goods. A pagan king, for example, may outdo everyone else in lust and luxury, pomp and pride, greed and wealth, and in violence, and is thus regarded as more successful than anyone else, since he has sunk deeper in this filth than anyone else and has been least touched by wisdom, temperance, sobriety, justice, and the other qualities that are truly valuable. In the second, by contrast, the most successful is the person who is least befouled by these coarse and commonplace goods, and has accumulated the largest stock of those true and spiritual riches. So why do you want a Christian ruler to be the sort of person whom even the pagan philosophers have always condemned and despised? Why should you maintain that his authority is enhanced

---

32. I Timothy 3:2–7.

by precisely those qualities that it has always been most admirable
to despise? Why burden an angel of god (for this is what bishops
are called in Holy Scripture) with things that are unworthy of any
man who can be called good? Why assess him according to the
amount of wealth he has, just because gold makes robbers rich and
tyrants powerful? There is supposed to be something heavenly
about a priest, something more than human. There is nothing worthy of someone in his elevated position except what is heavenly.
Why do you undermine his dignity by associating him with commonplace things? Why pollute his purity with the filth of this
world? Why do you not let him be powerful by exercising his own
kind of command? Why not allow him to be admired for his own
fine qualities, respected for his own authority, wealthy with his own
riches? This man was chosen out of a heavenly body, for that is
what the Church is, by the Holy Spirit to serve the highest purposes. Why do you drag him down into the petty conflicts and vicious rivalries of court life? Paul glories in the fact that he has been
separated from the world;[33] why do you drown my church leader in
the sewer, making him take after the lowest specimens of humanity? Why expose him to the anxieties suffered by someone behind
on his payments to a moneylender? Why drag a man of God into
business that would be degrading for any human being? Why measure the true happiness of Christian priests by whether they have
those things which Democritus laughed at as completely ridiculous, which Heraclitus wept over as entirely pathetic, which Diogenes scorned as frivolous, and Crates spurned as burdensome,
while the saints have always fled from them as if one could catch
plague from them? Why judge Peter's successor by how much
wealth he has, when Peter took pride in having nothing? Why do
you want the successors to the apostles as rulers of the Church to
seem important by surrounding themselves with those marks of
worldly distinction that the apostles trampled underfoot—which is
precisely why they are important? Why do you call "the patrimony
of St. Peter" something that Peter took pride in not having? Why
do you think the vicars of Christ should be entangled in riches,
when Christ himself called them thorns? The immediate responsibility and chief duty of a priest is to sow the seed of the word of
God; why then bury him in worldly possessions, which, more than
anything else, stifle the seed once it is sown? The priest should

---

33. Romans 1:1.

teach equity and define it for others; why then do you want him to be enslaved to riches, which embody unfairness? He dispenses the holy sacraments; why do you want to make him responsible for managing the vilest things? The Christian world looks to him to feed it with sound doctrine, to advise it on how to seek salvation, to provide consolation like a father, and to represent an example of how to live. Why would you imprison someone destined and devoted to such noble tasks on a treadmill of commonplace concerns? Thereby you both rob the bishop of his dignity and deprive the people of their bishop.

Christ has his own kingdom, one too fine to be contaminated by the kingdoms of the Gentiles, or rather, to speak more accurately, by their tyrannies. He has his own magnificence, his own wealth, his own delights. Why do we mix together things that are so at odds with each other? Earthly and heavenly, highest and lowest, pagan and Christian, profane and sacred: why do we confuse one with the other? The Spirit is both immensely wealthy and immensely generous, and its gifts are both numerous and valuable: gifts of languages, gifts of prophecy, gifts of healing, gifts of knowledge, gifts of wisdom, gifts of learning, the discerning of spirits, exhortation, consolation.[34] Why do you "bind together" these sacred offerings with the profane gifts of the world (I resist the temptation to say "strangle")? Why do you try to tie Christ to Mammon, and the spirit of Christ to Belial? Why should a miter be associated with a helmet, a sacred vestment with a martial breastplate, blessings with cannonballs, the shepherd with armed robbers? Why should priests wage war? Should someone who has the keys to the kingdom of heaven be busy knocking down town walls with cannon fire? How can it be right for the same person who keeps the people safe with the symbol of peace to declare war? How will he have the face to teach Christians in the streets and the marketplaces that wealth is to be despised, when money is the *a* to *z* of his own life? How can he have the cheek to teach what Christ both taught and showed by example, what all the apostles insisted upon, that evil is not to be resisted, that we must defeat the wickedness of evil men with goodness, that we must repay an injury with kindness, and overwhelm our enemies with generosity, when, in order to secure control of a market town, or to levy a tax on salt, he is prepared to have a tidal wave of war break over the whole world? How can he lead us towards

---

34. I Corinthians 12:4–10.

the kingdom of heaven (for this is the function Christ assigns to his Church), when he is entirely preoccupied with the kingdom of this world?

But perhaps you are excessively pious. You want to adorn the Church by adding worldly riches to her spiritual ones. I would approve, were it not for the fact that such a strategy has few benefits and enormous disadvantages. When you give a clergyman secular authority you give him at the same time the problems associated with accumulating money, you give him a tyrant's bodyguard, regiments of soldiers, spies, horses, mules, trumpets, warfare, slaughter, triumph, riots, treaties, disputes, in short all those things that are inextricably associated with government. Even if he has good intentions, when will he have the free time to fulfil his apostolic responsibilities, when he is swept away by so many thousands of different concerns; for the names of the men who have joined the army are being recorded; treaties are being negotiated and abrogated; those who undermine your authority are being brought under control, and those who would like to see a change of government are being persuaded to stay loyal; enemies are being crushed and garrisons reinforced; counselors are being listened to and secular ambassadors received; friends are being promoted to high office; and a whole host of other things are being done, far too many to remember, and yet each absolutely essential? Does it seem to you to indicate a proper understanding of the elevated status of the pope and of the cardinals to think that they should be dragged away to deal with these squalid matters, away from their prayers, during which they talk with God, from holy contemplation, which they perform in the company of angels, from the verdant meadows of Holy Scripture, in which they stroll in perfect happiness, from the apostolic task of spreading the Gospel, in which they most resemble Christ? Do you think anyone who really wishes them well would want to drag them away from the delightful and peaceful life they were enjoying in order to embroil them in these tempests and force them to bear these heavy burdens?

Moreover, not only is governing a state deeply unpleasant because of the unending hard work involved, but the results are much less satisfactory with the clergy than with the laity in charge. There are two reasons, I think, for this. In the first place, when it comes to politics, ordinary people are more willing to obey laymen than ecclesiastics. Second, secular rulers, since they expect their territories to be inherited by their children, do their best to make them as prosperous as possible. By contrast, ecclesiastics come to power late in life, and often when they are already old men. And they rule for their own benefit, not that of their heirs. Thus they are more interested in plundering their territories than in improving them; they behave more like an invading army than an established administration. Moreover, when a secular ruler comes to power he probably only has to fight once to secure his lands for himself and his heirs, and once he has promoted and enriched those he favors that task is done. With ecclesiastics, however, new struggles are always breaking out. Those promoted by the previous ruler have to be thrown out, and over and over again new men have to be enriched at the expense of those who are ruled. It is also not without significance that subjects are much more inclined to obey someone to whose rule they have become accustomed, even if his rule is harsh. And then, when he dies, he still seems to live on in his son and heir, so that the populace pretend to themselves that they have not exchanged one ruler for another but have retained the old in a new guise. Indeed, children are liable to take after their parents, not only in their looks but also in their behavior, especially if they have been trained by them. But it is very different when government is entrusted to men who are dedicated to the service of God: when the ruler changes there is a sudden and complete change in every aspect of government. Let me add that a lay ruler comes to the exercise of power having had some practice and after being trained for rule from the cradle; but a clergyman often finds himself occupying the supreme office contrary to all expectations, so that a man born by nature to pull on an oar is, against all odds, elevated to sit on a throne. Last of all, it is scarcely possible for one man to be equally good at dealing with two quite different but extremely difficult types of management, for even Hercules could not take on two monsters at a time. Nothing could be harder than to succeed at being a good prince. But it is much finer, and also much more difficult, to be a good priest. How can it be feasible to be both? These are the reasons why, if I am not mistaken, we see towns ruled by secular monarchs thriving as day by day they increase their wealth, their buildings, and their population, while the towns ruled by priests decline and fall into ruins.

What then was the point of linking together these two things, when their union results in so many disadvantages? Are you afraid that Christ, if he relies on his own resources, will have too little power, and that it is therefore necessary for a secular tyrant to share some of his strength with him? Do you think he will look in need of embellishment unless some worldly soldier makes him a present of some gold and a Phrygian embroiderer,[35] some French white horses, and a guard of honor—in other words, spatters him with some of his own pomp? Do you think he won't seem magnificent enough unless he is able to use those insignia that Julius Caesar, the most ambitious man the world has seen, rejected for fear of the hostility they would provoke?[36] Do you think him insignificant unless he is weighed down with secular authority, which, if he uses it to further his own interests, will make him into a tyrant, while if he uses it to serve the public good, there will be no end to his labors? Let men of the world concern themselves with worldly things; the lowest aspect of episcopacy is higher than the most exalted aspect of secular government. The more worldly goods you grant to the Church, the less of his own goods will Christ bestow upon it. The more completely her bishops are cleansed of the former, the more lavishly will they be enriched with the latter.

I believe you are now able to see how everything is transformed if you turn the Silenus inside out. Those who seemed to have the interests of Christian rulers closest to their hearts now seem the chief betrayers and enemies of such rulers. Those who you would have said were concerned to defend the dignity of the papacy you now discover were trying to defile it. I am not saying this because I think that any power or wealth that has come to the priesthood by any means whatsoever should be stripped from them, but I want them to remember and bear in mind their true greatness. Let them reject these commonplace, not to say unchristian, concerns and leave them to their inferiors; or at least, if they retain power and wealth, may it be while despising them, and, as Paul puts it, may they have them as if they did not have them at all.[37] Finally, I want them to be so adorned with the riches of Christ that whatever glory they acquire from this world will either be put in the shade by the light of higher things, or even seem sordid in proximity to them. The result will be that they will take more delight in what they possess and will feel less anxiety. Fear will not gnaw at them, as they worry that someone may rob them. They will not have to fight, facing uncer-

---

35. In classical times the Phrygians were experts at producing gold brocade.
36. Caesar refused the offer of a crown.
37. I Corinthians 7:29.

tainty and danger, to hold on to transitory and base possessions. They will not be deprived of what is rightly theirs while they rejoice as they grow rich at the expense of others. They will not lose the pearl of the Gospel while they hunt after the fake jewels of the world.

Meanwhile I make no mention of the fact that those things I wish they would despise will be theirs more abundantly if they have contempt for them. There is more honor in acquiring wealth while aspiring to have none than in chasing after it and snatching it up. What is the source of the Church's wealth, if not its contempt of wealth? What makes the Church glorious, if not its indifference to glory? The laity will be much more willing to give away their wealth, if they see that wealth is rejected by those whom they believe to be wiser than themselves.

Perhaps evil rulers should sometimes be tolerated. We owe some respect to the memory of those whose places we think of them as occupying. Their titles have some claim on us. We should not seek to put matters right if there is a real possibility that the cure may prove worse than the disease. But human affairs are really in a terrible state if those whose whole life ought to be a continuing miracle live such lives that the worst sort of men cheer them on, while the good sigh and groan over them. Their prestige is entirely dependent on the support they receive from the wicked, or (if you prefer) on the reluctance of ordinary people to abandon convention, or on the inexperience of those who are not worldly-wise, or on the tolerance they meet with from those who are good.

But my words have run away with me. I claim to be a mere compiler of proverbs, and I am turning into a preacher. It was that drunkard Alcibiades and his Sileni that drew me into this very sober discussion. But I will not feel too guilty for my mistake, if whatever has been out of place in a discussion of proverbs has been relevant in persuading people to amend their lives; if whatever contributed nothing to the advancement of learning served to incite people to piety; if whatever may seem beside the point, "nothing to do with Dionysius,"[38] in relation to the task I have undertaken may seem very much to the point in relation to the task we all face, that of living.

[1515]

---

38. *Adages*, II.iv.57.

Sir Thomas More, by Hans Holbein
(Copyright, The Frick Collection, New York)

Desiderius Erasmus, by Quentin Metsys (the Royal Collection)

The pair of paintings by Metsys was commissioned by Erasmus and Giles in May of 1517, a few months after the publication of Utopia, *as a gift for their friend More. They are sitting at opposite sides of the same desk, with the same bookcase in the background. Giles holds a letter in More's handwriting, while Erasmus wears a ring given to him by More. Erasmus is working on his paraphrase of* Romans, *but his eyes are on a book that Giles holds forward over the table edge, presenting it to the painting's owner. Lisa Jardine has argued that this is almost certainly the first edition of* Utopia, *which Giles and Erasmus had seen through the press. When he received this gift More replied with two Latin poems, of which one is entitled "The Picture Speaks":*

Peter Giles, by Quentin Metsys (private collection)

> *Such friends as once were Castor and Pollux,*
> *Such I present Erasmus and Giles to you.*
> *More grieves to be separated from them,*
> *Joined as he is to them by as great a love*
> *As anyone could have for his own self.*
> *They arranged to satisfy their absent friend's longing for them:*
> *A loving text represents their spiritual identity; I represent their*
>   *physical identity.*

The "loving text" (amans littera) *would seem to be* Utopia, *which
represents the spiritual identify of friendship because "friends have
everything in common."*

Map of Utopia (1516 edition, British Library copy)

196

VTOPIENSIVM ALPHABETVM. 13

a b c d e f g h i k l m n o p q r s t u x y

◌ ⊖ ① ⊙ ⊙ ⊙ ⊅ ⊖ ⊖ ⊕ ⊗ △ ⅃ Ⅼ ⌐ ⌐ ⊓ ⊟ ⊞ ⊟ ⊟ ⊡

TETRASTICHON VERNACVLA VTO-
PIENSIVM LINGVA.

Vtopos ha Boccas peula chama.

polta chamaan

Bargol he maglomi baccan

soma gymnosophaon

Agrama gymnosophon labarem

bacha bodamilomin

Voluala barchin heman la

lauoluola dramme pagloni.

HORVM VERSVVM·AD VERBVM HAEC
EST SENTENTIA.

Vtopus me dux ex non insula fecit insulam.
Vna ego terrarum omnium absq; philosophia.
Ciuitatem philosophicam expressi mortalibus.
Libenter impartio mea, non grauatim accipio meliora.

b 3

Utopian Alphabet (March 1518 edition, British Library copy)

197

Giles, Morus, Clement, and Hythloday in Conversation
(March 1518 edition, British Library copy)

Index